JUSTICE AND RECIPROCITY IN ARISTOTLE'S POLITICAL PHILOSOPHY

This book illustrates how Aristotle's ethical concepts such as justice, reciprocity and friendship offer a basis for his political philosophy. In particular, it points out the importance of Aristotle for articulating the concept of a civic relationship and developing a theory of integration, by exploring how he includes a wide variety of people within the deliberative and judicial processes. Comparisons between Aristotle's own thought and present-day 'Aristotelian' political theories, such as communitarianism, civic republicanism and the capabilities approach, are also among the unique approaches offered by the book and are used to illustrate his original vision of politics. They can also, however, offer new insights into the problems of how to read his texts appropriately in their context and why we now need to read them, not only out of an antiquarian interest, but also out of our concern for politics.

KAZUTAKA INAMURA is Lecturer in the Faculty of Education at Hirosaki University, Japan.

CAMBRIDGE CLASSICAL STUDIES

General editors

JUSTICE AND RECIPROCITY IN ARISTOTLE'S POLITICAL PHILOSOPHY

KAZUTAKA INAMURA
Hirosaki University

CAMBRIDGE
UNIVERSITY PRESS

CAMBRIDGE
UNIVERSITY PRESS

Shaftesbury Road, Cambridge CB2 8EA, United Kingdom

One Liberty Plaza, 20th Floor, New York, NY 10006, USA

477 Williamstown Road, Port Melbourne, VIC 3207, Australia

314–321, 3rd Floor, Plot 3, Splendor Forum, Jasola District Centre, New Delhi – 110025, India

103 Penang Road, #05–06/07, Visioncrest Commercial, Singapore 238467

Cambridge University Press is part of Cambridge University Press & Assessment, a department of the University of Cambridge.

We share the University's mission to contribute to society through the pursuit of education, learning and research at the highest international levels of excellence.

www.cambridge.org
Information on this title: www.cambridge.org/9781107110946

First published 2015

A catalogue record for this publication is available from the British Library

Library of Congress Cataloging-in-Publication data
Inamura, Kazutaka.
Justice and reciprocity in Aristotle's political philosophy / Kazutaka Inamura, Hirosaki University.
pages cm. – (Cambridge classical studies)
Includes bibliographical references and index.
ISBN 978-1-107-11094-6 (hardback : alk. paper)
1. Aristotle. 2. Political science – Philosophy. 3. Justice. 4. Political science.
I. Title.
JC71.A7153 2015
320.01′1 – dc23 2015012659

ISBN 978-1-107-11094-6 Hardback

CONTENTS

ACKNOWLEDGEMENTS

This book grew out of my PhD thesis (submitted to the Faculty of Classics, University of Cambridge). First of all, I am grateful to my supervisor, Malcolm Schofield. Supervision meetings with him are some of my best memories. He provided me with informative comments and encouraged me to develop my project on Aristotle's political philosophy. His continuing and considerable support for all aspects of my PhD life contributed immensely to my enjoyment of studying at Cambridge. I also wish to thank two examiners of my PhD thesis, Nicolas Denyer and Melissa Lane; an anonymous reader for Cambridge University Press; and two readers of the Cambridge Classical Studies series, David Sedley and Robin Osborne, all of whom offered me useful comments, criticisms and suggestions. Nick and David also kindly examined earlier versions of Chapters 5 and 6 in the reviewing processes of my PhD course. I hope that this book appropriately responds to their comments. I am also grateful to Noburu Notomi, who gave me an opportunity to concentrate on my research when I was a postdoctoral researcher of the Japan Society for the Promotion of Science at Keio University. Without his kind support, I could not have developed my research outside the Japanese context of political philosophy. Finally, I owe a deep debt of gratitude to Takashi Yamamoto. He introduced me to the study of ancient Greek philosophy and supported me during my undergraduate and postgraduate studies at Tokyo University.

Some of the materials in this book have already been published elsewhere in other forms. An earlier version of Chapter 6 was published in *History of Political Thought*, 32 (2011), and some arguments about the distribution of political authority in Chapters 2 and 3 appeared in *Polis*, 29 (2012). A concise version of Chapter 5 about civic friendship was published in the *Annual Review of the Philosophical Association of Japan*, 62 (2011). Earlier arguments about civic republicanism are partly based on my article in *The Japanese Journal of Political Thought*, 11 (2011), and arguments about citizenship education in Chapter 4 draw upon my Japanese article in *Studia Classica*, 4 (2014). My earliest idea of citizen reciprocity in Chapters 5 and 6 appeared in the *Annals of the Society for the History of Social Thought*, 34 (2010).

ABBREVIATIONS

Ath. Resp.	*Atheniensium Respublica* (*Athenian Constitution*)
DA	*De Anima* (*On the Soul*)
EE	*Ethica Eudemia* (*Eudemian Ethics*)
EN	*Ethica Nicomachea* (*Nicomachean Ethics*)
HA	*Historia Animalium* (*History of Animals*)
Met.	*Metaphysica* (*Metaphysics*)
MM	*Magna Moralia*
PA	*De Partibus Animalium* (*On the Parts of Animals*)
Pol.	*Politica* (*Politics*)
Rhet.	*Rhetorica* (*Rhetoric*)
Top.	*Topica* (*Topics*)

All the references to page, column and line numbers of the Aristotelian texts, except for the *Athenian Constitution*, are based on Bekker's edition. Similarly, references to Plato follow the pagination of Stephanus.

CHAPTER 1

ARISTOTELIAN POLITICAL THEORIES IN A LIBERAL DEMOCRACY

1.1 Aristotle and present-day 'Aristotelians'

In this book, I shall examine the characteristics of Aristotle's political philosophy with reference to his political works, such as the *Politics*, the *Nicomachean Ethics* and the *Eudemian Ethics*. In particular, it will address the problem of how his aristocratic way of thinking provides useful insights into the problems of political philosophy. Such problems include the distribution of political authority, the cultivation of civic virtue, the development of civic friendship and the arrangements for the economic conditions of citizens. I shall then explain the significance of Aristotle for considering the capacities, relationships and economic conditions needed for citizens to be integrated into political society and engaged in the governance of their society. Although in the past few decades Aristotle's political philosophy has become increasingly attractive to those developing democratic theories such as communitarianism, the capabilities approach and civic republicanism, I think that the original offers more useful insights into the problems of political philosophy than these 'Aristotelian' theories do. The present book therefore attempts to recapture Aristotle's original vision of politics to which present-day 'Aristotelians' have not been drawing full attention. I shall then argue for the importance of two major strains in Aristotle's thought neglected or underplayed in much contemporary writing about the *Politics*: (1) its aristocratic commitment; and (2) the key role of citizen reciprocity.

First, some scholars have tried to interpret Aristotle's political philosophy from a contemporary liberal democratic perspective, and thereby tried to make it compatible with and sympathetic towards the ideas of liberal democracy, such as human rights theory,[1] the deliberative democracy model[2] and the capabilities approach.[3] 'The democratic Aristotle', however, does not fit perfectly with Aristotle's 'aristocratic' idea that political authority should be distributed according to virtue (ἀρετή) (*Pol.* 3.9.1281a4–8).[4] Moreover, he excludes farmers, merchants and day-labourers from citizenship in an ideal polis (*Pol.* 3.5.1278a8–11, 7.9.1328b37–1329a2). It would thus seem to be a serious flaw that 'Aristotelian' scholars explore democratic theories based on Aristotle's political philosophy in spite of the fact that 'virtue' usually implies superiority, inequality and 'aristocracy'. I think that the democratic way of reading Aristotle's political works needs to be rectified not only by drawing attention to his aristocratic framework, but also by examining his theory of a mixed constitution, and showing how 'modern democracies' are actually, from Aristotle's perspective, one type of mixed constitution that needs the element of aristocratic governance to encourage ordinary citizens to participate in the deliberative and judicial processes.[5] Paradoxically, this reading of the aristocratic Aristotle will provide further fresh insights into the problems of political philosophy in democratic society, such as the distribution of political authority and the cultivation of civic virtue.

Second, I shall show how the concept of reciprocity, returning good for good (one element of the ordinary Greek view of justice, 'helping friends and harming enemies'), makes it possible for Aristotle to develop a political theory somewhat sympathetic towards democracy, even though he does not embrace the democratic idea that any free individual is entitled to participate in the political process. In Aristotle's view, the

1 Miller, *Nature, Justice, and Rights in Aristotle's Politics.*

2 Yack, *The Problems of a Political Animal.*

3 Nussbaum, 'Aristotelian social democracy', and more recently Nussbaum, *Creating Capabilities.*

4 As to the text of the *Politics*, I have followed Ross (ed.), *Aristotelis Politica*, unless stated otherwise. About translations, I have regularly consulted Reeve (trans.), Aristotle, *Politics*.

5 In *A Democracy of Distinction*, Jill Frank leaves this task aside and calls what Aristotle means by 'aristocracy' 'a democracy of distinction'. Clifford Bates looks not to Aristotle, but Polybius, who in his view originates the idea of a mixed constitution (see his *Aristotle's 'Best Regime'*).

reciprocal equality of governing and being governed in turn is the most important condition for the promotion of civic friendship among citizens. Furthermore, the concept of reciprocal equality enables us to acknowledge the priority of the civic, political relationship over other social or family relationships. This is because in Aristotle's view the citizens' reciprocal relationship of governing and being governed makes it possible for them to cultivate civic virtue and achieve full rationality or be open to 'reason' as practical wisdom instructs. I shall then show how extensive modification of the concept of democracy away from simple majority rule, or the sovereignty of the people, towards reciprocal equality in governing and being governed in turn is needed for us to recognise Aristotle's view of how to make a political system workable from ethical, political and economic perspectives. A focus on reciprocal equality, thus, reflects the key elements in his texts and enables us to offer a more realistic view of a civic relationship than the ones given by present-day 'Aristotelian' political theories.

In order to make clearer these crucial issues in Aristotle's political philosophy, I shall first describe what problems present-day 'Aristotelian' scholars raise in democratic theory and how they develop their political theories on the basis of Aristotle's political philosophy. As mentioned above, there have been three celebrated movements of thought that have attempted to use his political philosophy: communitarianism, the capabilities approach and civic republicanism. These three versions of 'Aristotelian' theory deal with the problems of political philosophy by exploring, respectively, Aristotle's conception of virtue with regard to the importance of a particular social community (communitarianism), the purpose of political distribution (the capabilities approach) and the significance of political participation (civic republicanism). None of these positions denies the importance of basic liberties, such as freedom of speech and assembly, liberty of conscience and freedom of thought. However, they raise questions about the liberal view of the role of society, the principle of distributive justice and the liberal valuation of political participation. In the scholarly literature on Aristotle's *Politics*, these 'Aristotelian' theories have been criticised, in that they depart from Aristotle himself, but I think that more constructive criticisms need to be made, by our considering whether these theories fully exploit Aristotle's arguments for developing political philosophy.

I shall clarify how these theories use Aristotle's conception of virtue to offer alternatives to modern liberal democratic theories and how they depart from Aristotle himself. Although present-day 'Aristotelian' scholars recognise some differences between Aristotle's and their own theories, they think that some essential elements in his political philosophy serve as a basis for their theories. As mentioned above, this book hopes to bring out the theoretical interest of Aristotle's original thoughts that present-day 'Aristotelian' scholars have not been illuminating fully. To this end, in what follows my first step will be to sketch what elements in his political philosophy have been treated as useful for developing political philosophy, and to point out how recent literature on the *Politics* does not adequately face the problem of reconciling the democratic elements excavated from Aristotle's text with his aristocratic commitment.

1.1.1 Communitarianism

Communitarian theorists find Aristotle's political theory attractive as promising a way out of the difficulty they perceive with modern moral theories and as enabling us to acknowledge the importance of an ethical community. In particular, they criticise the Kantian liberal understanding of the self, since it abstracts the self from any contingent characteristic and even from any particular understanding of human ends. I shall illustrate this point through Alasdair MacIntyre's arguments, since he is one of the most influential communitarians who rely on the tradition of Aristotle's ethics.

According to MacIntyre, there are three elements in ethical theories that serve to make the standard they propose intelligible:[6] (1) the concept of untutored human nature, or

[6] MacIntyre, *After Virtue*, 51–61.

man-as-he-happens-to-be; (2) human-nature-as-it-could-be-if-it-realised-its-*telos*; and (3) the concept of the precepts of rational ethics to instruct the transition from (1) to (2). Ethical theorists usually consider how to make the transition from (1) to (2). In this sense, they presuppose a certain account of the essence of man, or human *telos*, which is the purpose of this transition. In antiquity, reason plays this role in instructing us about both how to figure out our true essence and how to reach it. Modern moral theorists, such as Kierkegaard, Kant, Diderot, Hume and Smith, however, no longer assume that reason can play a role in identifying the essence of a human being. In their views, reason becomes calculative and accordingly can speak only of means, or how effectively to achieve an arbitrarily determined end, not of an end itself. Anti-Aristotelian science contributes to the rejection of the teleological role of reason, since it restricts the capacity of reason as fitted only for the logical assessment of the theories claiming to explain facts. The rejection of the idea of a human *telos* discernible by reason in modern moral theories then leaves two elements, an account of untutored human nature and a particular content for morality. These two, however, do not in general have a harmonious relationship with each other. In other words, the precepts of morality are likely to be ones that untutored human nature tends to disobey. In this sense, the project of modern moral theories was destined to be unsuccessful, since such theories attempted to seek a rational basis for their content of morality in an understanding of untutored human nature, as, for example, in the nature of desire or pleasure, without any account of human essence.

Against what MacIntyre regards as the unsuccessful project of modern moral theories, there are, he suggests, two alternatives – Aristotle and Nietzsche. MacIntyre criticises Nietzsche because the Nietzschean Man, the man who transcends, cannot find any good in society, but only within himself, by establishing the standard and authority of good.[7] This is because the Nietzschean Man transcends any social relationships and

[7] Ibid., 256–63.

activities from which 'objective' values are usually derived. According to MacIntyre, to cut oneself off from shared activities means to prevent oneself from finding any objective values outside oneself. John Rawls is taking the same line as Nietzsche when he assumes that any agreement about the good life is no longer expected to be made from a public standpoint. Furthermore, according to the liberal understanding of the self, I am what I myself choose to be. The self can always put in question what seem to be the merely contingent social features of existence, such as the membership of one's own family and a particular city in a particular time. This self cannot find any historically and socially meaningful role, which is what for MacIntyre provides the *telos* of an individual and explains the good for an individual.[8]

Instead, MacIntyre proposes that we need to return to the tradition of Aristotle's ethics, which he regards as representative of a long, continuing tradition of western ethical theories, and from which we can restore the context in which it becomes possible to understand how modern moral beliefs take the form they do.[9] In particular, MacIntyre explores the socialised element of virtue in order to identify the *telos* of a human being: in his view, what is good for an individual depends on the character of the narrative that provides his or her life with its unity. This narrative is always embedded in the story of those communities from which individuals derive their identity. In other words, the self has to find its moral identity through its membership in communities, such as family, neighbourhood, tribe and city. Human virtue then plays an important role in sustaining the social and historical community, which provides an individual's life with social and historical meaning. MacIntyre

[8] Charles Taylor also thinks that the essential characteristic of modern liberalism resides in the freedom to choose one's own form of life. In this view, no choices can be judged morally better or worse, and our obligation to belong to or sustain society, or to obey its authorities, is seen as being derived from our consent; Taylor, 'Atomism', 187–90, 196–7. Michael Sandel also characterises this liberal understanding of an individual as 'the unencumbered self', a self prior to and independent of purposes and ends, in his 'The procedural republic and the unencumbered self'.

[9] MacIntyre, *After Virtue*, 146.

therefore finds the asset of virtue in its capacity to preserve the tradition of morality.[10]

This understanding of the socialised element of virtue comes from MacIntyre's communitarian treatment of Aristotle's political philosophy.[11] According to MacIntyre, what Aristotle has in mind as civic friendship is virtue-friendship, not pleasure- or advantage-friendship. Citizens' relationships in a polis are considered to consist of a shared recognition of, and concern for, good. In this view, a political community is a common project of creating the life of the city and sustaining moral unity. MacIntyre thus emphasises the moral unity of a political community, from which an individual derives his or her identity. Although he casts doubt on Aristotle's project of identifying the essence of a human being in metaphysical terms,[12] he asserts that the essence of an individual can be defined within a historical and social context, so that the individual can find an objective standard of good.

There are, however, serious doubts among Aristotelian scholars as to whether we can use Aristotle's political philosophy as an intellectual resource for developing a communitarian theory. For example, Richard Kraut points out that what Aristotle regards as the ultimate arbiter of values and standards is not the community or tradition that citizens belong to, but rather the good without any qualification. In this view, a community abandons its own earlier practices when it realises how defective they are, and accordingly 'rational criticism brings about social change'. To be sure, Kraut argues, Aristotle may be called 'a communitarian', in that, in Aristotle's view, citizens need to be concerned not only with their own private

10 Concerning 'the socially and historically defined self', see ibid., 216–25, and Taylor, 'Atomism', 209.

11 MacIntyre, *After Virtue*, 155–9.

12 Ibid., 163, where MacIntyre states that 'any adequate generally Aristotelian account must supply a teleological account that can replace Aristotle's metaphysical biology'. Richard Kraut explains differences between Aristotle and modern evolutionary theory: Aristotle believes in the fixity and eternality of species, while evolutionary theory does not. Modern biology 'replaces the notion of what is good for an organism with that of its fitness, and fitness plays a purely explanatory role as a theoretical construct of evolutionary biology'; Kraut, *Aristotle*, 89–92.

interests, but also their fellow citizens' good lives, and a polis should play a larger role in cultivating citizens' character than does the political community we nowadays envisage. Their communal relationships are, however, not formed through an emotional, intimate friendship, but by sharing a single conception of the good and a single education.[13]

Bernard Yack also criticises communitarians (and civic republicans) because they lay very strong emphasis on the unity of a political community in which a consensus of moral beliefs is achieved. In his view, communitarians think that an individual cannot be privately happy when the state is afflicted and therefore embrace the idea of a 'communion', the active submergence of an individual's identity in the collective identity. Yack, however, argues that Aristotle's ideas of a political community include more serious possibilities of conflict than communitarians envisage. In defining a human being as a political animal, Aristotle implies that human beings form a political community based not on the consensus, or substantive agreement, regarding what is good and bad and what is just and unjust, but on 'reasoned speech and discussion'. What it means to be a political animal is, Yack argues, that citizens hold each other 'accountable' to the standard of political justice.[14] These debated standards bind citizens together even in large democratic republics in the modern world. In this sense, Yack thinks, Aristotle's political philosophy is useful not only in as small a community as an ancient polis, but also in a modern nation-state consisting of a large population with an extensive territory.[15]

MacIntyre, however, also admits that there is a serious possibility of conflict in a community and does not treat the standards of a community or tradition as the ultimate arbiter of ethical values. First, he is not reluctant to acknowledge

[13] Kraut, *Aristotle*, 353–6. Andrés Rosler also offers the same type of criticism of communitarianism as Kraut, in his *Political Authority and Obligation in Aristotle*, 167–77.

[14] Yack, *The Problems of a Political Animal*, esp. 51–71.

[15] Ibid., 71–85, for the applicability of Aristotle's political theory to a modern nation-state.

the role of conflict in ethics. He argues that conflict in Greek tragedy, such as that between Antigone and Creon, is 'the conflict of good with good embodied in their encounter prior to and independent of any individual characteristics', and regards highly the role of conflict in helping us understand the context of virtue and learn what our purposes are.[16] Next, MacIntyre's treatment of Aristotle's dialectic is not necessarily communitarian. In this view, the ultimate standards are justified in so far as they have vindicated themselves as superior to their historical predecessors by surviving the process of dialectical questioning.[17] In other words, progress in rational enquiry means not only transcending local and partial points of view, but also becoming able to explain how things appear to be from such local and partial points of view by appealing to how they really are.[18] MacIntyre therefore does not necessarily embrace the values that people hold without reflection in a local community.

MacIntyre also recognises the problems of using Aristotle's ethical theory in a different context. Aristotle's ethics is intended to formulate ethical values that citizens share in the polis. The social practice Aristotle has in mind is the practice of the ancient, relatively small city. There is, however, no longer a polis in our contemporary society. Accordingly, it is pointless applying Aristotle's ethics in a different context, although Florentine and Venetian Aristotelians of the fifteenth and sixteenth centuries did not find it difficult to use it, because they inhabited city-states, which were relatively similar entities to the ancient polis. MacIntyre then concludes that present-day Aristotelian theorists need 'to give an account of what kind of practice it is that, after the *polis* has disappeared, is able to supply the social context required for an Aristotelian ethics and politics'.[19]

16 MacIntyre, *After Virtue*, 163–4.
17 MacIntyre, *Whose Justice? Which Rationality?*, esp. 7–8, 360.
18 MacIntyre, 'Moral relativism, truth and justification', 68–73.
19 MacIntyre, 'Rival Aristotles: Aristotle against some renaissance Aristotelians', 5.

MacIntyre provides a basic outline of the social context that should be presupposed by present-day Aristotelian theory.[20] In an Aristotelian community, there must be sufficient agreement about goods and their rank ordering to provide shared standards for rational deliberation, although, of course, disagreements and conflicts can be allowed occasionally. Unlike the societies of modernity, MacIntyre thinks, this community requires a certain degree of agreement about moral standards in order to make public deliberation possible. Second, an Aristotelian community must be a small-scale local community in which people can call on one another to give an account of their views, so that shared deliberation is effective in decision-making. This type of community is not compatible with the centralised, large-scale nation-state and large-scale market economy, but it may be exemplified even in present-day societies in the form of various communities, such as households, farming cooperatives, schools or small towns.[21] Third, the practices of an Aristotelian community presuppose shared standards of rational justification that are independent of the de facto interests and preferences of its members. Importantly, MacIntyre rejects any notion of civic unity arising from some shared ethnic, religious or cultural inheritance, unlike other communitarians who treat cultural resources as essential for forming their identity. He then develops a theory of rational deliberation that can reach an agreement over cultural boundaries with reference to Aristotle's dialectic. In short, MacIntyre puts his hope in the establishment of the small community in which people can deliberate about ethical values publicly in a dialectical way.[22]

[20] MacIntyre, 'Rival Aristotles: Aristotle against some modern Aristotelians', 39.

[21] MacIntyre suggests the first and second points already in the conclusion of *After Virtue*, esp. 263, where he states 'what matters at this stage is the construction of local forms of community within which civility and the intellectual and moral life can be sustained through the new dark ages which are already upon us'.

[22] For the theoretical background of MacIntyre's arguments in detail, see Knight, *Aristotelian Philosophy*. Other philosophical works from a communitarian perspective are Walzer, *Spheres of Justice* and Taylor, *Philosophy and the Human Sciences*, although Michael Walzer takes a step towards liberalism in his 'The communitarian critique of liberalism', 96–112. Bernard Williams, in common with the communitarians, draws attention to the historical and cultural conditions

1.1.2 Capabilities approach

Martha Nussbaum's 'capabilities approach' is a particularly influential research programme not only in the interpretation of Aristotle's theory of distributive justice, but also in economics and development studies.[23] This approach takes the same line as communitarian theories, since it holds that Aristotle's conception of virtue gives us the objective standard of ethical goodness. Nussbaum, however, criticises communitarian interpretations because they are likely to lead us towards relativism, the view that the standard of ethical goodness can be valid only within a local community. In her view, communitarian theorists rely on the tradition and practices of local communities, which do not establish any universal criterion for human good.[24] By contrast, the capabilities approach aims to define a universally acceptable criterion for human good on the basis of 'grounding experiences' and 'our common humanity'. Although she admits that basic human experiences are interpreted differently from culture to culture, she argues that there must be common features of humanness across various societies, such as morality, dietary requirements, the negative response to bodily pain and a sense of fellowship with other people.[25] In particular, she stresses the ability of practical reasoning or choice, which plays an architectonic role in shaping human life, and regards it as the most essential characteristic of humanness.

Nussbaum refers to Aristotle's conception of the good or virtuous life to clarify this essential characteristic of humanness

of ethical beliefs, but he himself rejects classification as a communitarian because of his consciousness of the diversity of ethical beliefs in his 'Pluralism, community and left Wittgensteinianism', 29–39. See also Williams, 'Replies', 222, n. 19. For further debates between communitarianism and its critics, see Rasmussen (ed.), *Universalism vs. Communitarianism*, and for the relationship between Rawls and communitarians, see Mulhall and Swift, 'Rawls and communitarianism', 460–87.

[23] In her *Creating Capabilities*, 18, Nussbaum prefers the plural expression 'capabilities approach' to the singular 'capability approach', to emphasise the plurality of the important elements for measuring people's quality of life.

[24] For her criticism of communitarian theories, see Nussbaum, 'Non-relative virtues', 242–4.

[25] Concerning her concept of 'common humanity', see ibid., 263–6.

and thereby develop her social democratic theory of distributing resources. In particular, she draws inspiration from Aristotle's ideas that human happiness is involved with the exercise of the capacity for intellectual and ethical virtues, and that the aim of politics is to maintain the social environment in which people are able to live such a virtuous life. Based on these ideas, she stresses that we need a particular understanding of human happiness to distribute various resources in a community, and that human happiness is contingent upon the achievement of various human capabilities. Capabilities are to be understood as a particular set of basic 'functions' that a single person is able to develop, such as being in good health, having self-respect, thinking critically and taking part in a familial or social community.[26] When people are capable of achieving such functions, the social environment is in accordance with basic social justice. Politics should thus provide the social conditions in which people have opportunities or substantial freedom to achieve such a set of human functions at least up to some appropriate threshold level. In this respect, Nussbaum's list of capabilities is intended to suggest the general minimum requirements of social justice.

Nussbaum's social democratic ideas are based on her complaints about modern liberal political philosophy. She aims to define 'good' in more detail than liberals such as John Rawls or Ronald Dworkin do, and she criticises them for tending to treat income and wealth as indices of human happiness and for not recognising that those resources have a different impact on the people who receive them according to the conditions in which they live. For example, a person with a disability needs a greater amount of goods than other people in order to walk (one of the basic human functions). This is a case where we need to distribute unequal amounts of resources in order to maintain a social environment where all equally can walk. Liberals regard the good as an utterly subjective thing and accordingly

[26] Nussbaum enumerates ten central capabilities in her *Creating Capabilities*, 33–4, and *Frontiers of Justice*, 76–8. For its earlier version, see Nussbaum, 'Aristotelian social democracy', 70–1.

cannot socially assess how 'things' affect human happiness. Even if Rawls's 'primary goods' are equally distributed, the conditions under which people can exercise their functional capabilities will remain unequal. A theory of political distribution thus needs to draw attention to the 'persons' who receive the 'things' as well as the 'things' themselves, so that each and every person can exercise human functional capabilities up to some appropriate threshold level. Nussbaum's capabilities approach therefore raises a problem in the liberal understanding of good: liberals do not develop a theory of political distribution that can establish substantial freedom for human happiness.[27]

Nussbaum, however, is not proposing any radical abandonment of liberal political thought. In fact, she is anxious to give an account of how her ideas of human happiness fit in with the fundamental principle of modern liberal democracy. This is because, in accordance with its basic principle, modern liberal democracy cannot force people to comply with any particular idea of the good life that a government has decided upon, but rather assumes that individuals have the right to choose their own way of life.[28] Her strategy is to focus on the capacity for choosing, so that her 'social democracy' allows room for people's liberty. Repeatedly, Nussbaum stresses the ability of 'choice' as the most essential element in human functioning,[29] thereby making clear the role of a government as providing and maintaining the social environment where people are capable of choosing their own way of life. She then concludes that the

[27] For her criticisms of liberals, see Nussbaum, 'Nature, function, and capability', 150–5, 'Aristotelian social democracy', 53–62, and *Frontiers of Justice*, 164–8. More recently, in her *Frontiers of Justice*, 176–9, however, Nussbaum is somewhat sympathetic towards Rawls's theory of justice, in so far as, in her view, both her capabilities approach and Rawls's conception of justice as fairness embody the moral idea of human dignity.

[28] In his *A Theory of Justice*, 448, Rawls says: 'In a well-ordered society, then, the plans of life of individuals are different in the sense that these plans give prominence to different aims, and persons are left free to determine their good, the views of others being counted as merely advisory.'

[29] Nussbaum, 'Aristotelian social democracy', 80–6, 'Nature, function, and capability', 179–84, and 'Aristotle on human nature and the foundations of ethics', 118–20.

Aristotelian conception of goodness is open enough for people to make what Aristotle would allow as appropriate choices in a number of different ways.[30]

However, present-day Aristotelian scholars have been offering two types of criticism of Nussbaum's emphasis on the faculty of choice. The first type draws attention to a crucial difference between Aristotle's own theory and Nussbaum's treatment of Aristotle. To be sure, Nussbaum's argument is partly in accord with Aristotle's own view, since he mentions that 'choice (προαίρεσις)' is one of the defining characteristics of humans that other animals do not share (*EN* 3.2.1111b8–9, *EE* 2.10.1226b21–2),[31] and because of the lack of this ability, Aristotle asserts, other animals cannot form a polis (*Pol.* 3.9.1280a32–4). The problem with Nussbaum's position is, however, that the capacity for choosing does not necessarily lead an individual to live an ethical and political life. In Aristotle's view, a licentious person (ἀκόλαστος) chooses his way of life and lives a non-ethical life consistently (*EN* 7.3.1146b22–4). Even the person in the grip of vice has the capacity for choice, but this is not the capacity that Aristotle hopes people will cultivate in a polis. In this respect, Nussbaum's argument is not in line with Aristotle's

30 Nussbaum, 'Aristotelian social democracy', 81.

31 As to the text of the *Nicomachean Ethics*, I have followed Bywater (ed.), *Aristotelis Ethica Nicomachea*, unless stated otherwise, and about its translations I have regularly consulted Irwin (trans.), Aristotle, *Nicomachean Ethics*. As to the text of the *Eudemian Ethics*, I have followed Walzer and Mingay (eds.), *Aristotelis Ethica Eudemia*, unless stated otherwise, and about its translations I have regularly consulted Inwood and Woolf (trans. and eds.), Aristotle, *Eudemian Ethics*. Concerning the relationship between these two ethical treatises, I take the standard view that the *Nicomachean Ethics* were written after the *Eudemian Ethics*, and refer to the 'common books' (*EN* 5–7 = *EE* 4–6) as part of the *Nicomachean Ethics* (although the common books seem to have belonged originally to the *Eudemian Ethics* and have been later transposed to the *Nicomachean Ethics*). The *Politics* is supposed to have been written between these two ethical treatises. For details on the relationship of these three 'political' works, see Bobonich, 'Aristotle's ethical treatises', 12–36, Kraut, *Aristotle*, 16–19, and Miller, *Nature, Justice, and Rights in Aristotle's Politics*, 22–4. I refer to the *Nicomachean Ethics* more frequently than the *Eudemian Ethics*, primarily because in the former Aristotle recognises its relevance to the *Politics* more clearly, although I refer to the *Eudemian Ethics* occasionally in order to understand his political philosophy.

arguments for people's good lives as the purpose of political governance.[32]

Second, Nussbaum's Aristotle is criticised in that she does not draw enough attention to illiberal arguments in Aristotle's proposals for regulating an individual's life. In a liberal democracy, a government is supposed to be established primarily for the protection of 'negative liberty', which means the absence of impediment to the pursuit of one's own ends. In this society, an individual should have as much liberty as is compatible with all others having the same liberty. Within the area of individual rights, citizens are allowed to do as they want, or even to do the morally wrong thing. The right to choose our own way of life is unconditional, while the obligation to sustain our society is laid on us conditionally through our consent. Aristotle, however, does not address the problem of how far a government can intervene in an individual's life, but instead makes practical prescriptions that would violate the principle of basic liberties, such as freedom of expression (*Pol.* 7.17.1336b3–17) and the freedom to choose one's occupation (*Pol.* 7.9.1328b37–1329a2, cf. 3.5.1278a8–11). Nussbaum's Aristotle of liberal temper does not fit perfectly with those illiberal elements in Aristotle.[33]

In her reply, Nussbaum thinks it necessary for present-day Aristotelian theorists to depart from the historical Aristotle

[32] Originally, Williams offers this criticism of Nussbaum's argument in his 'Replies', 198. See also Mulgan, 'Was Aristotle an "Aristotelian social democrat"?', 96–7.

[33] For this type of criticism, see Charles, 'Perfectionism in Aristotle's political theory', 202–4, and Mulgan, 'Was Aristotle an "Aristotelian social democrat"?', 94–5. Fred Miller's attempt to introduce the concept of 'rights' in Aristotle's political philosophy also obscures this crucial distinction between Aristotle's and liberal political theory. What is essential for the 'rights-based' theory is to admit an individual's liberty, which a government cannot intervene in, but has rather the duty to protect. Although Miller correctly treats Aristotle's political theory as expressing the idea of 'moderate individualism' in the sense that Aristotle's conception of an individual's happiness includes other-regarding, friendly, cooperative interests, this treatment should have prevented him from introducing the concept of 'rights', since what the 'rights-based' theory seeks is to allow people the right to choose their own way of life as they want, whether it is morally good or bad, altruistic or egoistic. See Miller, *Nature, Justice, and Rights in Aristotle's Politics*, 87–139, 194–224, 373–8. For the criticism of Miller's thesis, see Schofield, 'Sharing in the constitution', 141–59. For the origin of the concept of 'rights', see Dagger, 'Rights', 292–308. I shall argue about Miller's Aristotle in the next chapter.

concerning the issue of personal liberty at least. She endorses Rawls's 'political liberalism', so that her list of capabilities should be used not as a comprehensive philosophical doctrine, but rather as an object of 'overlapping consensus' for political purposes only. In other words, she wishes to ground her capabilities approach not on the Aristotelian, metaphysical conception of human nature that is external to people's common beliefs, but on 'a partial ethical conception that can be accepted by people who hold different metaphysical views' (although she treats Aristotle's ethics as also giving an account internal to people's common beliefs).[34] In particular, in her reply to the first type of criticism, she maintains that the appropriate political goal is not to promote a policy by which people actually exercise the capacity for moral virtue, as Aristotle himself sees it, but to provide the social environment where people are given opportunities to choose one of the human capabilities.[35] Nussbaum therefore calls the political theory she wants to develop 'Aristotelian', not 'Aristotle's', simply because she makes use of Aristotle's ideas,[36] while recognising some arguments in Aristotle as useless for modern democratic theory. To point out the conceptual and contextual differences between Aristotle and Nussbaum with regard to personal liberty is therefore not crucial for criticising Nussbaum's 'Aristotelian' theory.

Nussbaum thinks now that her capabilities approach is 'Aristotelian' in the following three ways. First, she treats the pursuit of wealth not as the appropriate goal in politics, but rather as a means for achieving human happiness. Although gross national product (GNP) per capita is supposed to be a reliable index of people's welfare in any one nation, she thinks that quality of life needs to be assessed in terms of whether people can use resources for achieving a set of human capabilities. Second, Nussbaum treats the separateness of persons as a basic

34 Nussbaum, 'Aristotelian social democracy', 91. See also *Frontiers of Justice*, 163–4.

35 Nussbaum, 'Aristotle, politics, and human capabilities', 124. For Nussbaum's distinction between function as an active realisation of one or more capabilities and capabilities as freedom or opportunities to choose one or more functions, see Nussbaum, *Creating Capabilities*, 24–6.

36 Nussbaum, 'Aristotle, politics, and human capabilities', 105–6.

fact for political thought and rejects a totalitarian or holistic idea of society, in the sense that the appropriate goal of society lies in some total or average. Just as Aristotle criticises Plato's totalitarian idea of the happiness of a city, as distinct from the happiness of an individual, so she does not treat a utilitarian overall aggregate of happiness as a proper goal of politics, but instead wishes to promote the happiness of each and every individual. Third, Nussbaum again emphasises the capacity for choice and practical reason as the most important elements for enabling people to flourish. Just as Aristotle asserts that people cannot lead flourishing lives without choosing their own way of life, she wishes to provide the social environment where people have the freedom to choose their way of life.[37] In short, Nussbaum has been developing an 'Aristotelian' social democratic theory with reference to Aristotle's key ideas of human happiness, while acknowledging that in Aristotle's political philosophy there are illiberal elements which she does not think useful for developing a political theory in contemporary liberal democracy.[38]

1.1.3 Civic republicanism

Some civic republican theorists have found in Aristotle's political philosophy a resource that enables recognition of the significance of the political participation of citizens, unlike liberalism, which places high value on negative liberty and in consequence must value the liberty of non-participation in the political process. For other such theorists, Roman republican thought has often been seen as a more significant inspiration in the historical development of civic republican thought. Thus, in the scholarly literature two types of civic republicanism are usually identified, namely, 'Aristotelian' and what might usefully be called 'Machiavellian'. As I shall explain this distinction later in the present section, both encourage citizens to be engaged with

37 Nussbaum, 'Aristotle, politics, and human capabilities', 105–6, and *Creating Capabilities*, 125–9.

38 For the details of Nussbaum's and Amartya Sen's capabilities approach, see Alexander, *Capabilities and Social Justice*.

politics, but they differ to the extent that, in order to explain the significance of political participation, 'Aristotelians' appeal to the concept of human good, while 'Machiavellians', drawing on Roman republican ideology, appeal to the concept of liberty. In what follows, I shall focus on 'Aristotelian' republicanism to see how Aristotle's political philosophy has been used and reconstructed in civic republican arguments.

Hannah Arendt's *The Human Condition* was a pioneering work of contemporary civic republicanism supporting the view that the good life of a human being resides in public life, not in private life. Her strategy was to distinguish three fundamental activities – action, work and labour – within the *vita activa*, and to identify the significance of public life based on the concept of 'action', although 'the enormous weight of contemplation in the traditional hierarchy has blurred the distinctions and articulations within the *vita activa* itself'.[39] According to this distinction, 'action' is the only activity that corresponds to the human condition of plurality and depends on the constant presence of others, while 'labour' corresponds simply to the biological process of the human body, and 'work' corresponds to the unnaturalness of human existence and provides an artificial world of things, distinctly different from all natural surroundings. Arendt elaborates the concept of 'action' by following Aristotle's idea of man as a political animal in *Politics* I.2 and asserts that 'action' is essentially related to speech, in the sense that in a polis everything should be decided through words and persuasion, not through force and violence.

Arendt also identifies the importance of public life by illustrating the difference between public and private realms in antiquity. In her view, this difference precisely corresponds to the distinction between polis and household in Aristotle: the polis is the public realm of the equal, while the household is the private realm of the unequal. The polis is the sphere of freedom, while the household is the sphere of necessity, where its members have to work for the maintenance of their life. People can participate in the public realm and enjoy freedom only by

39 Arendt, *The Human Condition*, 17.

mastering the physical and economic maintenance of life. To be free means not to be subject to the hardships of life, namely, maintenance of the individual and the survival of the species. In Arendt's view, thus, freedom is exclusively located in the public realm. Given that freedom is an essential condition for leading a good life, then a good life is also exclusively located in public life. Politics is never related to the biological process of life, while the household is managed simply for the sake of life.[40] As the word 'economy' suggests, the management of economy is the business of the household (*oikos*), not of the polis. Arendt thus draws a clear contrast between the good life and the sustenance of life, and assigns the management of economy solely to the role of the private household. Moreover, she emphasises the politicised idea of virtue: 'Excellence itself, *aretē* as the Greeks, *virtus* as the Romans would have called it, has always been assigned to the public realm where one could excel, could distinguish oneself from all others.'[41] In this view, excellence is related, by definition, to other people, before whom one can show one's excellence. Only through 'action' and 'speech' can one become the best person in the public realm. In this sense, the presence of other people is indispensable for the exercise of the capacity for virtue.

According to Arendt, however, this clear contrast between the public and private realm in antiquity was subsequently blurred because of the rise of 'society'. She offers a completely negative view of society: it demands conformism, as if its members consisted of one enormous household, which has only one interest and one unanimous opinion. It rules out the possibility of 'action' by imposing various rules and normalising people's behaviour. In Arendt's view, 'society' is the extension of the business of the household, namely, housekeeping, which ancient Greeks never considered the business of the public realm. The birth of this conformism, or the assumption that men do not 'act' in front of each other, coincided with the rise of the modern science of economics, together with statistics. When men had become 'social' beings, economics had achieved

[40] Ibid., 28–37. [41] Ibid., 49.

its scientific character by reflecting their patterns of behaviour. Arendt attributes the cause of the rise of society to the emergence of the modern, large nation-state: the larger the population becomes, the more likely it is that the social rather than the political constitutes the public realm. By contrast, she argues, ancient Greeks were well aware that the polis could survive only if the population was restricted; otherwise, a large number of citizens would inevitably develop an irresistible tendency towards despotism.[42] Presumably, here Arendt has in mind Aristotle's argument in *Politics* 7.4 that the population should be limited in such a way as to ensure that citizens know one another. By developing this argument, she wishes to remind us of Aristotle's useful insight into the significance of political life for the good life, in order to protect against the gigantic, nationwide administration of housekeeping in modern democracies.

In his *The Machiavellian Moment*, John Pocock best illustrates the intellectual history of this Aristotelian type of republican theory, especially Aristotle's influence on the early modern Italian thinkers who were concerned about the universality and stability of civic life. Pocock also recognises the importance of the public realm, though somewhat differently from Arendt, in relation to its universality. According to his treatment of Aristotle, the polis is a universal community, in the sense that it requires citizens not to be absorbed in their private lives, but to pursue and distribute the common good.[43] In this view, political participation makes it possible for citizens to be engaged in the universal activity of self-governance by taking part in the decision-making process concerning the good of citizens and contributing to the achievement of other people's values. Citizens are thus required to pursue their own particular goods, which are perishable with time, in such a way that they relate themselves to one another and look after the good of the whole polis, which is less perishable. In other words, the polis is a primary locus where citizens can enjoy the universal good beyond their own private, perishable goods, and become beings in relation with the universal.

[42] Ibid., 38–43. [43] Pocock, *The Machiavellian Moment*, 67–8.

As a basis for the citizen's relation to the republic, Pocock emphasises the political dimension of Aristotle's conception of virtue: for Pocock's Aristotle, political life is the highest form of human life except for the contemplative life. As explained above, citizens need to relate themselves to one another and to be concerned with the common good. Virtue is expected to play a role in this, namely, to make it possible for a citizen to participate in the decision-making process in which all citizens look after the good of the whole polis. Pocock describes this political dimension of virtue as 'not the heroic manhood of a ruling individual, but a partnership of citizens in a polis'.[44] In this view, virtue is not only the excellence of an individual, but needs also to have been developed in such a way that it focuses on relationships with other people. Pocock draws attention to this relational character of virtue, especially when he says 'the good of citizenship – of ruling and being ruled – consisted in a relationship between one's own virtue and that of another. It was in this sense of the mutual and relational character of virtue that only the political animal could be a truly good man.'[45]

Michael Sandel develops this civic republican position further in a more present-day context, specifically by making clear the conception of liberty that his republicanism aims to achieve. According to Sandel, what is central to republican theory is 'the idea that liberty depends on sharing in self-governance',[46] or that liberty is 'internally connected to self-government',[47] as opposed to a liberal version of liberty in the sense of an opportunity or a capacity to choose one's own ends and values. In this republican view, we are free only in so far as we participate in the public life of a free republic that controls our own fate. To be sure, this conception of liberty is not incompatible with liberal freedom, in that participation in public life is one of the elements people may choose to pursue as a way of life. Sandel, however, thinks it essential, not optional, for achieving freedom that citizens are involved in public deliberation about the common good.

[44] Ibid., 78. [45] Ibid., 74.
[46] Sandel, *Democracy's Discontent*, 5. [47] Ibid., 26.

Usually, this type of liberty as self-governance is categorised as 'positive liberty' or the 'liberty of ancients', as opposed to 'negative liberty' or the 'liberty of moderns'.[48] It is then criticised on account of the fact that the idea of positive liberty *forces* people to be engaged with politics and thereby violates the principle of negative liberty, which protects the rights of an individual in a private sphere to choose their way of life.[49] It is also criticised because it encourages citizens to be dominant masters over the whole city without considering an appropriate form of restriction on popular participation.[50] Sandel, however, thinks that treating liberty as self-governance is a remedy for the problem of liberal neutrality about the concept of goods, because liberal liberty lacks the civic resources for sustaining self-government and impoverishes political discourse by banishing moral and religious arguments from the public realm for the sake of political agreement. In his view, the liberal understanding of a citizen as an object of treatment rather than an agent of self-rule concedes from the start a certain disempowerment or loss of liberty.[51] To make matters worse, the image of the freely choosing self may be simply 'a source of consolation for the eclipse of the public'.[52]

Furthermore, Sandel prefers Aristotelian republicanism to Machiavellian republicanism, which treats political participation as instrumental to the liberty of pursuing individual

48 See Berlin, 'Two concepts of liberty', 122–34, Constant, 'The liberty of the ancients compared with that of the moderns', esp. 310–11, and Taylor, 'What's wrong with negative liberty', 211–29. Isaiah Berlin first formulates 'positive liberty' not simply as political participation, but rather as self-mastery, the control of my 'empirical', 'heteronomous' self by my 'real', 'ideal', 'autonomous' self. This 'real' self, however, can be a social whole, such as a tribe, a church or a state. According to Berlin, this self can achieve 'higher' freedom, or positive liberty, by imposing its collective will on its members. Sandel's treatment of political participation as intrinsic to liberty is therefore one application of this idea, in the sense that an individual can achieve 'higher' freedom by participating in the political process and sharing in the will of the 'real' self, or the state.

49 Berlin, 'Two concepts of liberty', 162–72.

50 Pettit, *Republicanism*, 8, 17–19. For the debates between Philip Pettit and Sandel, see Pettit, 'Reworking Sandel's republicanism', 40–59, and Sandel, 'Reply to critics', 323–7. For the outline of the debates, see Besson and Martí, 'Law and republicanism', 3–36.

51 Sandel, *Democracy's Discontent*, 23, 27.

52 Sandel, 'Reply to critics', 323.

interests in the private sphere.[53] This is because unless citizens recognise sharing in self-rule as intrinsically important for their lives, their willingness to be engaged with public deliberation may be eroded by instrumental calculations about the costs and benefits of political participation. Aristotle's *Politics* is, then, a useful resource for Sandel to offer an alternative theory, since in this book Aristotle defines the purpose of governance with reference to the good life of a citizen.[54]

'Aristotelian' republicans, however, have been criticised for their inappropriate reconstruction of Aristotle and their nostalgic vision of present-day politics. As to the first point, Mulgan casts doubt on the civic republican treatment of Aristotle by arguing that Aristotle does not identify political participation with the essential element of human happiness.[55] According to Aristotle's arguments in Book I of *EN*, human happiness is not dependent on luck, and accordingly, Mulgan argues, the loss of political authority does not rule out the possibility of achieving happiness, since political success is simply a matter of luck. While a magnanimous man gladly accepts the offers of political office and honour when they come, he does not feel any loss even when they do not come. In Mulgan's view, what Aristotle regards highly are philosophy and social life involving family and friends, rather than the combination of philosophy and politics, to which ancient Greeks traditionally attached high value. Mulgan thus stresses the non-political dimensions of virtue and concludes that Aristotle should be seen as a predecessor of the Hellenistic moral philosophers who

53 Ibid., 323–7.

54 For Sandel's evaluation of Aristotle's *Politics*, see Sandel, *Liberalism and the Limits of Justice*, xi. Sometimes Sandel is regarded as a communitarian theorist, but he says that he would not identify himself as communitarian; Sandel, *Liberalism and the Limits of Justice*, ix–xvi. Walzer finds a difference between civic republicanism and communitarianism to the extent that the former conceives of the whole country as one community of citizens while the latter conceives of the whole country as a community of communities in his 'Michael Sandel's America', 175. Concerning the basic issues of civic republicanism and in particular Aristotle's influence on civic republicanism, see Skinner, *The Foundations of Modern Political Thought*, vol. I, 69–189, and Honohan, *Civic Republicanism*, 18–29.

55 Mulgan, 'Aristotle and the value of political participation', 195–215. See also Mulgan, 'Was Aristotle an "Aristotelian social democrat"?', 97–9.

propose retreating from public life, rather than as a spokesman of republican theorists who encourage people to engage in it.

From a 'Machiavellian' position, a criticism arises as to whether we can use Aristotle's conception of the good life as a basis for developing political theory in contemporary pluralistic society, where people have a wide variety of views on the good life. The two types of civic republicanism, 'Aristotelian' and 'Roman' or 'Machiavellian', both emphasise the importance of popular participation, unlike liberalism, but they differ in their conceptions of the purpose of political participation. In 'Aristotelian republicanism', as Sandel views it, political participation itself is an intrinsic good for the happiness of an individual. In this view, political life is the privileged locus in which we can attain our essential nature and enjoy the good life. By contrast, in 'Machiavellian republicanism', which Quentin Skinner explores with reference to Machiavelli's own *Discourses* or the Roman historian Livy, the purpose of the political participation of citizens is to promote the greatness of a self-governing republic, or a free state, which is able to act according to its own will without external servitude in pursuit of its own chosen end. In this view, citizens are required to engage in public life in order to uphold the freedom of their society. In 'Machiavellian republicanism', therefore, the purpose of political participation is to enjoy as much freedom as possible in a self-governing republic.[56] From this Machiavellian perspective, Skinner argues that Aristotelian political theories 'slip back into the womb of the polis',[57] because they rely on the idea of the good life to explain the significance of political

[56] See Skinner, 'The republican ideal of political liberty', 293–309. For the historical context of Machiavelli, see Skinner, 'Machiavelli's *Discorsi* and the pre-humanist origins of republican ideas', 121–41. For a discussion of a minor difference between Skinner and Pettit, see Pettit, 'Keeping republican freedom simple', 339–56. Recently, in his *Machiavellian Democracy*, McCormick develops Machiavellian republicanism further in considering the system in which citizens can be more actively engaged with politics. Although I draw a clear contrast here between Machiavellian and Aristotelian republicanism, Machiavelli's political philosophy is greatly influenced by Aristotelian civic humanism. For this point, see Viroli, 'Machiavelli and the republican idea of politics', 143–71, and Skinner, *The Foundations of Modern Political Thought*, vol. 1, esp. 152–86.

[57] Skinner, 'The republican ideal of political liberty', 308.

participation, in spite of the fact that we live not in a small, close-knit, moral community, but in a larger, pluralistic society, where we can no longer expect to come to agreement about the idea of the good life. In reply to 'Machiavellian republicanism', therefore, present-day Aristotelian scholars need to consider what insights Aristotle's political works provide into the problems of political philosophy in relying on the concept of the good life. To this end, there is a need to examine closely how the concept of the good life is operative in Aristotle's political philosophy.

1.2 Method and terminology

The 'Aristotelian' theorists I have been briefly considering draw attention specifically to Aristotle's ideas of the virtuous or good life to develop their theories as alternatives to contemporary liberal democratic theory. In the literature on Aristotle's *Politics*, some scholars criticise these 'Aristotelian' political theories by pointing out how these three versions vary from Aristotle's *Politics*, but present-day 'Aristotelians' also recognise the differences, and, accordingly, call their own theories 'Aristotelian'. I shall offer more constructive criticism of them, by considering whether they make the best use of Aristotle's arguments for developing their theories. Although each of the three approaches I have identified captures some of the characteristics of Aristotle's political thought, they do not fully illuminate his interesting vision of politics.

In particular, I think that the original is more convincing than the present-day 'Aristotelians' in considering the tensions between equality and inequality. As mentioned above, it is contradictory that 'Aristotelian' democratic theorists use the concept of 'virtue' to revitalise modern liberal democracy in spite of the fact that 'virtue' usually implies superiority, inequality and 'aristocracy'. In fact, there are serious doubts as to whether it is possible to reconstruct Aristotle's political philosophy in democratic theory. For example, Cynthia Farrar treats Aristotle as taking an aristocratic position simply because he excludes labourers and craftsmen, who are necessary to sustain a political community, from citizenship in an ideal polis. According to Farrar, Aristotle reserves the privilege of political participation for those who have practical wisdom, in order to secure the order of society.[58] Instead, she sheds light on neglected democratic theorists such as Protagoras, in reaction to the common supposition that there were no democratic 'theorists' (only politicians) in ancient Greece and that political philosophy began with two undemocratic thinkers, Plato and Aristotle.[59] It would thus seem to be a serious flaw that 'Aristotelian' scholars explore democratic theories based on Aristotle's political philosophy without any reflection on his arguments for aristocracy. I shall therefore consider how Aristotle's 'aristocratic' commitment offers a useful way of thinking about egalitarian politics.[60]

To be sure, Aristotle supports 'democratic elements' in some arguments, such as the defence of the wisdom of the multitude in *Politics* 3.11, and the clarification of political rule as the governance of free and equal citizens in contrast to despotic and domestic rule in *Politics* 3.6. How to understand Aristotle's ambivalent attitude towards democracy is thus one of the most crucial issues in research on his political philosophy. In particular, there is a need to consider how democratic elements in Aristotle's political philosophy can be reconciled with his aristocratic framework and to identify what conceptual framework makes it possible for him to develop a political theory somewhat sympathetic towards democracy, even though he does not embrace the democratic idea that the status of being free entitles anyone to participate in the political process. I shall clarify this framework with reference to Aristotle's conception of reciprocal equality and his emphasis on the importance of a wide variety of particular experiences that ordinary citizens have. It would seem to me that this ambivalent attitude towards equality and inequality provides interesting insights into the

58 Farrar, *The Origins of Democratic Thinking*, 266–74. 59 Ibid., 1–3.

60 David Riesbeck's forthcoming monograph, *Aristotle on Political Community*, addresses this problem – especially, how Aristotle's notion of a political community is reconciled with his defence of kingship. For his showing me an early draft of his monograph, I am grateful to him.

problems of political philosophy, because Aristotle is considering how to integrate a wide variety of people into the political process within his aristocratic framework, and to keep a sense of reciprocal sharing of political governance.

There are three remarks about method and terminology it will be useful to make at this point. First, I have been using the expression 'Aristotle's political philosophy', but some scholars doubt whether there is a unitary and coherent overall theory in Aristotle's *Politics*. For example, Werner Jaeger notes that 'for centuries, ever since the *Politics* has been systematically studied, close critical examination has revealed difficulties that make it improbable, and in fact impossible, that the treatise as we have it was ever planned as a whole or sprung from a single creative act of the mind'.[61] Famously, then, Jaeger seeks to demonstrate a development in Aristotle's political thought by acknowledging that in his earlier career Aristotle wrote the *Politics*, especially Books 7 and 8, in line with a Platonic conception of an ideal polis, and in his later career developed an empirical approach to actual poleis in Books 4, 5 and 6. Richard Robinson also points out that 'the *Politics* is a collection of long essays and brief jottings pretending to be a treatise . . . It makes a far less unified impression than most of his works except the *Metaphysics*.'[62] In this view, we should not assume that there is a unitary idea of 'Aristotle's political philosophy'. Robinson clearly states that '[i]t is useless to go to him [i.e. Aristotle] for political dogma and certainty'.[63] In the literature on Aristotle's *Politics*, then, it has been seen as a crucial task to reconcile its seemingly disparate qualities with one another and illustrate the characteristics of 'Aristotle's political philosophy' as consistently as possible, even though there may be some minor discrepancies. I agree with this way of responding to Jaeger. As Fred Miller says, I also am 'not convinced that there are major inconsistencies involving fundamental principles in the *Politics* requiring the postulation of different chronological strata to explain them away'.[64]

[61] Jaeger, *Aristotle*, 263. [62] Robinson (trans.), Aristotle, *Politics*, ix. [63] Ibid.
[64] Miller, *Nature, Justice, and Rights in Aristotle's Politics*, 24. See also Schofield, 'Equality and hierarchy in Aristotle's political thought', 100–14, where he

Second, the present book will reconstruct the unitary and coherent idea of Aristotle's political works in the context of political philosophy in general, even though this traditional type of approach to classical texts has been criticised by one of the most influential groups in the subject of political thought, 'the Cambridge School'. Traditionally, in the intellectual history of politics, people have been trying to interpret the classical texts of 'great' political philosophers by considering how they address the universal, perennial problems of politics. From this vantage point, if we are too seriously concerned with the social conditions or historical contexts in which they develop their theory, we shall lose sight of their timeless wisdom and lose contact with the value of studying them. This is a view shared by a good number of present-day Aristotelian scholars besides those I have already surveyed. They also treat Aristotle's *Politics* as offering a useful vision of politics for our contemporary society. For example, Eugene Garver thinks that 'we can do better in thinking about politics through the *Politics* than we could without the help of a great mind'.[65] Jill Frank 'seeks to make available his [i.e. Aristotle's] appreciation of the tensions and complexities of the world of politics so that we might rethink and reorganize our own political ideas and practices'.[66] Although she does not intend to apply Aristotle's political thought directly to our contemporary problems, she thinks that her book on Aristotle's *Politics* offers an ancient education for our time. Aristotle's *Politics* is, thus, considered to be a good guide for our politics in its scholarly literature as well.[67]

By contrast, the Cambridge School associated with the name of Quentin Skinner has been concerned with the contexts of debates in which political philosophers wish to support, criticise or oppose contemporary arguments and develop their own

identifies some of the principal projects in the *Politics* by developing three models: the rational, the political and the sociological.

65 Garver, *Aristotle's Politics*, 14. 66 Frank, *A Democracy of Distinction*, 16.

67 For a discussion of 'the method of reconstruction', see also Miller, *Nature, Justice, and Rights in Aristotle's Politics*, 21–2.

positions in their own day. This school aims to clarify what the author was intending to do in saying what is said in the text. To put it in Skinner's terms, 'we need to grasp not merely the meaning of what is said, but at the same time the intended force with which the utterance is issued' or 'what they are *doing in* saying it'.[68] The key point in this methodology is thus to find the historical meaning of a text and consider what the author intends to accomplish in his or her political context. In this view, 'there are no perennial problems in philosophy', and accordingly '[t]here are only individual answers to individual questions, and potentially as many different questions as there are questioners'.[69] Those who support this method would, then, criticise the traditional approach to Aristotle's *Politics* for losing sight of the historical contexts of his political philosophy and abusing him to justify its own ideology in present-day debates.

There is, however, the possibility of a convergence between the traditional approach and Skinner's method. Skinner also comes to recognise the relevance and significance of classical texts for our contemporary debates when he responds to the criticism of his method: out of an antiquarian interest, the Cambridge school sees history as a series of disconnected intellectual events and accordingly can demonstrate only the historical relativity of past thoughts, not their relevance to the present problems.[70] In his reply, Skinner develops his

68 Skinner, 'Meaning and understanding in the history of ideas', 82. Although this article was originally published in *History and Theory*, 8 (1969), I refer to the most recent version of it in his *Vision of Politics*, vol. 1, since Skinner modified this article considerably in this latest version. For the outline of Skinner's methodology, see Tully, 'The pen is a mighty sword', 7–25. Taylor summarises what is crucial in this methodology as 'Read the text as action in context' in his 'The hermeneutics of conflict', 219. For minor differences between Skinner, Pocock and John Dunn in the Cambridge School, see Tarlton, 'Historicity, meaning, and revisionism in the study of political thought', 307–28. MacIntyre also develops a historical-context-based approach to ethical and political theories in his *Whose Justice? Which Rationality?*, 1–11, 349–69, especially 9, where he argues that all doctrines 'have to be understood in terms of historical context'.

69 Skinner, 'Meaning and understanding in the history of ideas', 88.

70 See Mandell, 'The history of political thought as a "vocation"', 120–6, Rée, 'The vanity of historicism', 978–80, Tarlton, 'Historicity, meaning, and revisionism in

theory by arguing that his method makes it possible for us to situate our own system of beliefs in a particular historical context and consider possible alternatives to contemporary political theories. In particular, by incorporating Hans-Georg Gadamer's theory of hermeneutics, Skinner maintains that his method enables us 'to view our own form of life in a more self-critical way, enlarging our present horizons instead of fortifying local prejudices'.[71] In other words, reflections on the historical, alien character of beliefs we find in classical texts provide us with the potential to prevent our currently dominant political theory, namely, liberal democratic theory, from degenerating into uncritically accepted ideologies and thereby help us to obtain alternative views of the values embodied in our present life.[72]

I shall develop this line of hermeneutic method further not only by drawing attention to the historical contexts of Aristotle's political philosophy, but also by comparing it with modern political theories. A crucial insight of hermeneutics is that, although it is inevitable that we read classical texts first on the basis of our prejudices, reading classical texts creates the possibility of reinterpreting our conceptual framework in unfamiliar terms. In other words, we can take an opportunity to see the characteristics of both our own and the texts' conceptual framework, if we come to recognise differences between our and their 'horizons'. We then need to confront our own language of explanation with the language of the texts, and explore how our conceptual framework has been formed in the historical process and what alternatives the classical texts offer us. In particular, it would seem very informative to consider what Aristotle *would be likely to think* about modern 'Aristotelian' political theories, since this reflection enables us to illustrate

the study of political thought', 307–28, and Wokler, 'The professoriate of political thought in England since 1914', 134–58. For the existence of perennial problems in political philosophy, see Bevir, 'Are there perennial problems in political theory?', 662–75. In his 'Political theory and historiography', esp. 939, Howard Warrender thinks that Hobbes's political philosophy has relevance for all time.

71 Skinner, 'Interpretation of the understanding of speech acts', 125.

72 See Skinner, *Liberty before Liberalism*, 116–20, and Skinner, *Vision of Politics*, vol. 1, 6–7.

the positive characteristics of Aristotle's thought as well as the ideology of modern political thought.[73]

To that end, I am going to examine the differences in meaning between the terminology of Aristotle and that of modern political philosophy. This is, first, because political terms such as 'democracy' used in modern political theories have changed their meaning drastically since ancient Greek times, and, second, because modern political terms such as 'rights', 'constitution' and 'sovereignty' are theoretical terms, which Aristotle does not develop fully. If we use these modern terms to interpret his political philosophy without reflection, then we tend to attach an anachronistic conceptual framework to him. For this reason, it is very useful to compare Aristotle's and modern 'Aristotelian' political theories and thereby clarify what Aristotle has in mind in using his terminology. It is usually misleading for both present-day political theorists and classicists to analyse Aristotle's texts without reflecting on the differences between ancient and modern terminology. In this respect, a dialogue between Aristotle and modern democratic theorists is needed in order to read Aristotle's texts critically and correctly, as well as to recognise the unexamined assumptions of modern democratic theories. I shall therefore compare Aristotle's use of such terms as 'democracy', 'citizenship' and 'friendship' with modern political philosophers' use of those terms.

Third, as an example of terminology, a brief remark about the concept of 'polis (πόλις)' is in order. Usually, this Greek word is translated as 'state', but the present book transliterates it as 'polis'. This is, first, because the English word 'state'

[73] For a hermeneutic approach, see Gadamer, *Truth and Method*, esp. 235–45, R. Rorty, *Philosophy and the Mirror of Nature*, 357–65, and Taylor, 'The hermeneutics of conflict', 218–28. Taylor criticises Skinner's methodology by maintaining that to identify what the author of a text is doing is not enough, since we need to ask 'what our language of explanation entails about the truth of our subjects' beliefs'. In his reply, Skinner integrates hermeneutics into his methodology in his 'Interpretation of the understanding of speech acts', 124–7. With reference to Dilthey and Gramsci, Joseph Femia also develops a type of hermeneutic approach in arguing that we need to examine historical trends, make trans-historical comparisons, use general conceptions and draw out implications in order to uncover the historical meaning of past thought; Femia, 'An historicist critique of "revisionist" methods for studying the history of ideas', 156–75.

is a theoretical term, which was used by seventeenth-century political theorists, especially Thomas Hobbes, with a particular intent. According to Skinner, the modern concept of 'state' was originally developed when the need became pressing to detach sovereignty from the political authority of an individual ruler. In this view, the authority of a 'state' is a distinct form of political authority that is the only source of coercive power to regulate the whole community, and the ruler's duty is then to maintain this state apparatus, within which he is simply entrusted to administer political affairs. Furthermore, the modern concept of a 'state' is detached from the authority of the whole society or the people. In this view, a 'state' is something more than the expression of the power of the governed and is instituted not through trust, but by the absolute transfer of the people's sovereignty. Hobbes selectively uses this term, 'state', against the neo-scholastic understanding of political authority as vested in the people, in order to introduce a completely impersonal power distinct from both the ruler and the ruled, and to establish a single supreme authority to secure a people's peace against outside enemies. The crucial point of the modern concept of a state therefore lies in its impersonal character.[74] Because of this understanding of 'state', if we translate πόλις as 'state', Aristotle's basic claim is hardly intelligible from a modern perspective: his basic thesis would then be that a 'state' is an ethical community where citizens have a shared understanding of good and cultivate their virtue.[75] The 'impersonal' form of political authority cannot be expected to play this role, and, if it does, the coercive power of a modern state is never capable of enduring. It is, therefore, better not to use this theoretical term to understand ancient Greek political philosophy.[76]

74 Skinner, 'The state', 90–131.

75 Stephen Holmes harshly criticises the attempt to 'humanise' a modern-day state with a unifying purpose based on ancient Greek political philosophy, since a modern-day society presupposes a high degree of social differentiation, or a wide range of autonomous areas independent of politics; Holmes, 'Aristippus in and out of Athens', 1–26.

76 For differences and similarities between 'polis' and 'state', see Cartledge, *Ancient Greek Political Thought in Practice*, 11–24, and Hansen, *Polis and City-State*. Importantly, Hansen argues that in ancient Greece too there was a distinction

There is, however, a more positive reason for drawing attention to the role of the polis. The above explanation of the development of the concept of a 'state' shows that in the study of ancient Greek political philosophy, we need to analyse the role of politics at the level of the political ruler and the ruled. In particular, I shall focus on the element of 'action' in governance, and consider the necessary conditions for citizens to act or exercise political authority in a proper way and develop a friendly, cooperative relationship among themselves. In Greek, the word for political authority or public office (ἀρχή) literally means the 'beginning' of action. To 'govern' and 'be governed' is thus from this point of view another way of expressing the active and passive elements of action. This understanding of political authority will make it possible to draw attention to the role of a benefactor as well as a beneficiary, to burdens as well as benefits, and to the precept 'from each according to their virtue' as well as 'to each according to their needs'. It would seem that the most serious predicament for distributive theory in modern liberal democracy comes from the fact that the modern state apparatus tends to separate these elements into its own domain and focuses attention on the beneficiaries of governance only. In other words, the problem with modern political theory is not only that the modern state apparatus denies the possibility of action, as Arendt points out, but also that it makes citizens think of the role of governance from a passive perspective. By contrast, Aristotle's political philosophy integrates these elements in a comprehensive way and develops a general theory of

between state and civil society, and that both 'polis' and 'state' are closely linked to the concept of 'citizen' or 'citizenship'. Therefore, he concludes that 'city-state' is the closest equivalent to 'polis' (see Hansen, *Polis and City-State*, esp. 121–3). As I shall argue in Chapter 4, however, there is an important difference between the Greek concept of 'citizen (πολίτης)' and its modern equivalent. Furthermore, as discussed, the Greek concept of polis does not include the idea of an impersonal authority distinct from people's power. As Hansen himself points out, the concept of external sovereignty (independence from foreign countries) should be dissociated from the concept of polis (see Hansen, *Polis and City-State*, 77–83). The notion of external sovereignty is, however, an important basis for Hobbes to develop the concept of 'state' associated with the notion of internal sovereignty. Hence, I think it better to draw attention to the differences between 'polis' and 'state', since a few differences are enough to outweigh many similarities in conceptual analysis.

political distribution. It would seem to me that Aristotle's political works provide useful insights into the problems of how to integrate citizens into the political process, how to cultivate the civic virtue necessary for them to lead a public life and how to promote civic friendship between them. As with communitarians and civic republicans, I think that *Politica*, a work about the *polis*, sheds a positive light on the role of a local community in integrating people into society. In this book, therefore, I shall illuminate the significance of Aristotle's political works for articulating the concept of a civic relationship and keeping up a sense of sharing in self-governance.

1.3 Synopsis of chapters

Before moving on to examine the details of Aristotle's political philosophy, I offer here an outline of each of the following five chapters and their connections.

In Chapter 2, in order to clarify the role of the conception of the good or virtuous life in Aristotle's political philosophy, I consider how Aristotle uses the Platonic alternative conceptions of a good polis and how those conceptions are related to the notion of the good life of individuals. Although many scholars, such as Nussbaum and Miller, have drawn a distinction between Plato and Aristotle in terms of totalitarianism versus individualism, I emphasise the Platonic influence on Aristotle's conceptions of a good polis. To this end, in Section 2.3 I start by examining Aristotle's theory of distributing political authority in *Politics* 3, and show that his idea of aristocratic governance is a justified way of promoting his other idea that the purpose of political governance is to ensure the good life of people. In Section 2.4 I examine Aristotle's analogy between an individual and a polis in *Politics* 7, and show that the individual–polis analogy makes it possible to identify the goodness of a polis by explaining that a polis is good in so far as it performs its task, just as an individual is good in so far as he performs his own task. Overall in this chapter, I illuminate Aristotle's aristocratic notion of a good polis, according to which the distribution of political authority, property and other goods is arranged.

In Chapter 3 I address the issues of how Aristotle's 'democratic' arguments can be reconciled with his aristocratic framework, and how his theory of a mixed constitution provides useful insights into the problem of 'democracy'. To this end, in Section 3.2, with reference to Aristotle's definition of a constitution or political system (πολιτεία) in *Politics* 3.6 and 3.7, as well as his descriptions of constitutional change in *Politics* 4.13 and 6.7, I point out the difference between his typology of political systems and its modern equivalent – he classifies a political system in terms of who governs a polis or who actually exercises political authority, while modern political theories classify it in terms of who receives the benefit of governance or who is entitled to be a recipient of a governmental policy. For this reason, I argue that 'modern representative democracy' is not 'democracy' according to Aristotle's framework, but rather a mixed political system with monarchy, aristocracy, oligarchy and democracy. In Section 3.3 I examine in detail Aristotle's theory of the mixed constitution with reference to a crucial passage in *Politics* 3.12 (1283a14–22), as well as his general descriptions of a polity in *Politics* 4. In Section 3.4 I argue that Aristotle's arguments for the wisdom of the multitude in *Politics* 3.11 embody the idea of the mixture of democracy and aristocracy, to the extent that he identifies the virtue or merit of the multitude as a group to integrate them into some processes of deliberation and assessment. In Section 3.5 I demonstrate that modern political theories will find Aristotle's mixed constitution still useful in its implication that institutional arrangements in government need to be assessed in terms of whether they integrate the elements of governance properly, and not necessarily whether they mix various types of social class into the political system.

In Chapter 4 I turn to the issue of how Aristotle's political philosophy provides a relatively positive account of democratic or equal relationships between citizens. To this end, in Section 4.2 I examine Aristotle's conceptions of citizenship and civic virtue in *Politics* 3.1 and 3.4. In particular, although some

Aristotelian theorists identify the virtue of a citizen with the capacity for being actively engaged with politics, I find its point in enabling its possessor to exercise the faculty for both governing and being governed. In Section 4.3 I illustrate further the importance of civic virtue by exploring the difference between the virtue of a ruler and that of a servant in *Politics* 1.13, and examining the rule of law in *Politics* 3.16. I then argue that, in Aristotle's framework, the polis is more important than the family, because people can cultivate human virtue and achieve perfect rationality by establishing the reciprocal relationship of governing and being governed in a polis. In Section 4.4 I point out the important differences between Aristotle and 'Aristotelian' civic republicans: where Aristotle finds reciprocal equality important for the cultivation of an individual's virtue, Arendt finds no-rule, neither to rule nor to be ruled, essential for civic relationships; Pocock introduces the concept of the universal, imperishable good, which we do not find in Aristotle; and Sandel draws our attention solely to the active agency of governance.

In Chapter 5 I illustrate Aristotle's framework for the equal relationship between citizens through the lens of the concept of civic friendship. In Section 5.2 I examine his conception of friendship in general as depicted in *EN* 8 and 9, and point out that 'sharing' and 'reciprocity' are key conditions for forming friendship. In Section 5.3 I demonstrate that Aristotle applies this framework to his arguments in the *Politics*, as, for example, in defining a 'citizen' as one who shares deliberative and judicial authority (3.1.1275b18–20), and with regard to political governance as the reciprocal exchange of governing and being governed in turn (2.2.1261a30–7, 3.6.1279a8–16). I then refer to a crucial passage in *EE* 7.10 (1242b27–31), to point out that Aristotle clearly defines civic friendship as a reciprocal relationship between citizens for looking after each other's welfare through the exercise of political authority or public services. In Section 5.4 I address the issue whether civic friendship is a virtue- or an advantage-friendship, and demonstrate that it is basically an advantage-friendship, as clearly expressed in *EE* and *EN*, although in *Politics* 3 and 7 Aristotle emphasises concern for other citizens' virtue as an important condition for forming the polis. In Section 5.5 I examine Aristotle's criticism of Plato's *Republic* in *Politics* 2.2–5 in light of the concept of civic friendship. I then find its crucial point in the fact that Aristotle considers it wrong to expect that an intimate, emotional tie among citizens will ensure the unity of a polis.

In Chapter 6 I consider how Aristotle applies the concept of reciprocity to his arguments about the exchange and distribution of goods among citizens. First, I examine his arguments about commutative justice in *EN* 5.5. Unlike a Marxian treatment, I demonstrate that Aristotle does not offer here a scientific account of the exchange of goods in a market, but defines a fair or just exchange of goods between citizens, and, with reference to a relevant passage in *EN* 9.1 (1164b6–21), I argue that he has in mind an agreement on the benefit or pleasure of the recipient as a criterion for estimating the value of a product. In Section 6.4 I point out that Aristotle's criticism of commercial activity in *Politics* 1.8–11 is based not on the concept of reciprocity or 'commutative justice', as defined in *EN* 5.5, but rather on his teleological conception of nature. I demonstrate that he criticises people's desire to promote profits, rather than the civic relationship itself, in the exchange of goods. In Section 6.5 I examine Aristotle's arguments about the distribution of goods in a polis in *Politics* 4.11 and 6.5, and point out that by means of the policy of distribution he wishes to secure the reciprocal relationship of governing and being governed in turn. In short, I conclude that reciprocal equality is the key principle that Aristotle applies to the problem of how to preserve the equal relationship of citizens.

Although each of Chapters 2–6 can stand alone in focusing on a particular topic in political philosophy, they are closely related to each other and are mutually reinforcing. Chapters 2 and 3 can be considered a pair in examining Aristotle's aristocratic commitment and considering how he proposes distributing political authority according to his conception of a good polis. The last three chapters can be considered a group in demonstrating that the concept of reciprocity is the underlying principle that Aristotle applies in examining the relationship of citizens in his arguments about civic virtue, civic friendship and the exchange of goods. Arguments in Chapter 4 connect the first pair and the last three chapters in explaining that Aristotle finds the activities of governing and being governed essential for the cultivation of virtue.

In 'Conclusions', I summarise the importance of Aristotle for political philosophy. In particular, I point out that present-day scholars can find Aristotle's political philosophy insightful for its suggestions that (1) the multitude needs to be integrated into the deliberative and judicial processes not individually but collectively, based on the premise that they have the modicum of virtue necessary for judging correctly what public officials say and do; (2) that a distribution policy needs to take into account the equality of burdens or duties, as well as that of benefit; (3) that reciprocal equality rather than the sovereignty of the people should be the key principle for democracy; and (4) that a relatively small community plays an important role in enabling citizens to share their view of justice and good and to cultivate civic virtue. The book will conclude that Aristotle's political theory enables us to develop a model for integrating a wide variety of people into the political process on a local level, thereby fostering a sense of self-governance.

CHAPTER 2

THE GOOD LIFE AND A GOOD POLIS

2.1 Ambiguity in Aristotle's conception of a good polis

How does Aristotle use the concept of the good or virtuous life in developing his political theory? As explained in Chapter 1, Aristotle's political theory has been criticised for relying on the good life – a concept about which no one can seem to agree. In this chapter, I am going to examine the role of the good or virtuous life in Aristotle's political philosophy, thereby illuminating his aristocratic commitment. In particular, I shall consider the question, controversial in the current scholarly literature on the *Politics*, how Aristotle's conception of a good polis relates to his conception of the good life. The interpretation of this issue is crucial for evaluating how individualistic or totalitarian Aristotle's political philosophy is.

As is well known, Aristotle's ethics is intended to clarify the concept of human good with which political science is concerned and which a polis should enable its citizens to attain.[1] However, he offers an ambiguous account of the goodness of a polis in *EN* 1.2:

> Even if the good is the same for a polis as for an individual, still the good of a polis appears to be a greater and more complete good to acquire and preserve. For while it is satisfactory to acquire and preserve the good even for an individual, yet it is finer and more divine to acquire and preserve it for a people and poleis. (1094b7–10)

In the wider context of this passage, Aristotle explores the highest good, which we hope to attain for its own sake, and for the sake of which we hope to attain other things. He then considers it useful for our life to clarify what this highest good is and

[1] For a discussion of the relationship between ethics and politics in Aristotle, see Burger, *Aristotle's Dialogue with Socrates*, 207–11, Schofield, 'Aristotle', 310–15, and Striker, 'Aristotle's ethics as political science', 127–41.

which science deals with this good. In his view, the highest good is the subject of the art of politics or political science, because political science is the most controlling science that defines what subject an individual should study, and to what extent. Other sciences, such as general leadership, household management or rhetoric, are subordinate to political science in that the latter determines their purposes (*EN* 1.2.1094a26–b7). In the quoted passage, Aristotle argues that the good of a polis is more desirable than that of an individual, maintaining that political science deals with the highest good. His ethics is thus intended to explore this highest good and, accordingly, is called a sort of political science (πολιτική τις) (*EN* 1.2.1094b10–11).

There are, however, two ambiguous points in the passage. First, Aristotle clearly states that the good is the same for a polis as for an individual, but he does not explain how this is so. One might think that both the good of a polis and that of an individual amount to the same good, namely, the virtuous life of individuals. In this view, the same object is good for both a polis and an individual. Others, however, might think that the polis and the individual do not necessarily have the same object as their good, but both are good simply because they take the common form of goodness. Second, Aristotle maintains that the good of a polis is a greater and more complete good to acquire and preserve than that of an individual, even though both are the same. In particular, if the same object, that is, the virtuous life, is good for both a polis and an individual, it is unclear how the good for a polis is greater and more complete than the good for an individual. How does Aristotle differentiate the good of a polis from the good of an individual while maintaining that both are the same? Even though his account of the goodness of a polis is intended to give a framework for political science, it comes across as very ambiguous at the beginning of *EN*.[2]

[2] With regard to the passage *EN* 1.2.1094b7–10, Terence Irwin points out that 'Aristotle uses the singular "people [ἔθνος]" and plural "cities [πόλεις]" because he is thinking of the Greek people in the various Greek cities. In that case, he might be referring to the ambitions of Philip and Alexander of Macedon' (see Irwin (trans.), Aristotle, *Nicomachean Ethics*, 174). This interpretation would seem true, but I

In the next section, I shall first clarify the basic principle that Aristotle envisages as embodying the conception of a good polis in relation to the good life of its people. In the literature on the *Politics*, however, it is argued that Aristotle appears to hold somewhat contradictory notions of a good polis, and that some of those notions are the Platonic relics of the ideal polis in the *Republic*. I shall then argue that the crucial issues are how Aristotle is influenced by Plato's notions of an ideal polis, and how one might reconcile the seemingly disparate qualities. Overall in this chapter, I am going to consider how Aristotle develops his theory of a good polis using Plato's ideas of a good, happy or just polis, and to illuminate the basic framework of his constitutional theory, which I shall examine in the next chapter.

2.2 Alternative conceptions of a good polis

In general, Aristotle's ethics is intended to clarify the good of an individual in order to understand the good of a polis. He identifies the highest good with 'happiness' (εὐδαιμονία)[3] in *EN* 1.4 and 1.7, and aligns it with the activity of the soul in accordance with virtue through the human function argument in *EN* 1.7. Consequently, his ethics is dedicated to illustrating the virtuous life by examining many individual virtues: courage, temperance, justice, practical wisdom, etc. The highest good in ethics is thus explored in terms of the virtuous life of an individual, not directly from the perspective of the goodness of a polis, although certainly Aristotle says that a human being is by nature political in *EN* 1.7 (1097b8–11) as well as in *Politics* 1.2. The rationale for this exploration is that politics should be primarily concerned with the cultivation of people's virtue. In *EN* 1.9 (1099b29–32), Aristotle asserts that political science is concerned with the character of citizens, to make it

shall focus on the good of a single polis to illustrate the basic framework of his political philosophy, which is primarily concerned with the social arrangements within a polis, not over the whole range of Greek cities. A passage in *Politics* 7.7 (1327b29–33) may suggest the confederation of Greek cities.

3 I translate εὐδαιμονία as 'happiness', 'well-being' or 'flourishing'. I use these expressions interchangeably. For details on this concept, see, for example, Kraut, 'Two conceptions of happiness'.

possible for them to become good and do noble actions. In *EN* 1.13 (1102a7–12), he also points out that politicians in the true sense, such as the lawgivers of the Cretans or the Spartans, have been eager to work at virtue more than anything else. He thus argues that they must study a human soul in outline (1102a18–26). In this view, the purpose of politics is to cultivate citizens' virtuous character, which contributes to their individual good. The goodness of a polis, therefore, can be attributed to the good of individuals within the polis. This view is also expressed in the *Politics*. For example, in *Politics* 3.9, Aristotle maintains that what is genuinely called a 'polis' should be concerned with the cultivation of its citizens' virtue, unlike a military alliance or a commercial association, which are only anxious not to do wrong to, or be wronged by, other people (1280b1–12). More famously, at the very beginning of *Politics* 7, in which he explores the best polis under ideal conditions, he says that it is necessary to define what a most desirable life is before exploring what the best constitution is. This is because it is appropriate for those who live in the best constitution to lead a happy life, unless something unlucky happens to them (7.1.1323a14–21). Here Aristotle is not yet sure that the best life is the same for a polis as for an individual, but treats the best polis as one that promotes the best life of its members. In the basic framework for politics, thus, he considers the goodness of a polis from the perspective of the good of a wide range of its citizens.

This aspect of Aristotle's political philosophy is best explored, as already articulated in Chapter 1, by Nussbaum's 'capabilities approach'. Although Nussbaum's 'thinking has undergone numerous shifts'[4] since the 1970s, her article 'Nature, function, and capability'[5] is still the most important source for examining how she treats Aristotle's texts and draws inspiration from them for the development of her capabilities approach, or 'social democratic' theory. In reference to

[4] Nussbaum, 'Aristotle, politics, and human capabilities', 102.

[5] I refer to this paper published in *Oxford Studies in Ancient Philosophy*, supplementary volume (1988), 145–84. A similar version of this paper is published in Patzig (ed.), *Aristoteles' 'Politik'*, 152–86.

Politics 7.2 (1324a23–5), she defines Aristotle's distributive conception (DC), which is also the key principle of her capabilities approach, as follows: 'the best political arrangement is that arrangement according to which anyone whatsoever might do best and live a flourishing [i.e. happy] life'.[6] Referencing the very beginning of *Politics* 7.1 (1323a14–19), she also argues that Aristotle's theory of good political arrangement rests upon his theory of the good human life. According to Nussbaum, these two passages suggest that the task of politics is both broad and deep:[7] broad in the sense that it is concerned with the good lives, not of a small elite, but of the population at large, and deep in the sense that it is concerned with the totality of functionings that constitute a good human life. A theorist of distributive justice therefore needs to take into account not only various resources, but also the full picture of human happiness, which is the purpose of distributing resources.

According to Nussbaum, however, Aristotle's political theory contains two alternative conceptions of a good polis in the *Politics*: the holistic conception (HC) and the whole–part conception (WP):

> HC: A political arrangement is good (or virtuous in some concrete respect) in so far as it has the same structure as goodness (or some concrete virtue) in the soul of an individual human being.
>
> WP: A political arrangement is good as a whole in so far as its citizens are (each and every one?) good as individuals.[8]

Nussbaum defines HC with reference to the text in *Politics* 7.1 (1323b33–6), where Aristotle states that 'the courage, justice and practical wisdom of a polis have the same ability and structure, by partaking in which each human being is said to be just, practically wise and moderate'.[9] WP is extracted from arguments in *Politics* 7.9, in which Aristotle attributes the goodness of a polis to that of its citizens. In *Politics* 7.13, he also clearly states that 'a polis is excellent, because the citizens who participate in the constitution are excellent' (1332a33–4). Nussbaum

[6] Nussbaum, 'Nature, function, and capability', 146–7.
[7] Ibid., 149–50. [8] Ibid., 155–6, paraphrased.
[9] Unlike Ross, I do not add 'καὶ σωφροσύνη' at line 34 and 'ἀνδρεῖος καὶ' at line 36.

identifies the following difference between DC and WP: DC tells us that the task of a polis is to make it possible for its citizens to live well, while WP considers the goodness of the polis not in terms of something it does for its people, but in terms of the qualities of the people. Although DC suggests that we should engage actively in the improvement of the lives of the population at large, WP leads to the exclusion of some citizens, such as labourers and farmers, from citizenship, because they destroy the goodness of a polis due to their lack of virtue. Nussbaum also identifies a serious inconsistency between DC and HC: according to HC, we do not need to consider the good life of each and every citizen, but simply to ensure that in some way the polis as a whole realises each of the constituents of the good life in its overall structure, whereas in WP we need to look at the happiness of an individual who participates in the government. HC is concerned solely with the whole structure of a polis, whose goodness can be defined with reference to some general feature of goodness. Nussbaum maintains that WP and HC in Aristotle's *Politics* are the Platonic relics of the ideal polis in the *Republic*, and tentatively concludes that '*Politics* VII represents a more primitive stage in Aristotle's thinking on these issues',[10] and that 'when he does sort things out more perspicuously in *Politics* II–III, in connection with his criticism of Plato, he opts on the whole for DC'.[11]

Fred Miller also explores this anti-holistic perspective of Aristotle's political philosophy. Although Miller's attempts to introduce the concept of human rights into Aristotle's political philosophy have been criticised,[12] he draws a distinction between the two respective versions of holism and individualism to analyse Aristotle's political philosophy. In Miller's view,

[10] Nussbaum, 'Nature, function, and capability', 159.

[11] Ibid., 160. Originally, Werner Jaeger argues that Books 7 and 8 of Aristotle's *Politics* are written in his earlier career, influenced by Plato's notion of an ideal polis; Jaeger, *Aristotle*, 259–92. For a discussion of the composition of the *Politics*, see Rowe, 'Aims and methods in Aristotle's *Politics*', 57–74. Nussbaum formulates these various principles of a good polis based on Williams's classic paper about alternative conceptions of a polis in Plato's *Republic*; Williams, 'The analogy of city and soul in Plato's *Republic*'.

[12] For this criticism, see Schofield, 'Sharing in the constitution', 141–59, and for my comment, see Chapter 1, n. 33.

Aristotle's political philosophy is not holistic, but individualistic, because Aristotle does not hold that a polis has an end distinct from or superior to the ends of its individual members, but rather asserts that the best polis is concerned with the ends of its individual members, that is, the perfection of its citizens' lives. Miller does, however, draw a further distinction between extreme and moderate forms of these two positions, respectively: extreme holism, moderate holism, moderate individualism and extreme individualism. Miller then treats Aristotle's political philosophy as expressing the idea of moderate individualism, in the sense that Aristotle's conception of an individual's happiness is involved with the exercise of other-regarding virtues, such as friendship and generosity. This position is different from extreme individualism, such as Robert Nozick's libertarianism, which is anxious to secure the private rights by which individuals are at least not prohibited from engaging with the activities that they regard as good for their own life. In this extreme individualism, a polis or state has only an instrumental value for individuals to attain their own private good and does not have any inherent reason for looking after the benefit of other citizens.[13] In Miller's view, Aristotle's individualism takes a moderate position in identifying other-regarding activities as an essential part of the perfection of a human being.

Nussbaum and Miller offer these individualistic accounts in order to distinguish Aristotle's political theory from Plato's. Famously, Plato's Socrates in the *Republic* does not reduce the goodness, especially justice and temperance, of a polis to the goodness of its members, but treats the structure of a polis, or the relationships between the three social classes, as crucial for establishing a good polis. For example, in the beginning of *Republic* 4, Socrates argues that just as the beauty of a statue depends not on the beauty of any particular part, such as its eyes, but rather on the proportions of the whole statue, so the happiness of a polis depends on the structure of the whole

[13] Concerning his distinction between the moderate and extreme versions of holism and individualism, see Miller, *Nature, Justice, and Rights in Aristotle's Politics*, 194–224. For his criticism of modern extreme individualism, see ibid., 373–8.

(420c–d). This analogy suggests that the happiness of a polis can be defined in terms of its whole structure, since the proportion or structure of all parts of a polis are determined not by the aggregate of the conditions of its parts, but by their relationships. Nussbaum and Miller then hope to show that Aristotle does not provide this Platonic, holistic account of a good polis, but develops an individualistic position in reducing the goodness of a polis to that of its members.[14]

In what follows, I shall argue that Aristotle does not completely abandon the Platonic conceptions of a good polis (i.e. some moderate versions of WP and HC). To be sure, just as Miller argues in reference to Aristotle's criticism of Plato's *Republic* in *Politics* 2.2–5, Aristotle does not hold the extreme version of holism, a position that Karl Popper ascribes to Plato, which suggests that an individual must make himself subservient to the interests of a whole that embodies a higher order and has a noble aim completely independent of an individual's good.[15] In general, Aristotle's political philosophy is contrasted with Plato's in terms of individualism versus totalitarianism.[16] The two philosophers also differ concerning their views of the unity of a polis, and I shall examine this point through the lens of civic friendship in Chapter 5. Certainly, however, Aristotle holds some moderate Platonic ideas, such as a moderate version of holism wherein the goodness

[14] In his recent book on Aristotle's *Politics*, Kevin Cherry also argues that the key characteristic of Aristotle's political philosophy lies in defining the purpose of political governance as promoting the perfection of its citizens. Although I think it not plausible to draw a clear contrast between Aristotle and the Eleatic stranger in Plato's *Statesman* in terms of whether they regard politics as being primarily concerned with the good life or the preservation of life, Cherry maintains that Aristotle's view of the purpose of politics enables us to reflect more on the practices of our politics; Cherry, *Plato, Aristotle, and the Purpose of Politics*.

[15] See Popper, *The Open Society and its Enemies*, vol. 1, 86–119, esp. 90 and 107, where Popper argues that Plato considers justice as 'a property of the *whole state*, based upon a relationship between its classes', and that '[*t*]*he criterion of morality is the interest of the state*'. On page 86, Popper also treats '[t]he identification of the fate of the state with that of the ruling class' (WP in Nussbaum's term) as totalitarian.

[16] Some Aristotelian scholars tend to draw a distinction between Plato and Aristotle in terms of totalitarianism versus individualism; Miller, *Nature, Justice, and Rights in Aristotle's Politics*, 205–10, Nussbaum, 'Shame, separateness, and political unity', 395–435, Yack, *The Problems of a Political Animal*, 28, 83.

of a polis is determined primarily by its constitutional structure or the relationship of its citizens, and the notion of aristocratic governance wherein the goodness of a polis depends on the goodness of the governing class – David Charles calls this notion of aristocratic governance the narrow and shallow version of WP and formulates it as WP*: a political arrangement is good in so far as it ensures that positions of political power are held in a stable and secure fashion by those who are virtuous.[17] Usually, when Aristotle criticises the views of Socrates or Plato, he clearly formulates the target of his criticism as Socrates' or Plato's idea, although sometimes he does not demonstrate an accurate understanding of their views. By contrast, when he uses Plato's idea, he does not state that the idea relies on Plato's view. It is then more difficult to identify Plato's idea in the latter case than in the former. For this reason, when we examine the influence of Plato's idea on Aristotle's political thought, it is necessary to formulate Plato's conception as clearly as possible, and consider how it operates within Aristotle's argument. I shall, thus, illuminate the roles of the Platonic conceptions of a good polis in Aristotle's political philosophy, consider how these alternative conceptions can be reconciled with one another and explore how Aristotle applies the notion of goodness to an ideal polis.

To this end, in the next section, I shall examine Aristotle's theory of distributing political authority in *Politics* 3, and show that he justifies the notion of aristocratic governance in order to promote his other idea that the purpose of political governance is to ensure the good life of people. As William Newman says, Book 3 is 'the centre round which the whole treatise is grouped'.[18] I also think that this book expresses the core of Aristotle's political thought, not simply because the other books refer to it, but also because Aristotle develops a notion of the best polis that is more practical than his own view in Books 7 and 8 and therefore better suited to the practical aims of ethical and political philosophy as he sees it. As

[17] Charles, 'Perfectionism in Aristotle's political theory', 198, paraphrased.
[18] Newman, *The Politics of Aristotle*, vol. II, xxxi.

I shall argue in the next chapter, Book 3 develops a theory of the mixed constitution, the best constitution that is stable and practically achievable. Even in Book 3, however, Aristotle uses a Platonic notion of aristocratic governance (WP* in Charles's formulation) within his own framework for politics. Unlike Nussbaum, therefore, in Section 2.3 I shall explore the way it illustrates Aristotle's unitary and coherent idea of a good polis. In Section 2.4 I shall examine Aristotle's analogy between an individual and a polis in *Politics* 7 to clarify the role of moderate holism in Aristotle's political philosophy. As mentioned above, as well as in Chapter 1, Book 7 is generally considered to have been written in Aristotle's earlier career and thus been strongly influenced by Plato's notion of an ideal polis in the *Republic*. Certainly, Aristotle uses the Platonic notion of the best polis, but, as I shall show, he develops his own distinctive approach to the subject.

2.3 Distributive justice in political authority

Even Plato does not seem to develop as holistic or totalitarian a political philosophy as Popper, Nussbaum and Miller ascribe to him. This is because Plato's Socrates in the *Republic* does not argue that the happiness of a polis is *completely independent* of the happiness of an individual. In the context of the aforementioned argument regarding the happiness of a polis in *Republic* 4, Adeimantus criticises Socrates' view of an ideal polis (or what is called 'Callipolis' in the *Republic* (7.527c)) in such a way as to argue that the guardians in Callipolis are not happy because they are not allowed to have private property by which people ordinarily enjoy their life. In reply, Socrates reminds him that they have been constructing Callipolis not by trying to make one particular class very happy, but rather to make the whole polis (ὅλη ἡ πόλις) as happy as possible (420b, cf. also 7.519e–520a). Soon afterwards, Socrates clarifies the meaning of 'the whole polis' by saying that the well-organised polis should allow each class (ἑκάστοις τοῖς ἔθνεσιν) to share the form of happiness that is fit for its nature (421c). On the one hand, this view is not totalitarian in the sense that the whole polis is happy if and only if its structure is well organised, regardless of whether its citizens are unhappy.[19] When Socrates refers to the happiness of 'the whole polis', he means that the polis ensures that each class of its citizens shares an appropriate form of happiness by getting them to do their proper jobs. Although the term 'each class' does not necessarily mean each individual citizen in the polis, it is clear that Socrates is concerned about what form of life citizens lead in the polis. In his view, therefore, the happiness of a polis depends partly, if not totally, on the happiness of its citizens.

On the other hand, Socrates does not develop an individualistic view that the happiness of a polis can simply be reduced to the aggregate of individuals' happiness. In his view, we should not aim at promoting a kind of happiness that makes people reluctant to fulfil their own task. Rather, he formulates the happiness of individuals in terms of their contribution to the aim of the whole polis, namely, mutual benefit brought by the provision of foods and services. In particular, Socrates is very anxious to make the guardians do their own work, because it is vital to the happiness of a whole polis that rulers perform their jobs properly, since their proper work is to look after the whole polis (421a). Here Socrates has in mind the notion of aristocratic governance (or WP* in Charles's formulation), whereby the goodness of a polis is primarily determined by the nature of its governors.[20]

This idea is operative even in Book 3 of Aristotle's *Politics*. The following passage in *Politics* 3.9 is important for clarifying his basic idea of how to distribute political authority in a polis

[19] Christopher Taylor defines this position as follows: 'On the extreme totalitarian interpretation *polis* must be understood as "state", i.e. as an organization conceived as distinct from the individuals who compose it, and the aim of the founder of the ideal *polis* is to promote the well-being of that organization (conceived by Popper as its stability) in total independence from the welfare of its members'; Taylor, 'Plato's totalitarianism', 771.

[20] For a discussion of the role of the city-soul analogy in Plato's *Republic*, see Ferrari, *City and Soul in Plato's Republic*, Lear, 'Inside and outside the *Republic*', and Williams, 'The analogy of city and soul in Plato's *Republic*'. These sources discuss whether there is any inconsistency between Socrates' conceptions of a just city, and whether the analogy offers a causal account of the relationship between human soul and polis.

and addressing the question of what conceptions Aristotle uses in this book:

> A polis is the community of tribes and villages for the sake of a complete and self-sufficient life. This is, as we say, to live happily and nobly. We must thus think that the political community exists for the sake of noble actions, not for the sake of sharing lives. Hence those who contribute most to such a community have a greater share in the polis than those who are equal or superior in freedom or noble birth yet inferior with regard to civic virtue, or than those who exceed in wealth but are surpassed with regard to virtue. (1280b40–1281a8)

In the context of this passage, Aristotle aims to establish his aristocratic position that political authority needs to be distributed according to virtue, as opposed to oligarchic and democratic positions. In *Politics* 3.9 he criticises both the democratic and oligarchic treatments of distributive justice as one-sided: on the one hand, democrats wrongly suppose that when people are equal in one respect, i.e. being free, they are equal in all respects, implying the equal distribution of political authority among citizens. On the other hand, oligarchs wrongly suppose that when people are unequal in one respect, i.e. being wealthy or poor, they are unequal in all respects, including the distribution of political authority (see also *Pol.* 5.1.1301a28–35, b35–40). Aristotle then argues that virtue should be the primary criterion for acknowledging what people contribute to the polis, and that thus political authority needs to be distributed according to virtue.

To this end, in the quoted passage, Aristotle defines the purpose of political governance first, because distributive justice is originally defined in *EN* 5.3 as one kind of particular justice, according to which things need to be distributed in proportion to 'what people contribute (τὰ εἰσενεχθέντα)' to their common activity (*EN* 5.4.1131b27–32). In other words, it is 'just' that people receive things, such as profit, honour or political authority, in proportion to how much they contribute to the purpose of the business. In the case of political authority, in particular, it is in accordance with distributive justice that political authority is distributed according to merit (ἀξία), although there is in practice no general agreement on what 'merit' is

(*EN* 5.3.1131a25–9).[21] In *Politics* 3.9, therefore, Aristotle defines the purpose of political governance and considers what its positive contribution to a polis might be.

On the one hand, the quoted passage (*Pol.* 3.9.1280b40–1281a8) is not contrary to Nussbaum's idea of DC, since Aristotle asserts that the purpose of a polis is a complete and self-sufficient life, namely, living happily and nobly. Rejecting other ideas concerning the purpose of a polis – such as the acquisition of property, the sustenance of life, the exchange of goods or a military alliance – here Aristotle identifies the purpose of a polis with the happy, noble lives of citizens, as he does famously in *Politics* 1.2. On the other hand, it would seem that in the quoted passage he presupposes WP*, in the sense that a polis is good insofar as the governing citizens are good. He argues that civic virtue, or virtue, is the defining characteristic according to which we can judge who contributes to the polis in the fullest sense. In order to achieve individuals' happiness, he argues, the polis needs to be managed by virtuous people who exercise political power for the happiness of the whole community. In other words, the governance of virtuous persons is justified, because it contributes most greatly to people's happiness in the polis. WP* therefore plays a role that is complementary to DC.[22]

21 Concerning the conception of 'merit', Jeremy Waldron points out two aspects of distributive justice, a backward-looking aspect and a forward-looking aspect: that is, how a person has already contributed to the community, and how a person will contribute to the community in the future. He then contends that it is the latter that counts in the *Politics*. As Malcolm Schofield argues, however, this clear distinction is not particularly useful in understanding Aristotle's conception of 'merit'. For example, democrats regard liberty, or the status of being free, as the 'merit' according to which political authority should be distributed in equal measure. The status of being free, however, denotes neither prospective ability nor past performance. As to wealth and virtue, oligarchs and aristocrats can lay claim to political authority in proportion to both the forward-looking and the backward-looking aspects. Aristotle's conception of 'merit' does not therefore draw a sharp distinction between prospective ability and past performance. See Waldron, 'The wisdom of the multitude', 153–5, and Schofield, 'Sharing in the constitution', 152–4. Concerning the problem of how the conception of distributive justice lays the foundation for each political system, see Keyt, 'Aristotle's theory of distributive justice', 238–78.

22 In his 'Perfectionism in Aristotle's political theory', 192–3, 199, Charles also suggests that WP can be adopted in conjunction with DC, and that it is justified

These two perspectives on a good polis – the idea of aristocratic governance and the promotion of citizens' good lives – are also expressed in Aristotle's definition of aristocracy. In *Politics* 3.7 he indicates that aristocracy is the rule by a few – not many but more than one – who look to the common benefit, 'either because the best people rule, or because they rule with a view to what is best for a polis and those who share in it' (1279a34–7). Usually, according to Aristotle's typology, as I shall argue in the next chapter, a constitution is classified in terms of who governs a polis, and an aristocracy is defined as a constitution in which good persons hold supreme power in the polis (e.g. *Pol.* 3.18.1288a33–b2, 4.7.1293b1–7, 1293b40–1, 4.8.1294a9–11, *Rhet.* 1.8.1365b31–1366a2). In this respect, the title 'aristocracy' is somewhat misleading, since a political system in which hereditary nobles run the government permanently simply because of their wealth is not an aristocracy, but an oligarchy according to Aristotle's theory of constitutions. In general, thus, Aristotle regards aristocracy as political governance on the part of virtuous persons. In the quoted passage (*Pol.* 3.7.1279a34–7), however, Aristotle adds that a constitution is called aristocracy because the best people rule for the sake of what is best for the polis and the citizens. Here he points out that the object of political governance is also an important condition for aristocracy. Hence, his descriptions of aristocracy also fit well with the view that he considers the goodness of a polis from the two angles.

In *Politics* 3.12 Aristotle develops this idea of aristocratic governance further. Here he considers the possible objection that people can lay claim to the greater share of public office on the basis of any form of goodness, such as the colour of skin or height, but he answers this objection by way of analogy: 'When flute-players are equal in their art, people should not give the more or better flutes to those of them who are better born. For they will not play the flute any better. It is the

based on the fact that virtuous rulers contribute to the best life of all citizens in the polis. In her 'Reply to David Charles', 211, however, Nussbaum rejects Charles's suggestion and treats WP as exclusive to other principles.

better performers who should also get the better instruments' (1282b31–4). In this view, the criterion for the distribution of an instrument should not be based on the kind of goodness that makes no difference in the performance of the instrument. Soon afterwards, he also argues that noble birth and wealth do not make any substantial contribution to the performance of a flute-player. He dismisses the oligarchic idea that noble birth and wealth should be the defining characteristics of distribution (*Pol.* 3.12.1283a1–3). Hence, political authority should primarily be distributed to those who can work well in holding and exercising such authority, namely, to those who have the relevant excellence or virtue to make the best use of political authority.

Aristotle's aristocratic use of distributive justice, formulated in this flute analogy, is the material least compatible with Nussbaum's idea of political distribution. As Nussbaum herself admits,[23] Aristotle has in mind as a criterion for the distribution of resources not the potential capacity that people might cultivate in the future, but an already trained capacity that people can exercise in the present. Nussbaum wishes to establish a modern humanitarian position, that if a person has a potential capacity for human functions, then the government should be engaged with the cultivation of the potential capacity up to at least a certain threshold. Aristotle, however, argues that a resource needs to be distributed to those who have already acquired the capacity for making the best use of it, not those who might cultivate the capacity to use it in the future.[24] This is clear also from the definition of distributive justice in *EN* 5.4 (1131b27–32), in which, as discussed above, he considers it in accordance with distributive justice to apportion resources in proportion to what people contribute (τὰ

[23] Nussbaum, 'Nature, function, and capability', 167.

[24] Charles and Mulgan also point out this difference in Charles, 'Perfectionism in Aristotle's political theory', 195, and Mulgan, 'Was Aristotle an "Aristotelian social democrat"?', 92–3, but in her 'Reply to David Charles', 211, Nussbaum does not draw serious attention to this distinction in arguing that the flute distribution passage is 'a supplementary piece of evidence' for her view that a capability is the basis for a proper distribution.

εἰσενεχθέντα) to public funds. In consequence, the criterion for distribution is not aligned with people's needs, which the government should look after, but rather with 'merits', which make it possible for people to contribute to the community.

This distinction between an already acquired capacity and 'a capability' that can be acquired in the future can be illuminated more clearly with reference to a relevant passage in Aristotle's *On the Parts of Animals*:

> Just as an intelligent person, nature always distributes each instrument to the person who can use it. It is more appropriate to give flutes to the one who is a flautist (τῷ ὄντι αὐλητῇ), than to provide one who has flutes with the skill of playing them. For nature has given the lesser to the greater and superior, not the greater and more supreme to the lesser. If this is better, and nature does what is best among the possibilities, then it is not because a human being has hands that he is most intelligent, but because he is most intelligent among animals that he has hands. (*PA* 4.10.687a10–18)[25]

In the context of this passage, Aristotle offers a teleological argument that a human being has hands because he is intelligent, as opposed to Anaxagoras' causal explanation that a human being is intelligent because he has hands. Aristotle then applies his famous principle, 'nature does what is best among possibilities', which is the positive counterpart of the principle, 'nature does nothing in vain'. This principle supports his view that nature gives an instrument to the person who has the ability to play it, so that the instrument will be used properly.[26] Here Aristotle draws a clear contrast between a case in which an instrument is given to one who already has a capacity for using it and a case in which a capacity is given to one who has an instrument but does not have the capacity for using it. He endorses the former case.

Why then does Aristotle prioritise one who has already acquired the functional ability to perform over one who has

[25] The translation follows James Lennox (trans.), Aristotle, *On the Parts of Animals*, slightly modified.

[26] For details on the role of this principle in Aristotle's biology, see Lennox (trans.), Aristotle, *On the Parts of Animals*, 320–1, and Lennox, 'Nature does nothing in vain . . .', 205–23.

not? This is presumably because he has in mind the idea that the purpose of a thing is its use, rather than its possession. In *Politics* 1, he criticises the art of obtaining wealth, especially the art of money-lending, in that its purpose is the acquisition of money itself, not its use for life or good life, and regards it as contrary to nature (*Pol.* 1.10.1258a37–b8). Given that the purpose of a thing is its use, it is wise to distribute it to the person who can make the best use of it. In the same way, it is appropriate to distribute political authority to the person who has already attained the capacity for exercising it properly, rather than to the person who can cultivate it in the future if properly educated in favourable circumstances. Aristotle's conception of distributive justice, especially with regard to the distribution of political authority, therefore has a merit-based perspective, not an educational (or, in Nussbaum's term, a 'medical')[27] perspective.

On the one hand, Nussbaum captures an important characteristic of Aristotle's political philosophy, namely, the idea that a polis is established for citizens' good lives, and provides a substantive, detailed account of the purpose of political governance. She then uses Aristotle's conceptions of human happiness and human virtue to support her 'capabilities approach' and to lay the foundation for 'social democracy'. When it comes to the distribution of political authority, however, Aristotle does not argue that political authority should be distributed primarily for the cultivation of virtue in those to whom the authority is allocated. The conception of human virtue rather leads Aristotle to defend the idea of aristocratic governance, so that the government is managed for citizens' good lives. In other words, in reference to Aristotle's conception of the virtuous life, Nussbaum effectively introduces the Marxist conception of 'needs' into the distributive principle 'to each according to their needs', but Aristotle is better construed as applying the concept of virtue to the Marxist principle 'from each according to their ability'. In Aristotle's framework,

[27] Nussbaum, 'Reply to David Charles', 214.

therefore, the concept of virtue is also operative in the latter principle in order to secure the former principle.[28]

2.4 The role of the individual–polis analogy

I have been describing the role of Aristotle's notion of aristocratic governance for promoting the good of individuals, focusing mainly on *Politics* 3. Next, I am going to examine what conception of a good polis Aristotle has in mind when he draws an analogy between an individual and a polis in *Politics* 7. Here he draws this analogy repeatedly (*Pol.* 7.1.1323b40–1324a2, 7.2.1324a33–5, 7.3.1325b14–16, 30–2, 7.14.1333b37–8, 7.15.1334a11–12, cf. *Pol.* 4.11.1295a34–b1).[29] In this section, I shall not treat the individual–polis analogy simplistically as a remnant of the Platonic idea, but rather consider how Aristotle uses this analogy as a necessary element for developing his political thought. This individual–polis analogy may be seen as somewhat holistic in the sense that a good polis is defined with a view to its whole structure, with no necessary dependence on the goodness of each of its members. It does not, however, suggest the totalitarian or (in Miller's term) 'extreme holistic' conception that an individual must sacrifice his or her own interests for the sake of the whole polis. Rather, it draws attention to the whole structure of a polis as an entity that is called good or

[28] Although I do not explore the ideas of political distribution in Book 2, Aristotle presupposes WP in his criticism of Plato therein. Nussbaum refers to *Pol.* 2.5.1264b15–24 to show that Aristotle dismisses a Platonic holistic conception of a polis, and to defend her position that DC becomes predominant in Book 2. This passage, however, gives clear evidence that Aristotle has WP, not DC, in mind, since he argues that it is impossible to achieve the happiness of the whole without achieving the happiness of all parts, most parts or some parts (strangely, Nussbaum omits 'some parts' in her 'Nature, function, and capability', 159), and that if the governing class is not happy, no one will achieve happiness. Here Aristotle does not dismiss the idea that the goodness or happiness of a polis largely depends on the goodness or happiness of the governing class. See also Nussbaum, 'Aristotle, politics, and human capabilities', 112, in which she still maintains that the passage (*Pol.* 2.5.1264b15–24) supports her social democracy.

[29] Here Aristotle draws the individual–polis analogy also in one of the 'empirical' books, wherein he explores the best constitution and the best life for ordinary people, not under ideal circumstances. I shall argue about the middle constitution in Chapter 3 and the importance of the middle class in Chapter 6.

virtuous. I shall argue that this perspective is a necessary element for Aristotle to formulate the conception of a good polis as promoting the happiness of its members. The individual–polis analogy plays a relatively minor role in the *Politics*, but certainly it operates within Aristotle's framework for a good constitution.

For our consideration of the role of the individual–polis analogy, it is useful to examine the contexts in which Aristotle draws the analogy. The first example is the aforementioned passage (*Pol.* 7.1.1323b33–6), where he states that 'the courage, justice and practical wisdom of a polis have the same ability and structure by partaking in which each human being is said to be just, practically wise and moderate'.[30] In the wider context of this passage, Aristotle explores what the best or happiest life for a polis is, as well as for an individual. First, he defines the happy life for an individual as having and exercising virtue and practical wisdom rather than owning external goods, in line with his general framework of ethics. Then, he applies the same principle to the happiness of a polis, arguing that a happy polis needs not simply to possess something good, but also to do noble things, and that it is not possible for either a polis or an individual to act nobly without having virtue and practical wisdom. Soon after the above-quoted passage, Aristotle concludes that the best life for both an individual and a polis is a life of virtue sufficiently equipped with the resources needed to take part in virtuous activities (*Pol.* 7.1.1323b40–1324a2). Although he does not necessarily imply that the goodness or happiness of a polis is completely independent of that of an individual, at least he argues that a polis as an entity needs to have virtue and practical wisdom just as an individual does. In other words, the virtue of a polis is expected to contribute to its happiness just as the virtue of an individual does to his happiness.[31]

30 Unlike Ross, as mentioned above, I do not add 'καὶ σωφροσύνη' at line 34 and 'ἀνδρεῖος καὶ' at line 36.

31 Compare Kraut (trans.), Aristotle, *Politics*, 58–9, where he treats the quoted passage as expressing the Platonic whole–part conception, which means that 'a city's character derives from the character of some or all of its inhabitants'. I think that the passage suggests not this conception, but rather the holistic conception

Aristotle also draws this individual–polis analogy in his arguments about whether the happy life consists in a practical, political life or a theoretical, contemplative life. Although in *EN* 10 Aristotle famously prioritises contemplative life over political life (cf. 10.7.1177b12–26), in *Politics* 7.3 he acknowledges the significance of both of these two types of life.[32] Here he first makes a counterargument against the claim of those who propose theoretical life in such a way as to maintain that it is not correct to praise inaction more than action, because human happiness consists in action. However, he also recognises that theoretical life constitutes human happiness by enlarging the notion of action in the following passage:

> If these claims are correct, and we should assume that happiness is acting well, then the best life both in common for every polis and for an individual would be a life of action. Yet it is not necessary, as some suppose, for a life of action to involve relations with other people, nor are those thoughts alone active which we engage in for the sake of action's consequences; the study and thought that are their own ends and are engaged in for their own sake are much more so. For acting well is the end, so that action of a sort is the end too . . . Moreover, poleis that are situated by themselves and have deliberately chosen to live that way do not necessarily have to be inactive, since activity can take place among their parts. For the parts of a polis have many communal relationships with one another. (*Pol.* 7.3.1325b14–27)

Here again, Aristotle presupposes that the best life is the same for both a polis and an individual, and argues that both can lead a happy life without engaging in activities involving other people or other poleis. In particular, the happiness of a polis is considered to consist in the relational activities among smaller communities within the polis. The individual–polis analogy makes it possible to draw a picture of the happy polis that does not have relations with other countries.

that the virtue of a polis has the same feature as an individual's virtue in contributing to the happiness of a polis (or an individual).

[32] I follow Kraut's view that *Politics* 7 and 8 were written between *EE* and *EN*: 'the *Eudemian Ethics* does not explicitly compare the two lives [i.e. contemplative and political lives], the *Politics* does so but does not decisively come to a conclusion, and the *Nicomachean Ethics* fully explores the issue and champions the philosophical life'. See Kraut (trans.), Aristotle, *Politics*, 75–6.

This image plays a role in developing the arguments regarding the proper purpose of a good polis or legislator. In *Politics* 7, Aristotle displays an unfavourable attitude towards the constitutions of Sparta and other countries in describing how they organise their constitutions and laws for the sake of defeating and enslaving their rivals (7.2.1324b3–22, 7.14.1333b5–21, 7.15.1334a40–b2, cf. *Pol.* 2.9.1271a41–b6, 8.4.1338b11–16, 32–5). In *Politics* 7.2, for example, he points out that some people hope to rule other countries unjustly, even though they wish to govern themselves justly in their own country (1324b32–6). Soon afterwards, Aristotle argues that, given the possibility that a polis might live alone without any contact with other counties, the polis does not then aim to defeat its enemies in war, but a good legislator should think how people can partake of the good life and live happily (1324b41–1325a10). This argument is developed further in the later chapters. In *Politics* 7.14, Aristotle confirms that people engage in war for the sake of establishing a peaceful life, and that for this reason they need to be educated to have the capacity for enjoying their life in peace (1333a30–b5). More specifically in *Politics* 7.15, he treats philosophy, justice and temperance as the virtues that make it possible for people to enjoy the peaceful life and maintains that people need to cultivate those virtues, since it is difficult to be virtuous in peace while war compels them to be just and temperate (1334a22–40). Thus, in Book 7, Aristotle draws the individual–polis analogy to formulate the notion of the good polis that is situated alone, thereby suggesting that the role of a polis or rulers is to enable people to live a virtuous life in peace. Although he praises the Spartans, as mentioned above, for their public concern with the cultivation of virtue, he criticises them in that their concern is limited to a virtue needed in war, namely, courage. The analogy thus supports the claim that the best polis should aim to promote the perfection of its citizens, or what Nussbaum calls a distributive conception and what Miller calls 'moderate individualism'.

The individual–polis analogy in itself enables us to apply a functional approach to the goodness of a polis. This point can be clarified with reference to Aristotle's argument regarding the proper size and population of a polis in *Politics* 7.4. He maintains that we need to draw attention not to the number of its inhabitants, but rather to its ability, since a polis has a task (ἔργον) to perform (1326a12–14). In his view, it is not necessarily good for a polis to have as many people as possible, because an over-populated polis is difficult to govern well.[33] He explains that the magnitude of a polis has a certain measure, as do all other things, such as animals, plants and instruments, since each of these cannot maintain its own capacity when it is too small or large (1326a35–40). In this argument, he treats a polis as an agent that is engaged in its own work and draws attention to the function of a polis in order to clarify the goodness of a polis. Here he presupposes that a polis is good when it can perform its own task, just as an individual is good when he can perform his task. The texts that express the individual–polis analogy are thus reconciled with the view that the task of a polis is to contribute to the perfection of its individual citizens.

Although Nussbaum maintains that 'Aristotle's statements in *Politics* 7 are extremely close to Plato's actual expressions',[34] the role of the individual–polis analogy varies between Plato's *Republic* and Aristotle's *Politics*. In the former, Socrates draws an analogy between an individual and a polis in order to address the central topic of the *Republic*, namely, whether justice contributes to the happiness of an individual without bringing good reputation or reward. This is because it is easier to see justice writ large, or the justice of a polis, than justice writ small, or the justice of an individual, just as we can see letters writ large more easily than letters writ small or seen from a distance. Socrates then expects to identify justice with respect

33 In *Pol.* 2.6 (1265a10–17), Aristotle considers it difficult to obtain a territory large enough to keep 5,000 citizens in idleness, the population that the Athenian stranger proposes in Plato's *Laws* 5.737e. For the population of Athens in the fourth century BC, see Hansen, *The Athenian Democracy in the Age of Demosthenes*, 90–4, in which he estimates that there were at least 30,000 male adult citizens. For a discussion of the problem of the view that Athens was 'a face-to-face society', see Ober, *Mass and Elite in Democratic Athens*, 31–3.

34 Nussbaum, 'Nature, function, and capability', 158.

to an individual that resembles justice with respect to a polis (2.368c–369a). Socrates' argument therefore proceeds from the larger object to the smaller. Aristotle's analogy in the *Politics*, by contrast, proceeds from a good individual to a good polis. He first defines the best life for an individual in line with his own accounts in the ethical or external treatises, and applies the same definition to the best life or virtue of a polis. Even though the idea of the justice or happiness of a polis derives from Plato's Socrates, Aristotle does not define a good individual according to the characteristics of a good polis. Rather, he contends that the best life for a polis is one of virtue and peace even if there is no contact with other countries. Thus, the role of a legislator or politician is to make it possible for people to cultivate the virtues that contribute to a peaceful life. Clearly, this argument derives from Plato's *Laws* 1 (esp. 628a–e), in which the Athenian stranger argues that a politician in the true sense should legislate with a view to peace, not for the sake of defeating enemies in war. In this respect, a crucial difference between Plato's Socrates and Aristotle lies not necessarily in whether their accounts of a polis are holistic, but in the formulations of their arguments. In other words, some expressions of a good polis in Aristotle's *Politics* 7 are Platonic, as Nussbaum points out, but the way he uses these expressions does not parallel Socrates' argument in the *Republic*.

Miller does not shed enough light on the role of this Platonic individual–polis analogy in Aristotle's political philosophy. Miller categorises as moderate individualism Aristotle's argument that the same principle should apply to the good of both an individual and a polis,[35] but this idea can clearly imply the Platonic holistic idea that the virtue of a polis is defined in terms of the structure or relationship of its parts. Aristotle's aristocratic political theory allows for the minority of good people to occupy more important public offices than the majority of ordinary people do, just as the reasoning part of an individual's soul should play a more crucial role in deliberating upon and choosing the right action than the other parts of the

[35] Miller, *Nature, Justice, and Rights in Aristotle's Politics*, 213–14.

soul do. Although Miller expresses a reservation about whether Aristotle's criticism of Plato's *Republic* in *Politics* 2.2–5 is fair to Plato, he tends to draw a distinction between Plato and Aristotle in terms of holism versus individualism from Aristotle's perspective.[36] As discussed above, however, Aristotle's notion of an ideal polis is greatly influenced by Plato's, and cannot be treated simply as embodying the idea of individualism. In this respect, the antithesis 'individualism versus holism' does not help to distinguish Aristotle's political philosophy from Plato's. It is, then, more important to consider how the different Platonic perspectives on a good polis are integrated into Aristotle's political philosophy.

2.5 Conclusion

In this chapter, I have been considering how to reconcile Aristotle's alternative conceptions of a good polis and arguing that these conceptions are not simply the relics of Socrates' arguments in the *Republic*, but rather the necessary elements for Aristotle to define the good polis in which its people lead the good or virtuous life. Basically, Aristotle considers the goodness of a polis in terms of whether it promotes the good life of citizens. In this respect, the good is the same for both an individual and a polis, in that the good is defined in terms of the good life of an individual. The good of a polis is, however, a greater and more complete good to acquire and preserve than the good of an individual, because it is concerned with the lives of people at large.

In Aristotle's political philosophy, however, the concept of aristocratic governance is also a core principle for developing his theory of distributing political authority: a polis is good in so far as good or virtuous people shape the whole polis by

[36] See ibid., 205–10. In 205, n. 33, Miller notes that Aristotle attributes the extreme version of holism to Socrates' doctrine in the *Republic*, but Miller is concerned not with whether this doctrine is really what Plato's Socrates holds, but with what Aristotle's criticism reveals about his own views. See also Miller, 'Aristotle on the ideal constitution', 552–3, wherein he asserts that one of Aristotle's major contributions to subsequent ideal political theory is his 'articulation of an individualistic alternative to Plato's holistic ideal'.

exercising political authority, since this aristocratic governance contributes most to the good lives of citizens. In this view, who governs a polis is a crucial problem for securing good governance. This is because political authority is always dominant over other kinds of goods: usually, political authority imposes tax on citizens, distributes the wealth of citizens, regulates the policy of education and grants honour to eminent citizens. In this respect, political authority is a special kind of good to regulate the distribution of various other goods.[37] In arguing about equity (ἐπιείκεια) in *EN* 5.10, Aristotle asserts that even if the law is properly set up, equity is needed to deal with particular situations, since the law operates at a general level. In the same way, given that political rulers put the principles of justice into practice, any theorist of social justice needs to consider the system in which political authority is allocated to those who are virtuous and thereby exercised in line with the principles of social justice.

As I shall bring out in examining the theory of a mixed constitution in the next chapter, Aristotle asserts that virtuous people should be allowed to hold public office, while taking into account other bases for people to claim political authority, such as freedom, wealth and noble birth. This idea can also be seen as holistic, since Aristotle draws attention to the relationships among citizens, or the whole structure of a polis. Just as an individual needs to control his own soul by exercising the faculty of reason, so a polis needs to be governed by its reasoning part, the virtuous individuals. Aristotle's alternative conceptions of a good polis are thus not contrary to one another, since they simply express the different aspects of an ideal polis.

I have been illustrating the influence of a Platonic, aristocratic conception of a good polis on Aristotle's political thought. How then does Aristotle analyse democracy? How does he admit the political participation of ordinary citizens,

[37] In his *Polis*, 115, Hansen says, '[t]he nub of the *polis* was its political institutions, and through them the city-state regulated the various sectors that were important for the maintenance and furtherance of the society'. Michael Walzer also regards political authority as 'the regulative agency of social goods' in his *Spheres of Justice*, 15, 281–2.

even though he holds an aristocratic conception of a good polis? What perspectives make it possible for Aristotle to develop a more 'democratic' political theory than Plato? In the next chapter, I shall consider these problems, thereby illuminating a tension between aristocratic and democratic ideas in Aristotle's political thought. This tension or ambivalence in his attitude towards democracy and aristocracy would seem to serve as a basis for his theory of the mixed constitution. His constitutional theory, based on the aristocratic treatment of distributive justice, will give us an opportunity to think about democracy from an unfamiliar angle.

CHAPTER 3

DEMOCRACY, POLITY AND THE MIXED CONSTITUTION

3.1 Problems with the concept of 'democracy'

As mentioned in Chapter 1, Aristotle has an ambivalent attitude towards democracy. On the one hand, he does not embrace the democratic notion that any free individual should be allowed to participate in the political process. In his view, the ideal polis would not allow farmers, merchants or day-labourers to engage in politics, because they do not have the leisure time to cultivate the capacity for virtue (*Pol.* 3.5.1278a8–11, 7.9.1328b37–1329a2). According to his typology of constitutions, a democracy is classified as a deviant constitution of the multitude, since it is only concerned with the benefit of the multitude, not the benefit common to all citizens. As examined in Chapter 2, Aristotle embraces the idea of aristocratic governance in the sense that he believes political authority should be distributed to virtuous individuals, since they can make the best use of it for the benefit of the whole political community. On the other hand, he offers positive accounts of 'democratic practices' in some of his arguments, such as the defence of the wisdom of the multitude in *Politics* 3.11 and the clarification of political rule as the governance of free and equal citizens in contrast to despotic and domestic rule. In this chapter, I shall consider how these democratic elements in Aristotle's political philosophy can be reconciled with his aristocratic framework, thereby exploring why his political philosophy can be used as an intellectual resource for modern democratic theory, despite his clear support for an aristocratic political system.

It seems necessary to compare Aristotle's conception of democracy with its modern analogue, but this problem is not thoroughly explored in the existing literature on Aristotle's

Politics. For example, Jill Frank calls the constitution she wishes to explore in Aristotle's *Politics* 'a democracy of distinction', i.e. a democracy that requires the practice of virtue on the part of its citizens,[1] but she does not explicitly examine the difference between Aristotle's conception of democracy and our current conception of democracy. Richard Kraut treats Aristotle as 'a radically democratic thinker' who is concerned with the problems of 'democracy' as we now understand the concept, although Kraut recognises that '[t]he nations we now call democracies are in fact mixed regimes'.[2] Nussbaum also acknowledges that modern democracies are very different from the deviant constitution Aristotle attacks theoretically, and that her conception of 'social democracy' is based on his theory of a 'polity', not on a deviant form of democracy.[3] Kraut and Nussbaum, however, do not examine in detail the similarities and differences between Aristotle's mixed constitution and modern democracies, and do not consider how Aristotle's theory of the mixed constitution provides an intellectual resource for modern democratic thinkers. It would, then, seem misleading to argue about Aristotle's *Politics* without reflecting on the meaning of democracy based on his typology of constitutions.

Mogens Hansen offers an interesting argument regarding this problem by examining the characteristics of modern democracy in light of Aristotle's theory of a mixed constitution. In Hansen's view, a modern liberal representative democracy cannot be seen as a pure democracy from the perspective of ancient political thought. It is rather 'a mixed constitution' that integrates the elements of democratic, aristocratic and monarchical institutions into its political system. For example, the position of a prime minister or president comprises the monarchical element of modern democracy, in so far as this person has a number of prerogatives for taking action without the consent of parliament (i.e. the legislature). The parliamentary

[1] Frank, *A Democracy of Distinction*, 15–16, 178–80.
[2] Kraut, *Aristotle*, 461, 475.
[3] Nussbaum, 'Aristotle, politics, and human capabilities', 109–12.

system is, also, not necessarily based solely on the idea of democracy, since members of parliament are selected by election. This is because voting in an election is expected to be a method for selecting representatives who are more skilled and more intelligent than ordinary people. Hansen, therefore, argues that the ancient theory of the mixed constitution deserves to be revised in order to correct the prevailing simplistic view that modern democracy is simple rule by the people.[4] Hansen's argument implies that Aristotle's political theory can be interpreted as 'democratic theory', first, because modern representative democracy is not actually 'the democracy' that Aristotle classifies as a deviant constitution of the multitude, and, second, because Aristotle's theory of the mixed constitution instead serves as a basis for analysing and prescribing the combinations of various elements in modern democracy.

In the present chapter, I shall develop this line of Hansen's argument and add the following three points. First, Hansen observes that Aristotle's conception of democracy differs from its modern equivalent, but he does not explain in detail how it differs. I shall argue that Aristotle analyses a constitution from the perspective of who governs a polis, while modern thinkers tend to distinguish 'sovereignty' from 'government' and analyse a constitution from the perspective of who has the sovereignty to form the government or who is entitled to benefit from the government. This comparison will enable us to avoid giving an anachronistic interpretation of Aristotle's theory of democracy.

Second, Hansen's description of Aristotle's mixed constitution is problematic in that the mixed regime 'is a composite of two elements only: oligarchy and democracy. Monarchy is left out'.[5] This account is based on one of Aristotle's descriptions of a correct constitution of the multitude, a 'polity', and does not fully take into account Aristotle's theory of the mixed constitution. I shall identify the essence of his theory not

[4] Hansen, 'The mixed constitution versus the separation of powers', 524–30.
[5] Ibid., 520.

simply in the combination of two constitutions, but rather in the integration of three elements, namely, virtue, wealth and freedom, and more specifically in the defence of aristocratic governance with universal support from citizens. To clarify these points, in Section 3.3, I shall examine Aristotle's various descriptions of a polity and consider how he classifies the mixed constitution that includes the elements of virtue, wealth and freedom. In Section 3.4, I shall examine Aristotle's arguments for the wisdom of the multitude in *Politics* 3.11, which seems to me to combine the elements of virtue and freedom. Although these arguments have been thought to promote popular participation, I think that they can be illuminated more clearly in light of the idea encompassed in the mixed constitution.

Third, Hansen does not fully illustrate the influence of Aristotle's theory of a mixed constitution on the political theories of more recent generations in drawing a sharp contrast between Aristotle's theory of the mixed constitution and Montesquieu's theory of the separation of powers. I shall illuminate this influence by demonstrating, more specifically, that Aristotle's notion of distributive justice and his distinction between production and assessment in action play a very important role in the receptions of Aristotle's political thought, such as Montesquieu's theory of the separation of powers and John Stuart Mill's theory of representative government.

Overall, I shall clarify Aristotle's conceptual framework for analysing and organising a desirable constitution in comparison with some modern political theorists' equivalents. While the previous chapter examined Aristotle's notion of an ideal, aristocratic polis, this chapter is intended to illustrate his view of a desirable, practically workable polis that mixes the elements of aristocracy and democracy. He considers it necessary to integrate the claims of democrats into the political process to establish stable government. However, what has not been fully explored is how he reconciles the elements of democracy with his notion of aristocratic governance. I shall consider this problem by examining his theory of the mixed constitution in Books 3 and 4 of the *Politics*.

3.2 Democratic government and democratic sovereignty

In order to clarify Aristotle's conception of democracy, it is first necessary to examine his typology of constitutions – that is, his classification of various constitutions into six types. He classifies various constitutions in terms of who actually exercises political authority, not who is potentially entitled to exercise it. This perspective enables him to provide a realistic account of changes in the constitution or governmental system, and so analyse democracies with a view to social class.

For our consideration of these issues, his definition of 'constitution [or political system] (πολιτεία)' is of special importance:

> a constitution is an arrangement of a polis with respect to its offices, particularly the one that has authority over all matters. The citizen-body is supreme in every case, and the constitution is the citizen-body. I mean, for example, that in democracies the people are supreme, while in oligarchies the few are supreme, and we say that the constitution too differs between them. (*Pol.* 3.6.1278b8–14)[6]

Although 'politeia (πολιτεία)' in Greek could mean citizens' rights, grants of citizenship, the daily life of citizens or, metaphorically, the soul of the polis,[7] here Aristotle defines it as the ordering of the supreme political offices over all matters. In his view, it is possible to classify various constitutions based

[6] In English, 'constitution' sometimes means the most basic laws by which the authority of a government is restricted. In addition, 'constitution' is used as a theoretical term based on the modern distinction between 'sovereignty' and 'government'. For example, in his *Rights of Man*, 93, Thomas Paine states: 'A constitution is a thing *antecedent* to a government, and a government is only the creature of a constitution. The constitution of a country is not the act of its government, but of the people constituting a government. It is the body of elements, to which you can refer, and quote article by article.' In translating πολιτεία as 'constitution', 'political system' or 'regime', I do not mean to refer to this modern conception of 'constitution': what Aristotle has in mind as πολιτεία is not the basic set of laws antecedent to a government, but the ordering of a government itself. I use 'constitution', 'political system' and 'regime' interchangeably as translations of πολιτεία.

[7] See, for example, *Ath. Resp.* 54.3, *Pol.* 4.11.1295a40–b1, Demosthenes, 19.184, 23.89 and Isocrates 7.14, 12.138. For more on this point, see Hansen, *The Athenian Democracy in the Age of Demosthenes*, 65.

on who has the supreme power in the polis. Democracy is the system in which the people occupy the most important role of governing the polis, while oligarchy is the system in which the few run the government. According to his typology, who governs a polis is the defining characteristic of a constitution, and various constitutions are classified with regard to the number of rulers: one, the few or the many (*Pol.* 3.7.1279a25–8).

Although this threefold division can be traced back to Pindar,[8] Aristotle draws a further distinction between 'correct' and 'deviant' constitutions. In his view, a correct constitution is one that looks after the common benefit (τὸ κοινῇ συμφέρον, τὸ κοινὸν συμφέρον) of citizens, while a deviant constitution is one that looks after the benefit of the ruling people only (*Pol.* 3.6.1279a17–21, 3.7.1279a28–31, 3.13.1283b40–1284a3). Aristotle then classifies kingship, aristocracy and polity as correct constitutions of one, the few and the many, and tyranny, oligarchy and democracy as the respective deviant constitutions (*Pol.* 3.7.1279a32–b10). Famously, he calls the specific type of the correct constitution of the many a 'polity (πολιτεία)', using exactly the same term as its genus, constitution, although Plato draws a distinction between positive and negative types of democracy – Polybius calls its positive type 'democracy' and its negative type 'ochlocracy (ὀχλοκρατία)'.[9] In Aristotle's *Politics*, a democracy is deviant from a polity, because it is only concerned with the benefit of the ruling poor majority, while a polity is concerned with the common benefit of the many and of the few.[10]

8 Pindar, *Pythian*, 2.86–8 (see Hansen, *The Athenian Democracy in the Age of Demosthenes*, 66).

9 See Plato, *Statesman* 302d–e, and Polybius 6.4.6, where they basically distinguish between the correct and deviant constitutions of the many in terms of whether the constitutions respect the rule of law. For the details of Aristotle's conception of a polity, see the Section 3.3.

10 Concerning the problem of whose benefit the common benefit theory is concerned with, Donald Morrison ('Aristotle's definition of citizenship', 156–61) proposes the interpretation that the governing class comprises citizens in the full sense, namely, those who participate in deliberative and judicial office, and the governed class comprises citizens in a qualified sense, namely, metics, children, the retired elderly, exiles and the disenfranchised, and thereby maintains that a correct constitution looks after the common benefit of citizens both in the full sense and in the qualified sense. It is, however, implausible in Aristotle's theory that a

In *Politics* 3.8, however, Aristotle argues that the number of the rulers is not crucial for distinguishing between oligarchy and democracy. In most cases, the rich happen to be few in society, while the poor happen to be many. The crucial factor is, then, wealth or poverty, because people claim political authority according to wealth or freedom (since even the poor have freedom). Aristotle thus defines oligarchy as the system in which the rich rule a polis, and democracy as the system in which the poor rule a polis, whether they are few or many (*Pol.* 3.8.1279b17–19, 1280a1–4, 4.4.1290b1–4, 17–20). In this view, the nature of the rulers is crucial for classifying various constitutions, since they determine the nature of a polis as a whole. A more precise criterion in his typology of constitutions is, therefore, which people govern a polis, not necessarily how many people govern a polis.

In line with this perspective, Aristotle analyses and classifies many types of contemporary democracy with a view to the nature of the multitude. In his view, the nature of democracy also varies according to which people govern a polis, e.g. farmers, craftsmen or labourers (*Pol.* 4.4.1291b17–28, 4.12.1296b26–31, 6.1.1317a24–9). In *Politics* 6.4 he more

constitution is primarily concerned with the benefit of metics, children and so on. This false interpretation is simply attributable to the fact that Morrison does not recognise that Aristotle's terminology distinguishes between a citizen (πολίτης) and a free person (ἐλεύθερος), as I shall argue in the next chapter. Based on this distinction, a constitution can be considered correct because it looks after the common benefit of the rulers and the ruled or free persons. Aristotle clearly states that political rule is the governance of free and equal persons (*Pol.* 1.7.1255b20, 1.12.1259b4–6, 3.4.1277b7–9). Children are therefore not primarily the beneficiaries of political rule, although they are the beneficiaries of paternal rule. In this respect, John Cooper's interpretation is more plausible in its claim that a correct constitution looks after the benefit 'common to all the citizens, i.e. all the free, native-born residents', although Cooper also fails to make anything of the distinction between a citizen and a free person in his 'Political animals and civic friendship', 228–9. See also Collins, *Aristotle and the Rediscovery of Citizenship*, 134, and Simpson, *A Philosophical Commentary on the Politics of Aristotle*, 150–3. Concerning the development of the common benefit theory from Aristotle to Aquinas, see Keys, *Aquinas, Aristotle and the Promise of the Common Good*, esp. 63–86. It would seem that Aristotle's argument about man as a political animal who shares the view of justice and goodness in *Politics* 1.2 plays a more important role in the development of Aquinas's theory of 'the common good' than does Aristotle's distinction between a correct and a deviant constitution in terms of whether it looks after 'the common benefit'.

clearly ranks four types of democracy according to the type of people; the best type of democracy is the polis governed by farmers. This is not because its constitution grants as many people as possible the equality of political participation in line with the principle of democracy, but, on the contrary, because farmers are busy working to sustain their livelihoods in the country and thus do not frequently come to the city to take part in the popular assembly. As a result, in this agrarian democracy it is possible, and beneficial for the polis, that qualified persons take up important public offices while the multitude are not short-changed (*Pol.* 6.4.1318b6–1319a4). The second-best type of democracy is governed by herdsmen, who get their living from livestock, mainly because they are physically fit for military activities and live in the open (*Pol.* 6.4.1319a19–24). The third type is a democracy ruled by other free persons, such as craftsmen, merchants or labourers, because these people are, in Aristotle's view, not able to cultivate their virtue due to their vulgar work (*Pol.* 6.4.1319a24–30). Finally, the worst type of democracy is the polis in which anyone, even if they are illegitimate citizens or those whose fathers or mothers are not citizens, may participate in rule (*Pol.* 6.4.1319b1–11).[11] Aristotle, thus, classifies many types of democracy based on the characteristics of the people who actually participate in the democratic political process.[12]

How, then, does Aristotle address the problem of which class is going to form a government? It would seem that his account of constitutional change is very realistic, in the sense that he analyses the power-relations of the people in a polis. In particular, although he takes into consideration wealth and popularity as influential elements in power-relations,[13] he draws serious attention to the influence of military power in determining the power-relations in a polis, especially in *Politics* 6.7 (1321a5–21, cf. 4.3.1289b31–40, 4.13.1297b12–25, 5.4.1304a17–33): when

[11] For a detailed illustration of this worst type of democracy, see Section 3.3.

[12] For a contrast between Aristotle's 'class analysis' of democracy and an 'elite theory' developed by Thucydides and Isocrates, see Eucken, 'Der aristotelische Democratiebegriff und sein historisches Umfeld', 277–91.

[13] See, concerning the advantage of ostracism, *Pol.* 3.13.1284a17–22.

the main military force is the cavalry, the constitution becomes an oligarchy, because it is only the wealthy who are able to feed horses. When hoplites are important, then the constitution becomes a polity, because individuals in Greece had to provide their own armour, which the poor could not afford.[14] When the army relies on light-armed or naval forces, it becomes a democracy, because a male adult can take part in the army as a light-armed soldier or a rower of a warship regardless of financial resources. Based on historical evidence, Aristotle explains why a constitution gets changed in relation to the main military force.

Aristotle's typology of constitutions based on the analysis of actual power-relations is significantly different from any modern political theory that assumes that a constitution is determined by the will of a sovereign. Jean-Jacques Rousseau was the first to completely separate the theory of sovereignty from that of government. According to Rousseau, which constitution is established is determined not by actual power-relations, but by the will of a sovereign, or by the assembly of the entire people.[15] In this view, it is conceivable that the people could establish a monarchical government through exercise of their own sovereignty. Even though this situation seems somewhat contradictory from the viewpoint of Aristotle's political philosophy, it is a consequence of the theoretical assumption that a sovereign selects the type of government. In contrast, Aristotle's political theory does not hold the conception of 'sovereignty' as distinct from the type of government. The modern theoretical conception of 'sovereignty' is thus somewhat misleading with regard to the interpretation of Aristotle's conception of 'supremacy (τὸ κύριον)'.[16] Aristotle distinguishes

[14] In *Pol.* 6.7.1321a12–13, however, the constitution in which hoplites play an important role in defending the country is described as 'the next kind of oligarchy', not a polity. As I shall argue about property qualifications in a polity in Section 3.3, 'the next kind of oligarchy' is just another expression for a polity. In *Pol.* 4.13.1297b1–25, a hoplites' constitution is clearly described as a polity.

[15] See Rousseau, 'Of the social contract', Book 3, Chapter 18.

[16] As to the translation of 'τὸ κύριον' in *Pol.* 3.6.1278b8–14, Barker, Pellegrin, Robinson, Schütrumpf and Sinclair translate it as 'sovereign (souverain, soveräne)', Everson and Jowett as 'highest', 'sovereign' and 'supreme', Tricot as 'suprême' and 'souverain', and Reeve and Lord as 'to have authority'.

various constitutions not in terms of who is allowed to elect the government, but in terms of who actually exercises political power in the society. His political theory therefore does not leave the construction of a constitution to the will of the people, but aims to classify various constitutions based on an analysis of power-relations.

This understanding of a constitution on his part explains a difference between ancient and modern democracy. The modern conception of democracy presupposes the sovereignty of the people, namely, the idea that a democracy's legal basis should be rooted in the people. It does not necessarily mean that people take part in government and exercise political power. Political equality in modern democracies basically means equal application of the right to elect representatives.[17] The people do not necessarily decide political issues or exercise political power, activities which are the business of their government, although there is occasionally a referendum in which people are allowed to decide political issues on their own. Democratic sovereignty, which only allows people to choose a government, is significantly different from democratic government, in which individuals themselves exercise political authority in attending the assembly or holding public office in turns. In fact, Rousseau, who advocates the sovereignty of people, criticises democratic government in which all citizens govern the state on their own, sitting permanently in the assembly to deal with public affairs.[18]

In ancient Athenian democracy, by contrast, people were able to decide political and judicial issues on their own.[19] In the popular assembly, any citizen was permitted to make a proposal about a political issue and express his own opinion in

[17] Walzer expresses the same view of modern democracy and regards a citizen as 'a potential participant': 'Democracy requires equal rights, not equal power. Rights here are guaranteed opportunities to exercise minimal power (voting rights) or to try to exercise greater power (speech, assembly, and petition rights)'; Walzer, *Spheres of Justice*, 309–10.

[18] See Rousseau, 'Of the social contract', Book 3, Chapter 4.

[19] For descriptions of the ancient Athenian democracy, I primarily refer to Hansen, *The Athenian Democracy in the Age of Demosthenes* and Sinclair, *Democracy and Participation in Athens*.

front of the audience, although many participants simply listened to what other people said and cast a vote on the proposal. In the popular court, any citizen also had the right to judge every lawsuit as a juror and dole out punishment by choosing between the respective proposals for punishment made by the accuser and the defendant. There, people were also able to accuse political leaders, for example through the process of indictment for making an illegal proposal (γραφὴ παρανόμων), and to assess the work of public officials at the end of their tenure (εὔθυναι). Moreover, many public officials, such as the 500 members of the council and 600 other officials, were selected by lot from among citizens over 30 years old. Only about 100 magistrates, including all the military commanders and some important financial officials, were selected by election, i.e. by a show of hands in the popular assembly (*Ath. Resp.* 43.1, 61.1–7). Usually, people other than military officials were forbidden to hold the same office twice in their life (or, for council members, three times), although it was possible to hold a different office (*Ath. Resp.* 62.3, *Pol.* 6.2.1317b23–4). This arrangement allows citizens to hold different public offices in turn and in consequence guarantees democratic equality not just of the political right to select representatives, but also of the political authority to govern a polis. In this respect, the ancient Athenian democracy consisted of a democratic government in the sense that people (i.e. male adult citizens) made decisions on public issues and exercised political power on their own.

Aristotle's criterion – who governs a polis – also offers an interesting view of election. Usually, the defining characteristic of modern democracy resides in the free and fair election of rulers by the people. From a modern perspective, election is understood as a democratic method for selecting officials. Surprisingly, however, in Aristotle's work election is described as one of the defining characteristics of oligarchy: he clearly states that the election of public officials by vote is oligarchic (*Pol.* 4.9.1294b7–10, 31–3), presumably because the wealthy are likely to win an election by taking advantage of their resources and leisure. At the same time, he also admits that it is characteristic of the aristocratic constitution that public officials are selected by election (*Pol.* 4.7.1293b7–12, 4.14.1298b5–11). To be sure, election is more democratic than hereditary succession and can be integrated into the democratic constitution (e.g. *Pol.* 4.14.1298a24–8), but the democratic method for choosing public officials is, as mentioned above, not to elect them but to draw lots or to take turns (*Pol.* 6.2.1317b19–21).[20] In this respect, from the viewpoint of Aristotle's political theory, modern democracy is a system that incorporates oligarchic or aristocratic elements. At the same time, it also includes a democratic element concerning election, in that it does not set a property requirement for someone to be a candidate for public office. In Aristotle's typology of constitutions, therefore, modern democracy would not necessarily be a deviant constitution, 'a democracy' which oppresses the few and only looks after the benefit of the ruling poor majority, but rather a mixed system including elements of aristocracy, oligarchy and democracy.[21]

Hence, although Aristotle criticises a 'democracy' in which the multitude actually exercise political power as they want without any restriction, calling it a deviant constitution, it remains possible to treat Aristotle's political theory, especially his theory of the mixed constitution, as a 'democratic' theory that provides intellectual resources for analysing representative democracy. It is, then, misleading to read Aristotle's criticisms of 'democracy' without recognising that he is using the criterion of who governs a polis, not of who is entitled to select a government, the latter of which criteria generates a different account of democracy. Usually, modern democratic theorists hope to establish a government that aims to be concerned

[20] See also *Pol.* 4.15.1300a31–b5, where it is very ambiguous whether the election of public officials embodies the idea of aristocracy, oligarchy or democracy.

[21] For the aristocratic elements of election, see Manin, *Principles of Representative Government*, 134–45. Benjamin Barber discusses the merits and applicability of 'election by lot' in modern democracy as curbing the oligarchic tendency of representative democracy; Barber, *Strong Democracy*, 290–3. Peter Simpson offers an interesting account of the American political system as oligarchic from an Aristotelian perspective in his 'Aristotle's *Regime of the Americans*', 109–27.

with the benefit of all citizens and that is responsive to their claims; as discussed in the previous chapter, Nussbaum develops her social democratic theory in this way with reference to Aristotle's idea that a good polis should look after the happiness of its citizens.[22] This notion of a desirable government also fits well with Aristotle's standard for a correct constitution, since a correct constitution needs to look after the common benefits of free people (*Pol.* 3.6.1279a17–21, 3.7.1279a28–31, 3.13.1283b40–1284a3). However, this standard does not, in particular, support the 'democratic government' in which all citizens exercise political authority, but rather supports any form of correct constitution, including the aristocratic government in which virtuous rulers most carefully look after the common benefit of the people. Aristotle's theory of the mixed constitution can therefore be used as a democratic theory that enables us to consider how to distribute political authority in order to create a government that is responsive to the needs of citizens. In the next section, I shall examine his mixed constitution in detail to consider how he integrates the element of democracy into the aristocratic governance.

3.3 Polity and a theory of the mixed constitution

In his theory of the mixed constitution, Aristotle illustrates the characteristics of what he sees as a desirable, practically workable political system. As mentioned above, Hansen's account of Aristotle's mixed constitution is problematic in his assertion that it 'is a composite of two elements only: oligarchy and democracy'.[23] This account is based on one of Aristotle's descriptions of a correct constitution of the multitude, a 'polity', and does not fully represent Aristotle's theory of the *mixed* constitution. It seems important here to recognise a difference between Aristotle's description of a polity and his

22 Nussbaum, 'Aristotelian social democracy', 53, and 'Nature, function, and capability', 149, 156–7.

23 Hansen, 'The mixed constitution versus the separation of powers', 520.

theory of the mixed constitution that aims to integrate the elements of oligarchy, democracy and monarchy or aristocracy, although a polity embodies one of the ideas of the mixed constitution. In particular, one point in his theory of the mixed constitution is the mixture or integration of the 'elements' necessary for organising a polis, in addition to the mixture of the various types of 'social class'. To illustrate this point, in this section I shall consider, first, what constitution Aristotle actually means when he refers to a polity, and, second, how he develops his theory of the mixed constitution within his aristocratic framework.

In Aristotle's *Politics* there are two descriptions of a polity as a specific type of constitution: one is the polity that consists of the middle class, or hoplites, and the other is the polity that is organised simply by the mixture of democratic and oligarchic elements. On the one hand, according to Aristotle's typology of constitutions in *Politics* 3.7, a polity is classified as a correct constitution of the many (1279a37–9). He points out that only a very few people, and maybe only one individual, can ever attain a high standard in all forms of virtue, while the many cannot, but military virtue is an exception, because it can be acquired by the many. Regarding the problem of whether 'the many' here means 'all citizens', Aristotle mentions that 'those who defend the polis are most supreme in this system, and those who possess weapons participate in this system' (*Pol.* 3.7.1279b2–4). This sentence implies that 'the many' who have political power in a polity are those who possess weapons, namely, hoplites. This description of a polity can be found in other books as well as in Book 3. In *Politics* 4.13, for example, he argues that a polity should consist of hoplites only, because hoplites are the middle class between the wealthy and the poor, and they balance the claims of the wealthy and those of the poor (1297b1–6). In *Politics* 2.6 he asserts that the constitution the Athenian stranger (whom he takes to be Socrates) puts forward as a desirable constitution in Plato's *Laws* is what people call a polity because it consists of hoplites (1265b26–9). Aristotle, thus, regards one type of 'polity' as a political system that consists mainly of the middle class, or a so-called 'hoplite democracy'.[24]

On the other hand, in *Politics* 4.8 and 9 Aristotle has a different description of 'polity' when he states that a polity is a mixture of democracy and oligarchy (*Pol.* 4.8.1293b33–4, cf.1294a15–17), and analyses the three methods for uniting democratic and oligarchic systems (*Pol.* 4.9.1294a35–b13). The first method is to take something from the laws of both: in an oligarchy the wealthy are punished with a fine if they fail to perform their duty of serving on a jury, and in a democracy the poor are provided with an allowance if they carry out their duty of serving on a jury. A polity imposes a fine on the wealthy and provides the poor with an allowance. The second method is to adopt the mean between the laws of each: in an oligarchy political participation is limited to the wealthy who have a large amount of property, while in a democracy there is no limitation. A polity qualifies those who have a medium amount of property to participate in the political process. Here, 'hoplite democracy' can be seen as adopting this method for uniting democratic and oligarchic systems, since the hoplites are the middle class: neither the rich, who can be cavalry, nor the poor, who cannot afford their own weapons. The third method is to accept some elements from each of these constitutions: in an oligarchy public officials are elected by vote, and candidates are subject to a property qualification, while in a democracy there is no property requirement, and public officials are selected by lot. In a polity there is no property requirement and public officials are elected by vote. This type of polity bears a close resemblance to modern democracy: the modern democratic practice, the election of public officials without a property

[24] In his 'Polity, political justice and political mixing', 210, Thornton Lockwood argues that there are *three* types of polity in Aristotle's *Politics*, but his third version of a polity is the middle-class regime, which is basically the same as the hoplite democracy (Lockwood's first version of a polity). Hence, it is possible to classify Aristotle's descriptions of a polity into two, not three, types. For the terminology of the middle class in Aristotle, see Ober, 'Aristotle's political sociology', 119–20. In Chapter 6, I shall discuss why Aristotle attaches importance to the middle class.

qualification is, from the viewpoint of Aristotle's theory, an effective method for balancing the claims of oligarchs and democrats. To sum up, by 'polity' Aristotle basically means the political system that integrates the elements of both democracy and oligarchy, and 'hoplite democracy' is one specific type of polity that is a compromise between the claims of oligarchs and democrats, as described above under the second method.[25]

A polity, the regime in which oligarchy and democracy are mixed, embodies one of the important ideas in Aristotle's theory of the mixed constitution, namely, his recognition that both democracy and oligarchy in their respective extreme forms tend to destroy their own systems. He offers a piece of practical advice to address this problem: 'we should not forget the mean, which the deviant constitutions now forget, and many practices which appear to be democratic destroy democracies and many practices which appear to be oligarchic destroy oligarchies' (*Pol.* 5.9.1309b18–21, cf. 4.9.1294b14–36, 6.5.1319b37–1320a4). On the one hand, it is not hard to provide an account of how an oligarchy in its extreme form will destroy its own system: when fewer and fewer people have an enormous amount of resources in society, and finally only one magnate comes to monopolise most of the resources, the magnate comes to have political power like a tyrant's (*Pol.* 4.11.1296a1–4, 5.8.1308a19–24). On the other hand, it is not immediately clear how a democracy in its extreme form destroys its own system. According to Aristotle, the principle of democracy is liberty, which has two characteristics: the supreme power of the majority and licentious living (*Pol.* 6.2.1317b2–17). He describes democracy that relentlessly pursues these ideals as 'extreme democracy' (*Pol.* 4.4.1292a4–37, cf. 4.6.1292b41–1293a10, 4.14.1298a28–33, 6.4.1319b1–11): in this political system, the many have complete power and are not even restricted by laws.

[25] For Aristotle's view of 'polity', see Rowe, 'Aristotelian constitutions', 378–86. For the issue of how the political relationship between mass and elite was institutionalised and balanced in the history of classical Athens, see Ober, *Mass and Elite in Democratic Athens*, 53–103.

Just as a tyrant likes flatterers, the many are fond of the demagogue who proposes what they want in the assembly. In criticising public officials, the demagogue insists that the people should judge everything for themselves, and the people are pleased to accept this. In consequence, the majority, and finally the demagogue, rule the polis as they want. What Aristotle considers dangerous here is the resemblance of democracy to tyranny. Extremism in democracy thus results in the despotic rule of the majority, which destroys social harmony with the wealthy. He therefore repeatedly suggests that in a democracy there is a need to look after the benefits of the wealthy and to achieve social harmony between the free majority and the few wealthy (*Pol.* 5.8.1309a14–20, 6.5.1320a4–17). A polity is thus classified as a correct constitution because it integrates both oligarchic and democratic elements, and thereby aims to concern itself with the common benefit of the many and the few.

Aristotle's theory of the mixed constitution is, however, not limited to the mixture of democracy and oligarchy, but also aims to integrate the element of aristocracy or monarchy. In the following passage, to start with, he does not leave out monarchy, but rather asserts that it is better to integrate as many types of constitution as possible:

> Some people claim, indeed, that the best constitution is a mixture of all constitutions, which is why they commend the Spartan constitution. For some say that it is made up of oligarchy, monarchy and democracy . . . But in the *Laws*, it is said that the best constitution should be composed of democracy and tyranny, constitutions one might well not consider constitutions at all, or as the worst constitutions of all. Therefore, the proposal of those who mix together more constitutions is better, because the constitution composed of more elements is better. (*Pol.* 2.6.1265b33–1266a5)

To criticise the view of the Athenian stranger in Plato's *Laws*, here Aristotle cites the claim that the best constitution is the mixture of all constitutions, namely, oligarchy, monarchy and democracy. At the end of the quoted passage, he himself accepts that the constitution made up of more constitutions is better than the constitution made up of democracy and monarchy only. Generally, in his view, in order to sustain a polis, it is necessary for every part of the polis to wish the constitution to be preserved (*Pol.* 2.9.1270b21–2, 4.9.1294b34–40), or at least for the part that wishes the constitution to continue to be stronger than the part that does not (*Pol.* 4.12.1296b14–16, 4.13.1297b4–6, 5.9.1309b16–18, 6.6.1320b26–8). This idea is one of the bases for his theory of the mixed constitution, as a polity integrates the claims of both democrats and oligarchs, while the extreme form of democracy or oligarchy excludes many parts of the polis. In this view, the better strategy is for a polis to avoid excluding any element of the constitution, in order to gain support from all its citizens and stabilise the constitution. The Spartan constitution, Aristotle also argues (*Pol.* 2.9.1270b21–6), embodies this idea in establishing the systems of monarchy (the kings), oligarchy (the senate) and democracy (the overseers). Clearly, thus, the element of monarchy is not left out as an element necessary for establishing a stable constitution.

Aristotle's theory of the mixed constitution, however, is developed not only for the purpose of constructing a stable polis, but also for that of constructing a good polis. In his view, the element of monarchy or aristocracy should be mixed with other elements in order for the polis to be managed well. This idea is best expressed in the following passage:

> The dispute about political authority has to be a dispute among the elements out of which a polis is constituted. Hence the high-born, free individuals and the wealthy reasonably lay claim to honours [i.e. offices], since there must be free individuals and those who pay tax (for one could no more make a polis only out of the poor than out of slaves). But if these are necessary, it is clear that justice and military[26] virtue are also necessary. For without these additions it is not possible for the polis to be managed. More exactly, whereas without the former [i.e. free individuals and the wealthy] there cannot be a polis at all, without the latter [i.e. justice and military virtue] it cannot be managed nobly. (*Pol.* 3.12.1283a14–22)

[26] Here I read πολεμικῆς, consistently with many manuscripts (as Dreizehnter, Newman, and Susemihl and Hicks read), not πολιτικῆς (as Ross reads). This is because Aristotle regards those who are engaged in war as a part of a polis rather than a necessary element of a polis (*Pol.* 4.4.1291a22–8, 7.9.1329a2–5). Compare Schütrumpf (trans.), Aristoteles, *Politik*, Bücher II–III, 515–16, where he reads πολιτικῆς, not πολεμικῆς, because the concept of 'military virtue' is, he thinks, more relevant to the existence of a polis than the good governance of a polis.

Here Aristotle argues that we need to distribute political authority by taking the constituents of a political community into consideration. He then proposes a pragmatic compromise between oligarchs and democrats, and admits that both wealthy and free individuals have a reasonable claim to political authority. He adds, however, that even though the wealthy and the many are all allowed to take part in the government, men of justice and military virtue should have the highest authority in the polis. Here he classifies elements such as wealth and the status of being free as necessary conditions for a polis to survive, and identifies justice and military virtue as essential elements for a polis to be managed nobly. In other words, he supports not just the mixture of political constituents, but also the governance of a polis by men of virtue. His theory of the mixed constitution, thus, integrates the element of aristocracy or monarchy, as well as the elements of democracy and oligarchy, in order to support his idea of aristocratic governance, in which men of virtue take up the most important, supreme authority.[27]

The passage quoted is also important for identifying Aristotle's theory of the mixed constitution as it is developed in Book 3 of the *Politics*. As mentioned in Chapters 1 and 2, Werner Jaeger maintains that in Book 3 'Aristotle is working up to the best state',[28] and his attitude there is 'as theoretical and conceptual as that of the actual description of the best state in Books VII and VIII'.[29] The passage, however, shows that Aristotle is developing his theory of a mixed constitution that takes into account the claims of oligarchs and democrats to construct a stable and good constitution. He does not simply introduce his ideal constitution that is only concerned with citizens' virtue. Book 3 can thus be treated as demonstrating his notion of a desirable, practically workable constitution, although certainly it is different from Books 4, 5 and 6, to the extent that

[27] Compare Charles, 'Comments on M. Nussbaum', 201, where he maintains that Aristotle does not address the problem of conflicting values in the *Politics*. In the passage quoted, however, Aristotle does address the problem of conflicting values: freedom, wealth and virtue.

[28] Jaeger, *Aristotle*, 267. [29] Ibid., 269.

Book 3 is also concerned with the cultivation of citizens' virtue in a polis while Books 4–6 are primarily concerned with the stability of the constitution.

With which constitution – polity or aristocracy – does Aristotle then identify this mixed system? The following remark is helpful: 'since there are three grounds for rival claims of the equality in a political system, liberty, wealth and virtue (the fourth, what people call noble-birth, follows from these two, since noble-birth is a combination of old wealth and virtue), it is evident that the mixture of the two, the wealthy and the poor, should be called a polity, and the mixture of these three should be most genuinely called an aristocracy among other systems after the true, first aristocracy' (*Pol.* 4.8.1294a19–25, cf. 4.7.1293b7–21, 5.7.1307a5–12). Clearly, Aristotle suggests that the mixed constitution encompassing liberty, wealth and virtue should be called an aristocracy, in addition to the true aristocracy that takes only virtue into account. This is because in this type of mixed constitution virtuous citizens are allowed to hold the highest offices. By contrast, as discussed above, a polity is defined essentially as the constitution that combines the elements of democracy and oligarchy only, and accordingly it is obviously not as ideal a constitution as an aristocracy.[30] If a constitution is established on the basis of citizens' virtue, it should thus be classified as an aristocracy or aristocratic polity from the viewpoint of Aristotle's theory.

To sum up, there are two important principles in Aristotle's theory of the mixed constitution: first, a polis needs to integrate as many types of constitution as possible to form a stable constitution or avoid being overthrown by those who are excluded from its government; second, a polis needs to establish the 'second-best' aristocracy, in which men of virtue take up the most important offices in order to govern a polis nobly, while the wealthy and the free individuals are allowed to participate

[30] One passage in *Politics* 3.18 (1288a32–7), however, seems to describe the correct constitution of the multitude as an ideal system, although the descriptions are very brief and ambiguous. See Schmitt, *Constitutional Theory*, 237, in which he regards a polity as an ideal political system.

in the political process. How, then, does Aristotle more concretely propose distributing political authority among various types of people to embody this idea of the mixed constitution? In other words, how does he integrate the element of aristocratic governance into a polis while considering the stability of the polis? In the next section, I shall consider these problems in examining his arguments for the wisdom of the multitude in *Politics* 3.11, since these arguments seem to follow his basic idea of the mixed constitution, or the establishment of a stable and good government. *Politics* 3.11 is another piece of evidence for proving that in Book 3 Aristotle is developing his theory of a mixed constitution that integrates the elements of aristocracy and democracy.

3.4 The wisdom of the multitude

Aristotle's arguments for 'the wisdom of the multitude' in *Politics* 3.11 are usually represented as a democratic element in his political philosophy, in that they promote the political participation of citizens in general.[31] I think, however, that these arguments can be illuminated more clearly in light of his theory of the mixed constitution, and that they actually come from his efforts to integrate the multitude into the political process within his framework for aristocratic governance. According to his conception of distributive justice, we need to take seriously the following analogy, which seems to be paradoxical for people living in a democratic society. If a medical licence, for example, should be distributed to a person medically knowledgeable and adept at surgery, and a general should be chosen from among people excellent at commanding an army, then political authority should, similarly, be distributed only to individuals fit for political authority, and ordinary citizens should not be allowed to participate in the political process

[31] See Ober, 'Aristotle's political sociology', 129–31, Schofield, 'Aristotle and the democratization of politics', 292–300, and Waldron, 'The wisdom of the multitude', 145–65. By contrast, a recent study draws attention to undemocratic elements in these arguments; Bouchard, 'Analogies du pouvoir partagé', esp. 174–6.

in equal measure. In fact, Aristotle gives some attention to the claim that the multitude is not suitable even to exercise the authority to choose officials and assess their work (*Pol.* 3.11.1282a7–14). Although he does not necessarily support this claim, as we shall see later in the present section he considers the idea that an expert is better than a layperson at assessing anything that another skilled person has created. Once we assume that virtue is the primary criterion for the distribution of political authority, it becomes difficult to commit ourselves to a democratic distribution even with regard to the election and assessment of officials. The first issue concerning Aristotle's arguments for the wisdom of the multitude is, thus, how he integrates democratic elements into his aristocratic framework for politics. In contrast to a democratic reading of *Politics* 3.11, I shall illustrate the mixture of both aristocracy and democracy in these arguments, and demonstrate that these arguments provide a justification for popular participation through their identification of the multitude's virtuous capacity for exercising political authority, not through maintaining that the status of being free entitles the multitude to participate in politics.

The second issue is, then, what capacity Aristotle has in mind as comprising the advantage of the multitude over the few good individuals. In the scholarly literature, Jeremy Waldron most famously argues that Aristotle expects ordinary citizens to demonstrate deliberative and dialectical ability. Waldron refers to the famous passage about man as a political animal in *Politics* 1.2 (1253a7–18) and offers an interpretation that the wisdom of the multitude is a kind of model of our human nature as 'speaking beings': through conversation in the popular assembly, people can share and dynamically improve their insights, so that they attain a higher level of practical wisdom than the few excellent individuals. In Waldron's view, therefore, Aristotle's arguments for the wisdom of the multitude provide a basis for a deliberative democracy model.[32]

[32] The following recent articles and book also treat Aristotle as developing a deliberative democracy model; Wilson, 'Deliberation, democracy, and the rule of reason in Aristotle's *Politics*', 259–73, Ober, 'Democracy's wisdom', 104–22, and

Daniela Cammack, however, criticises Waldron's treatment of Aristotle as a supporter of deliberative democracy and instead draws attention to moral capacity as the merit of the multitude, thereby arguing that 'the presence of others would cause individuals to amplify socially valued characteristics and repress those that are disapproved, leading groups to act better and do more than single men'.[33] In Cammack's view, thus, it is not the variety of the multitude's epistemic capacity, but rather the common exercise of the multitude's moral capacity that fosters better decisions in politics, since this common exercise reinforces the multitude's moral behaviour in society. In what follows, *pace* Cammack, I shall develop an argument for the variety of the multitude's epistemic capacity as their merit. However, I shall do so not by drawing attention to their deliberative capacity, as Waldron does, but rather by drawing attention to their perceptive faculty for recognising particular situations. I think that Aristotle's notion of practical wisdom serves as a basis for acknowledging this positive characteristic of the multitude.

For our consideration of these issues, the following passage, in which Aristotle acknowledges the cumulative potency of virtue and practical wisdom in the multitude, is of special importance:

> The many, who are such that each individual is not a good man, when they meet together, are, however, able to be better than those [i.e. the few best], not as an individual, but as a collective, just as a feast to which all contribute is better than one provided at one person's expense. For each of the many has a part of virtue and practical wisdom, and when they get together, just as the multitude become one man with many feet, hands and perceptions, they

Kraut, *Aristotle*, 404–6. In his 'The wisdom of the many', 10, John Bookman takes a similar approach in arguing that the wisdom of the multitude is involved with their collective understanding of their way of life, their constitution. Elsa Bouchard, however, criticises Waldron's treatment by pointing out that juries in the Athenian popular court did not argue about their own views, but simply listened to the claims of an accuser and a defendant (see 'Analogies du pouvoir partagé', 170–1). As I am going to argue, I also do not think that a deliberative democracy model is what Aristotle envisages here. Presumably, the many are expected to properly evaluate the speeches of orators, the reports of public officials, and the claims of an accuser and a defendant.

33 Cammack, 'Aristotle on the virtue of the multitude', 188.

become one man with regard to their character and intellect. Therefore the many judge the works of music and those of poets better. For each individual among them judges a different part and all of them judge all the parts as a whole. (*Pol.* 3.11.1281a42–b10)

Although soon afterwards Aristotle casts doubt on the validity of this argument for some groups of people and admits that certain people are not markedly different from beasts, here he acknowledges the merit of the multitude in the field of politics. In this respect, he clearly does not argue in a democratic way that all should share in government because all humans are by nature equal, but rather identifies good character in the multitude as a group. However, there are two particular interpretative problems in this passage: how to understand the implications of the feast analogy for the positive characteristics of the multitude in politics, and how Aristotle considers that the multitude can combine disparate parts of practical wisdom into one in his framework for the unity of virtue.

First, there are two types of interpretation of the feast analogy. According to Josiah Ober, this feast analogy is concerned with the variety of the dishes the multitude can bring to the dinner, which implies that the multitude can deliberate better than the few by pooling diverse knowledge.[34] According to Cammack, by contrast, the feast analogy is concerned not with the diversity of the dishes, but with the total amount of financial contribution the multitude can make towards the dinner.[35] In this view, the feast analogy suggests that the many can contribute more to the polis than the few in terms of wealth, countering the claim of oligarchs that the poor majority do not contribute financially to the polis and so should not be vested with political authority (cf. *Pol.* 3.11.1282a39–41, 3.13.1283a40–2). It would seem to me, however, that Aristotle contemplates both of these points in his use of the feast analogy. This is clear when he uses the feast analogy again to claim the superiority of the multitude in *Politics* 3.15. Here Aristotle says 'a polis consists of many people, just as a feast to which many contribute is

34 Ober, 'Democracy's wisdom', 110–11.
35 Cammack, 'Aristotle on the virtue of the multitude', 181–4.

better than one simple meal. That is why a crowd can also judge many things better than any single individual' (1286a29–31). The contrast is drawn between the feast to which many contribute and 'one simple (μιᾶς καὶ ἁπλῆς) meal'. Hence, Aristotle has both the amount and variety of the food in mind as the advantage(s) of the feast to which the multitude contributes. The feast analogy, then, implies that both the diversity and the large population of citizens contribute to their making better decisions in the political and judicial processes.

Second, given that Aristotle has the variety of the capacity of the multitude in mind, it is not clear what he means when he refers to the diverse parts of practical wisdom. According to his framework for the unity of virtue, when it comes to 'natural virtue' (i.e. character traits without practical wisdom), on the one hand, it is possible for someone to have some part of natural virtue but not to have another part. For example, an individual may be naturally brave but not temperate, and another person may be just but not brave (*EN* 6.13.1144b32–6). It is, then, also possible to combine those parts of natural virtue so that the multitude as a whole has all the character traits necessary for action. If, on the other hand, one has practical wisdom, Aristotle holds that one necessarily has all virtues (*EN* 6.13.1145a1–2). It is not clear, therefore, what is meant by a part of practical wisdom or how to combine all of the parts of practical wisdom possessed by the multitude into one.

Aristotle seems to provide a clue to this problem in the following passage: 'when they all come together they have enough perception (ἱκανὴν αἴσθησιν), and when mixed with their betters, they benefit their poleis, just as a mixture of coarse foods with refined makes the whole diet more nutritious than a small amount of the latter. Taken individually, however, each of them is an imperfect judge' (*Pol.* 3.11.1281b34–8). Here Aristotle suggests that the multitude can combine what they perceive when they come together. If we explore the feast analogy further, we see that the diversity of perception is what the multitude can contribute to collective activity. Why then does Aristotle draw attention to the faculty of perception as one of the merits of the multitude, particularly with regard to the political process, but not with regard to other fields, such as mathematics?

His understanding of practical wisdom seems particularly helpful in approaching this problem. Just before *EN* 6.8, where he treats legislative and political understanding as one type of practical wisdom, Aristotle maintains that practical wisdom is concerned with particulars, which are the object of perception, and that for this reason people without knowledge can be more practical than those with knowledge (*EN* 6.7.1141b14–18). Generally speaking, he maintains, knowledge is concerned with universals, and accordingly one who has knowledge does not necessarily have the information about particulars that is necessary to behave correctly. In this respect, perceptions about particulars play a greater role in action than knowledge about universals.[36] This understanding of practical wisdom, especially the importance of perception (αἴσθησις) in action, underlies his arguments for the wisdom of the multitude: in the passage quoted above (*Pol.* 3.11.1281b34–8), Aristotle mentions that the multitude as a group has sufficient perception. Given that perception regarding particulars is the defining characteristic of practical wisdom, a wide variety in the perceptions of the multitude contributes to appropriate action more significantly than the perceptions of the few. In referring to the combination of parts of practical wisdom, therefore, Aristotle means the combination of diverse perceptions about particulars.[37]

This argument fits in very well with Aristotle's notion of the rule of law. In the context of the feast analogy, he considers

[36] See also Aristotle's *Metaphysics* 1.1 (981a12–24), where he draws a distinction between experience (ἐμπειρία) and skill (τέχνη), and argues that experience regarding particulars is sometimes more useful for action than skill or knowledge about universals.

[37] In *Pol.* 3.16.1287b25–30, the rule of the many is justified by the fact that they have more perceptive faculties, so that they can see and judge an object better than an individual can. Here Aristotle simply summarises a claim of those who oppose kingship, but this passage is also helpful in revealing that many perceptive faculties are seen as contributing to judgement. For the difference between mathematics and politics with regard to particulars, see Aubenque, 'Aristote et la démocratie', 255–64.

whether it is better for the best person or the multitude to govern matters that laws cannot determine and marshals the argument for the wisdom of the multitude to support the rule of the multitude (*Pol.* 3.15.1286a24–31). In *Politics* 3.16 (1287b15–25), the argument for the rule of the multitude is formulated as part of the defence of the rule of law, namely, the claim that under the rule of law the multitude should govern particulars that the law cannot determine. Aristotle himself does not adopt this claim in this context, but he develops the same argument in *Rhetoric* 1.1, where he argues that a law should leave as few things as possible to the discretion of members of an assembly or a judicial court because: first, it is easier to find a few people who are capable of legislating than a large number who are so capable; second, laws are made after lengthy consideration; and third, the decision of a legislator is not particular but rather prospective and general (*Rhet.* 1.1.1354a31–b16). Here Aristotle does not regard the multitude's intellectual capacity positively, because they are easily affected by their emotions or likes and dislikes,[38] but acknowledges their important role in judging particular cases– namely, determining whether something happened or not, whether something will be or will not be, or whether something is or is not – because a legislator cannot foresee these particular problems. In Aristotle's view, thus, the multitude is expected to perceive a particular situation properly under the rule of the laws enacted by the better people under careful consideration regarding universals; this is the case irrespective of whether Aristotle is regarding the wisdom of the multitude relatively positively, as he does in *Politics* 3, or negatively, as he does in *Rhetoric* 1.1.

After considering the aforementioned claim that the multitude is not suitable even for the selection and audit of public officials, Aristotle argues that the multitude displays its nature not in the process of carrying out governmental or administrative actions, but in assessing the proposals and work of public

[38] In *Politics* 3.15 (1286a31–5), however, Aristotle argues that the multitude is less easily corrupted than the few.

officials. He then draws a distinction between the action of production and that of utilisation, likens the performance of work to production and the assessment of work to utilisation, and argues that a person who uses a product judges it better than the person who makes the product:

> concerning some skills, the producer would not be either the only or the best judge, but also those who do not possess the art know the products. For example, knowledge about a house does not belong only to the builder, but one who uses it also judges the product better (and it is the household-manager who uses it). So too a helmsman judges a rudder better than a carpenter; and it is the guest, not the cook, that judges a dinner. (*Pol.* 3.11.1282a17–23)[39]

In this view, one who uses the product of an art can assess the product properly without having made the product. Based on this premise, Aristotle implies that although the many do not possess the art of politics, they are able to assess the work of political governance with which public officers are engaged.

This distinction between production and utilisation provides an interesting insight into the relationship between an administrative office and an assembly. An example is the role of a general, which should be assigned to a person adept at leading an army. How we can win a battle is a matter of how we 'produce' victory, and the solution to this problem requires special skill and knowledge about military matters. In addition, a general on the battlefield needs to cope with a chaotic, risky and complicated situation and decide what to do immediately. An extraordinary tactical skill is thus needed to perform this task. It is therefore terribly dangerous to choose a general democratically by lot or in turn, since this might result in fighting against enemies under the command of a general who has no knowledge of military matters. In contrast, the questions of whether the battle is or has been useful for the community or how we should 'use' the skill of generalship for the benefit of the community are a matter for assessment. In this case, people can consult a general about military matters if they need to, and

[39] See also Plato's *Republic* 10.601c–d.

take time to assess what they perceive and hear from the general and other experts in the popular assembly. The many themselves, then, need not possess special skills or the capacity for great foresight in order to confront this type of problem; rather, they must have sufficient perception to review the proposals and work of public officials. Aristotle's distinction between production and utilisation therefore enables him to support the political participation of the many more specifically in some collective evaluation processes (cf. *Pol.* 5.9.1309b3–8).[40]

Concretely, how does Aristotle propose distributing political authority to the multitude? He suggests that the many should be allowed to participate in deliberative and judicial authority (*Pol.* 3.11.1281b31), especially in the council, the assembly and the court, in which citizens examine political and judicial matters not individually, but collectively (*Pol.* 3.11.1282a34–41). As an example of this practice, he supports Solon and other legislators' policy of assigning to the multitude the role of electing officials and calling them to account, but not allowing the multitude to serve as officials individually (*Pol.* 3.11.1281b32–4, cf. 2.12.1274a15–21). This policy is supported by Aristotle's aforementioned arguments for the wisdom of the multitude: in the passage quoted first (*Pol.* 3.11.1281a42–b10), he does not expect them to create great music or compose remarkable poems individually, but argues that they are able to judge the works of musicians and poets collectively. In the passage about the distinction between production and utilisation (*Pol.* 3.11.1282a17–23), he presupposes that the many do not

[40] In his 'Aristotle and the democratization of politics', 298, Schofield argues that the multitude's capacity for collective judgement is what Aristotle calls 'comprehension (σύνεσις)', not practical wisdom, in *EN* 6.10. To be sure, comprehension is very close to the wisdom of the multitude, to the extent that a person of comprehension judges well what other people say, just as the multitude is expected to judge well what public officials say. There is, however, a difference between comprehension and the wisdom of the multitude in the sense that the former is not prescriptive and thus does not determine what action we must do or not do (1143a6–10), while the latter is presumably prescriptive and concerned with collective action, such as whether the society must participate in war or not. It therefore seems that the wisdom of the multitude that Aristotle has in mind in *Politics* 3.11 does not perfectly fit with 'comprehension' in *EN* 6.10.

have the capacity for the art of creating a product but, rather, have an eye for assessing the product. These arguments imply that in politics we need to divide various processes into planning, deliberation, decision, execution and assessment of policies. On the one hand, the many are suitable to participate in the processes of deliberation, decision and assessment, because in these collective decision-making and evaluation processes they can combine their positive characteristics into one perfect virtue and practical wisdom in mixing with the better people. The authority for these processes can be allocated to the popular assembly or judicial court. On the other hand, it is appropriate to distribute the authority for other processes to administrative officials based on the virtue necessary for the associated work.

This concept clearly shows that Aristotle does not abandon his aristocratic idea of political distribution in his defence of the wisdom of the multitude. According to his aristocratic use of distributive justice, political authority should be distributed based on virtue, and he acknowledges the virtue of the many, or an assembly, which provides a wide variety of character traits and perceptions and combines them into one perfect virtue with the help of the better people. At the same time, he holds that we should distribute each administrative office to the person who has the capacity for working well in that office individually. The key idea in Aristotle's distributive theory is therefore that we should consider the characteristics of the distributed 'things' and those of the 'persons' (or groups), and distribute 'things' to the 'persons' (or groups) most suitable for them. Based on this idea, Aristotle proposes both integrating the many into the political process and limiting their roles to collective decision-making or assessment processes. Moreover, in the passage quoted (*Pol.* 3.11.1281b34–8), he maintains that the multitude benefit their polis when they mix with the better people. This passage is a clear piece of evidence that Aristotle holds an aristocratic idea not only in his opinion that political authority should be distributed according to people's virtue, but also in his opinion that the better people should play a proper role in the political process, namely, by holding important public offices individually. Furthermore, in *Politics* 3.11 he integrates the multitude into the political process, not because the multitude has the right to participate in politics, but simply because it is dangerous for a polis to have a large number of people who are excluded from public office (*Pol.* 3.11.1281b28–30). This is clearly an application of his idea of the mixed constitution, or the principle that it is strategically better for establishing a stable constitution to include as many people as possible in the political process.

A contrast between Aristotle and Protagoras also illustrates a less democratic element in Aristotle's argument for the wisdom of the multitude. As Schofield suggests, Aristotle's argument seems to be 'reminiscent of the defence of democracy attributed to Protagoras in Plato's *Protagoras*'.[41] Famously, Protagoras there assumes that Athenian citizens have enough virtue to offer opinions in the assembly when he asserts that, compared with barbarians – who lack education, judicial courts, laws, punishment and any concern with virtue – an individual who is brought up in a lawful society is inherently just, even if he is the most unjust person in that society (*Protagoras* 327c–d). Protagoras also argues that everyone is a teacher of civic virtue, just as everyone is a teacher of Greek, and that accordingly people should assume that a person with a modicum of virtue is capable of teaching civic virtue (*Protagoras* 327e–328a). In Protagoras' political philosophy, thus, the concept of virtue does not support governance by experts, or aristocratic government, but rather supports Athenian democracy based on the premise that every Athenian is virtuous enough to participate in such democracy.[42] Aristotle, however, takes a somewhat different approach from Protagoras in that he not only regards the multitude as a better judge than a few best individuals, but also endorses popular participation by identifying

[41] Schofield, 'Aristotle and the democratization of politics', 295. Furthermore, Schofield there points out that in Thucydides 6.39.1 Athenagoras claims that it is the intelligent who give the best advice, but that it is the many who are the best judges of what they hear from the intelligent.

[42] In her *The Origins of Democratic Thinking*, 81–7, Farrar describes what Protagoras has in mind as 'competence' as opposed to 'excellence' (Socrates' conception) and resolves the difficulties that Plato presents to Protagoras.

the multitude's virtuous character as a group, not on an individual basis. Aristotle's view of ordinary citizens' virtue is, thus, less democratic than Protagoras', in that Aristotle specifically expects the citizenry as a whole, mixing with the better, to be virtuous enough to judge political and judicial matters, whereas Protagoras assumes that every citizen is virtuous enough to speak in the assembly.[43]

All of these points considered, then, it is imprecise to call Aristotle's arguments for the wisdom of the multitude simply 'democratic', since he does not offer a democratic argument that the status of being free entitles any citizen to participate in the political process in any role they wish. Although Aristotle has Athenian democracy's policies and institutions specifically in mind in *Politics* 3.11 (e.g. 1281b32–4, 1282a26–32), his argument for the wisdom of the multitude should rather be seen as an effort to provide a positive account of Athenian democratic practices consistent with his aristocratic idea of political distribution. Hence, his theory of the mixed constitution, especially the combination of aristocracy and democracy, serves as a basis for his theory of the integration of the multitude.

3.5 Receptions of Aristotle's theory of the mixed constitution

In order to consider how Aristotle's aristocratic political theory provides useful intellectual resources for modern democratic theories, I am going to examine the influence of Aristotle's theory of the mixed constitution on the political theories of more recent generations, such as Montesquieu's theory of the separation of powers and J. S. Mill's theory of representative government. Montesquieu and Mill inherit Aristotle's theory of the mixed constitution together with his arguments for the wisdom of the multitude in considering how a government should distribute political authority to its political institutions. In particular, they aim to combine well the elements of both aristocracy and democracy, take the characteristics of

43 On this point, see Nancy, 'Aristote devant les objections de Socrate à la démocratie', 282.

the multitude into consideration, and distribute a limited role to the multitude while allowing administrative officials to play appropriate roles. I shall illustrate this point first by describing Montesquieu's theory briefly, and second by examining Mill's theory, especially his view of the multitude in comparison with Montesquieu's, in detail.

A widespread interpretation of Montesquieu's theory highlights his suggestion that the checks and balances among the legislative, administrative and judicial powers are indispensable for preventing tyrannical rule. For example, Ernest Barker maintains that while the defining characteristic of Aristotle's theory of a mixed constitution is the union of social classes, that of Polybius' and Cicero's theories is the checks and balances among social classes, which in Montesquieu's theory takes the form of the division of powers. Barker then draws a clear contrast between Aristotle and Montesquieu in such a way as to argue that Aristotle maintains that 'the different departments will work harmoniously together, because each is permeated by the same spirit as the rest', while Montesquieu asserts that the division of power helps to secure liberty by hampering authority. Barker asserts that in Montesquieu's theory, therefore, we can find something more akin to Polybius and Cicero than to Aristotle.[44] Hansen also draws a very sharp contrast between

44 See Barker, *The Political Thought of Plato and Aristotle*, 484–5. John Pocock emphasises the checks and balances even in Aristotelian theory, especially in stating that '[t]he evil to be avoided was the situation in which any group was able to exercise an unshared power over the whole... there might even be a despotism of the good or the wise, if the good which they pursued were less than the good of the whole'. There are, however, no arguments concerning the despotism of virtuous people in Aristotle. It seems, rather, that the good that the virtuous people pursue, namely, the cultivation of virtue, cannot be anything other than the good of the whole. As discussed above, Aristotle does not dismiss the ideal of governance of virtuous persons, even when he supports the integration of other social classes. Therefore, he would say to Pocock that good people by definition never govern a polis despotically. Pocock's treatment of Aristotle's theory of a mixed constitution is strongly influenced by Polybius' argument; Pocock, *The Machiavellian Moment*, 71–2. For ancient theories of the checks and balances of political power, see Plato's *Laws* 3.691d–692c, Polybius' *Histories* 6.15–18, and Cicero's *Republic* 1.54, 69. Concerning the origin of the theory of a mixed constitution, compare Bates, *Aristotle's 'Best Regime'*, 117–21, where Bates looks to Polybius, who in his view originates the idea (but of whom he provides an idiosyncratic interpretation).

Aristotle's theory of the mixed constitution and Montesquieu's theory of the separation of powers. In Hansen's view, the latter is an outdated theory, because each function of government, such as legislation, the implementation of laws or adjudication, is not performed by one branch of government only, although the theory suggests that such separation is necessary to prevent the abuse of power. Hansen points out many exceptions to the separation of powers, such as the legislative process initiated by an executive branch of government, not by a parliament, and the constitutional court denying a law enacted by a parliament. Instead, in his view, Aristotle's theory of the mixed constitution best explains the actual practices of modern democracy in seeking cooperation among different parts of government with regard to the various functions of government.[45]

There is, however, an important way in which Aristotle influenced Montesquieu's theory, namely, the idea that in order to construct a good government we should distribute only limited power to each political organ, taking the various characteristics of each organ into consideration.[46] Montesquieu argues that the political participation of the people should be restricted to the election of representatives and criticises the ancient assembly in which the people themselves passed decrees on political issues. He defines the characteristic feature of representatives – legislative power – as debate on political affairs, but does not maintain that they should pass decrees. The role of representatives should therefore be limited to the enactment of laws and the monitoring of the laws' implementation. Furthermore, the authority for administration needs to be delegated to a monarch, because a government needs to resolve issues swiftly and effectively, and administration is not a suitable matter for the deliberation of the masses. In taking over Aristotle's

[45] Hansen, 'The mixed constitution versus the separation of powers', esp. 510–17. On 524–8, Hansen describes how constitutional arrangements in modern democracy, such as elective presidency and a constitutional court, embody the idea of the mixed constitution. Hansen's argument is descriptive, but I shall illustrate how a theory of the mixed constitution can also develop an evaluative argument for assessing whether a given institutional arrangement contributes to the elements of governance.

[46] See Montesquieu, *The Spirit of Laws*, Book 11, Chapter 6.

ideas in this way, Montesquieu regards legislation as the work of assessment and administration as the work of production, and distributes each role to an appropriate political organ.[47]

A similar view appears in J. S. Mill's theory of representative government. Although he provided intellectual resources for the development of a theory of liberal democracy, articulated mainly in his 'On liberty', his 'Considerations on representative government' presents a traditional idea of the mixed constitution. I shall examine the background of this work in detail to consider how Aristotle's theory of the mixed constitution serves as a basis for Mill's theory of modern representative government. The underlying problem in this book is how we can support the role of parliament in refuting the claim that members of parliament cannot play an important role in contemporary democracy because legislation and administration in contemporary society require highly specialised skills and professional knowledge. On the one hand, Mill admits the positive characteristics of bureaucracy: bureaucracy accumulates knowledge and provides appropriate practical know-how to those who are actually engaged in public affairs. On the other hand, Mill treats 'routine' as a serious disease of bureaucratic government, in the sense that bureaucracy does not allow the energy of the individual mind to flourish and wastes the talents of its distinguished members. Bureaucracy thus requires popular control to enable the man of original genius to prevail over the obstructive spirit of trained, mediocre bureaucrats.[48] How, then, can we integrate popular control into bureaucratic government?

To address this problem, Mill also draws a clear distinction between 'controlling the business of government and actually doing it'.[49] In this context, he argues that we need to consider what kinds of business a parliament or the body of the people at large is competent to do properly. On the one hand, in his view, a body of men is not fit for action unless it is organised

[47] For Aristotle's further influence on the founders of America, see Biondi, 'Aristotle on the mixed constitution and its relevance for American political thought', 190–6.

[48] Mill, 'Considerations on representative government', 289–92.

[49] Ibid., 271.

and under command. Even if the body consists only of a few select members, it needs to be commanded by one chief, reducing all the other members to his subordinates. This is because a group of people at large tends to weaken a sense of responsibility among its members, whether it is a joint-stock company or a government. The management of a company or government therefore requires an executive manager who will feel responsibility for action. On the other hand, Mill treats deliberation and discussion as activities that can be done by a body better than by an individual. In his view, a body of the many can play a vital role in hearing and considering many conflicting opinions. Mill argues that deliberation and discussion thrive in an equal relationship in which people take others' opinions into account, while action requires an unequal, hierarchical relationship in which action is organised and commanded by one director. From this perspective, he asserts that the proper role of a representative assembly is to watch and control the government, ask it to explain and justify its policy, and reveal the desires of the people – making it the place of discussion for all opinions related to public matters. He thus identifies the role of a body of the people in the process of deliberation and assessment by distinguishing talking from doing.[50]

Mill does, however, make two negative points about the capacity of a parliament. First, he does not expect a parliament to be able to properly appoint public officers in the government, including members of the cabinet, and would allow it to nominate only the prime minister, who would have the authority to appoint senior public officers. This is, Mill argues, because people must nominate public officers based on a strong

50 Ibid., 282–4. Here Mill does not quote Aristotle's *Politics* explicitly, but in his 'Grote's Aristotle', 505, he regards it as presenting us with the mode of thinking of a moderate aristocratic politician in Athens. Mill's arguments about the relationship between government and parliament seem to be based on this moderate aristocratic way of thinking. However, there is of course a great difference between Aristotle and Mill: Aristotle considers the governance of virtuous citizens important for making the polis ethically good, while Mill's arguments about the necessity of bureaucracy do not incorporate ethical considerations. In Mill's view, bureaucracy is necessary for efficient and stable government that will counter the claims of popular control.

sense of responsibility, and the special qualifications required for special duties can be recognised only by those who are accustomed to examining a person based on their own experiences of those duties. A public body, however, does not recognise the special qualifications, but rather tends to appoint a person just because he is popular on a personal level.[51] Aristotle and Mill therefore differ in that the former supports the system that allows the assembly to nominate public officers, while the latter does not assert that a public body has the capacity for assessing special qualifications that special public officers must possess.

Second, unlike Montesquieu, Mill casts doubt on the capacity of a parliament to legislate. In his view, the process of making laws involves the intellectual work that needs to be performed by trained minds after long and serious study. Every provision of a law needs to fit consistently with all the existing laws, and should be framed based on the most accurate and long-sighted consideration of its effect. These conditions are not fulfilled when laws are voted on clause by clause in a miscellaneous assembly. Mill therefore argues that debate by the many is not a suitable way to propose legislation, and that the authority to draft and revise laws should be delegated to a body of the few, a commission of legislation.[52]

Mill borrowed this idea from the ancient Athenian commission of legislation (νομοθέται). The Athenians drew a distinction between law (νόμος), which is generally applicable to similar cases, and decree (ψήφισμα), which is a temporary agreement on an issue. The Athenian assembly in the fourth century BC could not pass laws or decrees that contravened or contradicted existing laws; if anyone proposed a decree that was held to contradict an existing law, he was liable to be denounced before the popular court. When new laws were required, the assembly chose five advocates for the old law over the new law. The advocates and the person proposing the new law would then discuss its necessity, and finally the members of the commission would

[51] Mill, 'Considerations on representative government', 275–7. [52] Ibid., 277–80.

vote on it.[53] Aristotle regards a situation in which the people pass decrees without any respect for laws as one characteristic of 'extreme democracy' (*Pol.* 4.4.1292a4–13).[54] In referring to this practice, presumably based on what he had learned from George Grote's *History of Greece*, Mill proposes that although a parliament should have the authority to sanction or reject a proposal from the commission of legislation, as well as the authority to send a bill back to the commission for reconsideration, a parliament should allow the commission to draft, revise and examine laws. What is useful for Mill's theory of representative government is thus an idealised formulation of Athenian democracy, which includes good constitutional arrangements for modern representative democracy.[55]

To be sure, these theories of the mixed constitution contain a serious problem in their idealised pictures of the relationship between administrative office and assembly, especially in Mill's view of a parliament as the place for deliberation and discussion, when in an actual parliament there may be little deliberation that contributes to the improvement of governmental policies. These theories do, however, seem to have an important implication for modern democracy, for they propose avoiding putting political power completely in the hands of the people, preferring the construction of political organs that ensure careful deliberation or effective administration.

From the time of ancient Greece until the eighteenth century, democracy had been held in deep contempt because it had attempted to distribute supreme power to the many without any restrictions, ignoring the nature of the many.[56] Today,

[53] For a detailed discussion of the Athenian legislative process, see Canevaro, '*Nomothesia* in classical Athens', 139–60, Hansen, *The Athenian Democracy in the Age of Demosthenes*, 161–77, Jones, *Athenian Democracy*, 52–3, Rhodes, '*Nomothesia* in fourth-century Athens', 55–60, and Sinclair, *Democracy and Participation in Athens*, 83–4.

[54] See also Andocides 1.87 and Demosthenes 23.86. In (ps.) Plato's *Definitions* 415b, the law is defined as a political judgement of many people, not limited to a certain time, and decree as a political judgement limited to a certain time.

[55] For this point, see Urbinati, *Mill on Democracy*, esp. 60–4.

[56] For example, James Madison indicates that 'a pure democracy, by which I mean a society consisting of a small number of citizens, who assemble and administer the government in person, can admit of no cure for the mischiefs of faction . . . such

however, democracy in a different sense is seen as the only source of legitimacy for a constitution. This is primarily because people have gradually gained power in the name of democracy since the middle of the nineteenth century. As this process developed, the criterion for democracy changed from who governs a state to who is the beneficiary of governance. Although, from ancient Greek times, 'democracy' had meant that form of government in which a specific class of people predominated, the image of the class-divided society has faded, as 'class' has come to be understood in terms of consumption rather than type of production.[57] To be sure, as Hanson points out, '[t]he fact that democracy is no longer understood in class terms does not mean that classes have disappeared...it does mean that we no longer understand the relationship between political power and social class as a central problem of democracy'.[58] As the image of the class-divided society has faded away, the long-standing tradition of theories of the mixed constitution has also become exhausted, since one feature of such theories is in fact the checks and balances between various groups within a class-divided society. There remains the problem of how to allocate political power to various different political organs, but liberal political theory cannot provide any ideas about this problem except in relation to securing basic liberties.

By contrast, Aristotle's theory of a mixed constitution helps us to consider how to establish what we now call 'democracy', because the key points in his theory include not only the mixture of 'social class', but also that of the 'elements' of aristocracy, oligarchy and democracy: virtue, wealth and freedom. In effect, his theory shows that the requirement for the successful functioning of democracy is to separate political powers according to the characteristic capacities of each organ, and

democracies have ever been spectacles of turbulence and contention; have ever been found incompatible with personal security or rights of property'. Madison instead calls his representative democracy 'a republic'. See Hamilton et al., *The Federalist Papers*, No. 10.

57 For the conceptual displacement of 'democracy', specifically in the history of American politics, see Hanson, 'Democracy', 68–89.

58 Ibid., 85.

to make it possible for the multitude, or the people at large, to be involved in the political and judicial processes of deliberation and assessment. Even though the roles of 'production' and 'assessment' of a governmental policy cannot be assigned separately to a government and an assembly,[59] we still need to balance the various requirements of governance between an aristocratic element taking the initiative in legislation and implementing the laws effectively, on the one hand, and a democratic element examining and criticising the business of the government, and thereby drawing public attention to the issues, on the other. In this respect, the origin of the long-standing theories of the mixed constitution is still useful if we wish to assess institutional arrangements in terms of whether they play their expected roles properly in representative democracy.

3.6 Conclusion

In this chapter, I have considered how Aristotle integrates democratic elements into his aristocratic framework for politics by examining his typology of constitutions, his theory of the mixed constitution and his arguments for the wisdom of the multitude. I have demonstrated that he classifies a constitution in terms of who actually exercises political authority, not who is entitled to form a government or receive benefit from a government, and that for this reason the democracy that he criticises as a deviant constitution is not necessarily what moderns see as their representative democracy, which he would classify as a mixed constitution integrating the elements of aristocracy, oligarchy and democracy. I have also considered more specifically how his theory of the mixed constitution provides useful intellectual resources for modern democratic theorists, by drawing attention to his methods for integrating the multitude into his aristocratic framework, such as his emphasis on

59 On this point, see Hansen, 'The mixed constitution versus the separation of powers', 514–17. Today, the relationship between the executive branch of government and parliament has been changing: the task of proposing a governmental policy is undertaken mainly by ruling parties, and the task of assessing it is undertaken mainly by opposition parties.

the variety of perceptions that the multitude have and his distinction between production and assessment. These ideas seem to have provided a basis for modern constitutional theorists to contemplate a proper distribution of political authority among various political institutions. Thus, Aristotle's aristocratic theory provides insights into the problem of distributing political authority even in the context of modern democracies.

CHAPTER 4

CIVIC VIRTUE

4.1 Arguments about civic virtue

In the previous chapter, I examined Aristotle's aristocratic way of thinking about politics and considered how he integrates what we see as 'democratic elements' into his aristocratic framework. In the present and following chapters, I shall turn to the issue of what conceptual framework Aristotle uses to analyse and cultivate the ideal of equality among citizens. Given that Aristotle does not embrace the modern democratic ideas that the status of being free entitles all citizens to participate in the political process or that human rights are inalienable, what features of his political philosophy make it nonetheless somewhat sympathetic towards democratic governance? I shall address this problem by examining his conceptions of civic virtue (Chapter 4), civic friendship (Chapter 5) and commutative justice (Chapter 6), and demonstrate that he regards the reciprocal equality of governing and being governed in turn as the key element that enables citizens to cultivate their virtue and build friendly relationships among themselves.

In this chapter, I shall consider what Aristotle's conception of civic virtue implies regarding relationships with other people. Although 'virtue' is usually concerned not with relationships among individuals, but with the internal structure of an individual's character, a primary reason for addressing this issue is to consider what character traits Aristotle maintains will enable the development of a free and equal relationship among citizens in the political sphere. In fact, during the past few decades, Aristotle's conception of civic virtue has provided a resource for Aristotelian republicanism to draw on in developing arguments about the importance of political participation and building a conceptual framework for forming a civic relationship. For example, Michael Sandel asserts that civic virtue enables citizens to be engaged in political activity as agents, not as passive subjects of governance, and thereby achieve an ideal of freedom as self-governance. What is essential in civic republican politics is thus to cultivate in citizens the qualities of character that the ideal of self-governance requires, such as knowledge of public affairs, concern for the whole and a moral bond with the community that goes beyond the capacity to respect others' rights while pursuing one's own ends.[1] In this view, civic virtue thus enables citizens to participate in the political process and look after the common good beyond their own private interests.

The same view of civic virtue is expressed in the final report of the Advisory Group on Citizenship, or what is called 'The Crick Report'. This report proposes reforming citizenship education in the UK in such a way as to foster not the 'subject' who passively obeys the law, but the 'active citizen' who participates in the political process and responsibly changes the law when it is necessary to do so.[2] Aristotle's political thought offers a background to this educational reform in providing the view of such active citizenship. The chairman of this advisory group says:

> To the Greeks and the Romans citizenship was both a legal term and a social status: citizens were those who had a legal right to have a say in the affairs of the city or state, either by speaking in public or by voting, usually both . . . Active citizenship was believed to be a prime moral virtue: no human being could be themselves at their best without participating in public life. Aristotle remarked that whoever could live outside the *polis* – the city, or the civic relationship or the community of citizens – was either a beast or a god. Although both the Greek city states and the Roman Republic were destroyed, the memory and the ideal of free citizenship endured.[3]

Here Bernard Crick maintains that Aristotle's view of a human as a halfway being between beast and god in *Politics* 1.2 means that participation in public life is essential for human

1 Sandel, *Democracy's Discontent*, 5.
2 Advisory Group on Citizenship, *Education for Citizenship and the Teaching of Democracy in Schools*, esp. 2.1–2.9.
3 Crick, *Essays on Citizenship*, 4.

happiness, and that active citizenship is a prime moral virtue. He thus introduces this ideal of civic virtue into the present-day context of citizenship education, thereby suggesting that citizens need to be encouraged and educated to cultivate the civic virtue that enables them to be actively engaged in politics.

In the literature on Aristotle's *Politics*, however, there are serious controversies about whether Aristotle really encourages citizens to participate in the political process, and how he relates political activity or the exercise of virtue in the political sphere to an essential element of human happiness. On the one hand, Terence Irwin argues that in Aristotle's framework political activity is not only concerned with the provision of resources, which is simply a necessary condition for achieving human happiness, but is also more directly related to happiness itself.[4] In Irwin's view, a virtuous person has a reason to regard another virtuous person as another self, and extend the scope of practical reason and deliberation to the good of other people.[5] Irwin thus thinks that cooperative activity provides an individual with a good that is intrinsic to their happiness, because the good of their friends can be understood as their own good.

There are many other scholars who shed light on the politicised dimension of virtue in Aristotle, thereby implying that the exercise of virtue in the political sphere is part of human happiness. Usually they see this dimension through the arguments regarding the difference between the virtue of man and that of a citizen in Book 3 of the *Politics*. David Keyt does not find any conflict between a good man and an upright citizen in an ideal political system.[6] This is because in an ideal political system a good man is permitted to govern a polis through the exercise of his practical wisdom, which is also the mark of a good man. Keyt identifies the difference between the virtue of a man and that of a citizen only in non-ideal political systems, since virtue or practical wisdom is not respected in these

4 Irwin, 'The good of political activity', 74–6. 5 Ibid., 94.

6 Keyt, 'The good man and the upright citizen in Aristotle's *Ethics* and *Politics*', 220–40.

systems, and other values, such as liberty or wealth, are the aims of these systems. Likewise, Jean Roberts sees no conflict between a good man and a good citizen, especially between moral virtue and civic virtue.[7] She strongly supports the view of man as a political animal, and identifies the differences between the virtue of a man and that of a citizen only in terms of the variations in citizens' roles to sustain a polis and in terms of the variations of political systems.[8]

On the other hand, some Aristotelian scholars assess the non-political nature of virtue and do not give priority to political activity. As mentioned in Chapter 1, Richard Mulgan treats Aristotle not as a spokesman of civic republicanism, but rather as a predecessor of the Hellenistic philosophers who propose retreating from politics. In Mulgan's view, Aristotle stresses the importance of philosophy and social life involving personal friends and family, not the combination of philosophy and politics.[9] Gisela Striker also casts doubt on Irwin's arguments in such a way as to argue that the significance of the sharing of political authority is not based on the concept of friendship, but simply on a demand on the part of justice that it is fair to treat equals equally. According to her interpretation, throughout the *Politics* Aristotle describes practical wisdom as a capacity for ruling, and this narrow idea of practical intelligence makes it possible for him to presuppose that participation in government is an indispensable part of human happiness. Striker, however, casts doubt also on this narrow understanding of practical wisdom itself, since the rational capacity can be exercised in many other different professions. She therefore concludes that Aristotle's identification of political participation with human happiness does not have a firm basis in his theory.[10]

7 Roberts, 'Excellences of the citizen and of the individual', 555–65.
8 Malcolm Schofield also sheds light on the political dimensions of virtue, especially courage, justice and practical wisdom, in Aristotle (see Schofield, 'Aristotle's political ethics', 305–22).
9 Mulgan, 'Aristotle and the value of political participation' and 'Was Aristotle an "Aristotelian social democrat"?'.
10 Striker, 'Comments on T. Irwin', 99–100.

In sum, the issues relating to Aristotle's conception of civic virtue are how he integrates the exercise of civic virtue within his framework for human happiness, and how he prioritises political activity over other social, familial activities. First, some scholars as well as civic republican theorists treat Aristotle as encouraging citizens to exercise their practical wisdom in the political process, and identifying the virtue of a citizen with the capacity for being engaged in politics. Clearly, in Aristotle's framework, political activity can be recognised as part of human happiness, in that it is the exercise of practical wisdom. Aristotle, however, offers a more complicated view of the characteristics of civic virtue. In particular, although in *Politics* 3.1 he defines citizenship by drawing attention to the 'activity' of citizens, namely, public deliberation and judgement, in *Politics* 3.4 he identifies 'passivity', that is, the role of being governed, as one of the crucial elements of a citizen's virtue. What we need to explore, then, is how Aristotle identifies this passive element with a citizen's happiness, and how to understand the apparent contradiction between his definition of citizenship and his definition of civic virtue. In the next section, I shall identify the significance of the elements of both governing and being governed, not only as they relate to the demands of justice, as Striker points out, but also from an educational perspective, in order to see the connection between civic virtue and human happiness.

Second, there is also a controversy as to how Aristotle considers the polis to be more important than the family is for achieving the good life. In a civic republican view, the polis is the primary locus for citizens to achieve human happiness, whereas in a communitarian view, as well as in Mulgan's view, the family is also one of those important communities where citizens cultivate a sense of belonging and moral character. To be sure, in Aristotle's view the highest form of life lies not in public life, but rather in contemplative life, as Hannah Arendt and John Pocock recognise. Famously, in *EN* 10.7 Aristotle suggests that a human being should assimilate to the immortals and perform theoretical activity as much as possible. By contrast, political activities are classified as the secondary activity, since they fall short of leisure (σχολή) and sometimes aim at other ends, such as political power or honour (1177b12–26). In Aristotle's view, thus, the exercise of virtue is not limited to political activity. As examined in Chapter 2, however, he treats the good of a polis as finer and more divine than the good of an individual (*EN* 1.2.1094b7–10). Although he does not here propose a totalitarian conception of a good polis, at the least he prioritises the good of a polis over the good of an individual. What we need to explore, then, is what conceptual framework makes it possible to place a higher value on a polis than on an individual or private family. Given that virtue can be used for private activities that, from a modern perspective, seem to be more significant for an individual's happiness, how does Aristotle give priority to the political dimension of virtue? In Section 4.3 I shall consider this problem by drawing attention not to the concept of freedom (Arendt) or the universal good (Pocock), but to the scale of rationality. In other words, I shall consider how Aristotle acknowledges the difference between the civic and private uses of virtue by examining the way virtues and individuals' capacities for them vary with the capacity for rationality.

Although civic republican theories capture some important points in Aristotle's political theory, in Section 4.4 I shall point out differences between Aristotle's own and 'Aristotelian' civic republican political theory. In particular, I shall demonstrate these differences by examining Arendt's oversimplified picture of the relationship between polis and family, Pocock's ambiguous concept of 'the universal good' and Sandel's concept of positive liberty. Overall, this chapter is intended to consider, somewhat differently from civic republican perspectives, how Aristotle identifies the significance of political activity for human happiness. I shall then conclude that Aristotle's political philosophy does provide a basis for a republican conception of civic virtue, although not without important qualifications.

4.2 The virtue of a citizen

Aristotle's definition of citizenship is in line with the civic republican conception of what it means to be a citizen, to the extent that he analyses citizenship based on citizens' activities. In *Politics* 3.1, he explores what the essential element of citizenship is, first defining it as participation in the judicial process and in public office (μετέχειν κρίσεως καὶ ἀρχῆς) (1275a19–23). He does not hold the defining characteristic of being a citizen to be residence within a polis (1275a7–8) or access to the legal processes of prosecuting and being prosecuted (1275a8–11), but the fact that a citizen issues judicial decisions as a judge and holds public office. This definition, however, leaves open the question of what public office actually means. Aristotle then divides various kinds of public official into those with limited tenure and those (such as members of a jury or members of the popular assembly) with unlimited tenure. Refuting the criticism that membership of such bodies does not count as holding public *office*, Aristotle treats such membership as nonetheless constituting public office on account of its supreme power, and calls it 'unlimited office'. In making this argument, he is thinking of jurymen and assemblymen in particular as those who participate in public office, and this argument is therefore best suited to citizenship in a democracy. In other constitutions, their tasks, namely, judgement and deliberation, are vested in public officials with limited tenure. In order to make his definition workable for various constitutions, Aristotle defines a citizen as one who is entitled to share deliberative and judicial office (κοινωνεῖν ἀρχῆς βουλευτικῆς καὶ κριτικῆς) (*Pol.* 3.1.1275b18–20).

The manner in which Aristotle subsequently develops his idea of citizenship effectively involves an important distinction between a citizen (πολίτης) and a free person (ἐλεύθερος) in his terminology. In *Politics* 3.5, Aristotle considers whether a craftsman or manual worker (βάναυσος) counts as a citizen, and argues that in the best polis a craftsman cannot be admitted to be a 'citizen' because craftsmen cannot acquire virtue unless they are freed from necessary work (1278a8–11). In an aristocracy, Aristotle says, where public offices are given to citizens according to virtue, craftsmen and labourers cannot be 'citizens' (1278a15–21), although they are still free persons. This argument shows that Aristotle does not fully embrace the type of democratic practice in which any free, male, native-born adult is enrolled as a citizen even if he is not virtuous at all.[11] While in a democracy such free persons are coterminous with citizens, in an oligarchy only the wealthy and in an aristocracy only the virtuous can be 'citizens'. In Aristotle's terminology, therefore, a free person, who lives freely in a private sphere, is different from a citizen, who by definition decides public issues and exercises political power.[12]

How, then, does Aristotle define the virtue of a citizen? The following passage is of especial importance in *Politics* 3.4, where he considers whether the virtue of a good man and that of a citizen are the same by analogy with a sailor:

Just as a sailor is one of a number of members of a community, so, we say, is a citizen. And though sailors differ in their capacities (for one is an oarsman, another a captain, another a lookout, and others have other sorts of titles), it is clear both that the most exact account of each sort of sailor will be peculiar to his virtue, and similarly that there will also be some common account that fits them all. For the safety of the voyage is a task of all of them, since this is what each of the sailors is trying to achieve. In the same way, then, the citizens too, however different they may be, have the safety of the community as their task. But the community is the constitution. Therefore the virtue of the citizen must be in relation to the constitution. Consequently, if indeed

[11] For a discussion of this undemocratic element of Aristotle's arguments about citizenship, see Frede, 'Citizenship in Aristotle's *Politics*', 167–84.

[12] Because of his strong interest in ancient political theory, Jean-Jacques Rousseau draws a distinction between a bourgeois and a citizen (*citoyen*), the latter of whom is a participant in the sovereign authority, and argues that '*houses make the city [ville] but Citizens make a City [cité]*'; Rousseau, 'Of the social contract', Book 1, Chapter 6. Pierre Pellegrin translates ἐλεύθερος and πολίτης into 'homme libre' and 'citoyen', respectively, in the passage (*Pol.* 3.5.1278a8–11). For a difference between the ancient and modern concepts of 'citizenship', see Walzer, 'Citizenship', 211–19, in which he illustrates that a citizen in ancient Greece is one who is engaged in lawmaking and administration, while a citizen in modern society is one who is protected by the law and entitled to the protection of life, liberty and property. It would seem that the conceptual displacement of 'citizenship' from an active political actor to a passive recipient of the benefits of governance corresponds to that of 'democracy', from describing the system of the people as 'the actors of governance' to describing the system of the people as 'the recipients of the benefits of governance'.

there are several kinds of constitution, it is clear that there cannot be a single, perfect virtue of an excellent citizen. In contrast, we say that a good man is good according to a single, perfect virtue. It is then clear that it is possible to be an excellent citizen without possessing that virtue according to which a man is excellent. (1276b20–35)

At first sight, this passage seems to be problematic, since here Aristotle notes that there are various tasks of citizens as well as those of sailors, while he defines a citizen as one who participates in deliberative and judicial office. According to his definition, the task of a citizen seems to be simply to participate in deliberative and judicial office. How can we identify the variety of citizens' tasks? It would seem that in the quoted passage Aristotle simply focuses on the specific types of citizens' tasks: in *Politics* 6.8 he enumerates these tasks, such as the regulation of the market, the wardenship of a city, the administration of the treasury, the execution of a sentence, the defence of a polis and the worship of gods. Although there is a common feature of civic virtue, namely, the preservation of a political system, Aristotle notes the variety of citizens' tasks.[13] This argument presupposes his characteristic viewpoint when identifying virtue: here as elsewhere, he defines the virtue of a citizen with reference to his work (ἔργον). The virtue of a citizen is in this passage considered to be the ability to work on a specific task for the security of a community. This focus on a specific task leads Aristotle to consider that the virtue of a citizen is different from the virtue of a man. Soon afterwards (*Pol.* 3.4.1276b37–1277a5), he argues that, since it is impossible to establish a polis with only good men, and all the citizens do not have the same quality, each member should do his own work well, and the virtue of a citizen is thus different from that of a good man. Based on the diversity of citizens, Aristotle maintains that the

[13] Roberts asserts that the variety of citizens' tasks comes from the differentiation in the jobs necessary to sustain a city, such as farming, making tools, trading, fighting and so on, in his 'Excellences of the citizen and of the individual', 557. However, given that Aristotle does not necessarily consider those who engage in the jobs necessary to sustain a city to be 'citizens' or a part of the city (*Pol.* 3.5.1278a2–3, 7.8.1328a21–5, 7.9.1329a34–8), a more plausible interpretation is that the variation in citizens' jobs comes from the wide variety of public work. For this point, see Keyt, 'The good man and the upright citizen', 222–3.

virtue of a citizen varies from work to work, although the virtue of a good man is a single, perfect virtue.

Moreover, in the passage quoted above (*Pol.* 3.4.1276b20–35), he argues that the virtue of a citizen varies from constitution to constitution. For example, in an oligarchy, where public office is allocated to citizens according to the amount of wealth, a citizen is required to contribute to the task of increasing the wealth of a polis. The virtue of a citizen in an oligarchy is thus the ability to deliberate about how to increase wealth in a polis. In contrast, in an aristocracy, where public office is allocated to citizens according to virtue, the virtue of a citizen is the ability to deliberate about how to achieve the good life of citizens. In this case, the virtue of a citizen can be the same as the virtue of a man. In fact, Aristotle asserts that the virtue of a man and that of a citizen are exactly identical in the ideal polis (*Pol.* 3.18.1288a38–9, 4.7.1293b3–7, 7.14.1333a11–12). Thus, while the second distinction between the virtue of a citizen and that of a man lies in a difference in the principle governing a political system, he admits that these are identical in the ideal polis.

Next, Aristotle more specifically considers how the virtue of a citizen is the same as the virtue of a man for some individuals, namely, rulers (*Pol.* 3.4.1277a13–25). The rationale for this identification comes from Aristotle's understanding of practical wisdom: he considers the practical thinking engaged in by a ruler to be one demonstration of the capacity for practical wisdom. In his view, practical wisdom and the art of politics are the same disposition, although their objects of use are different (*EN* 6.8.1141b23–33). In developing the view that a good ruler is also a good man, he presupposes this politicised understanding of practical wisdom, which is also one of the defining elements that make a person ethically good.[14]

In the aforementioned definition of citizenship (*Pol.* 3.1.1275a19–23) and civic virtue (*Pol.* 3.4.1276b20–35), Aristotle focuses on the activity of a citizen, but he considers a

[14] For a discussion of the relationship between practical wisdom and ethical virtue in detail, see McDowell, 'Virtue and reason', 50–73, and Sorabji, 'Aristotle on the role of intellect in virtue', 201–19.

citizen to be one who is governed as well as one who governs, and defines the virtue of a citizen as the capacity for both governing and being governed (*Pol.* 3.4.1277a25–32). He argues that the virtue of a citizen is different from that of a good man, since whether a man is good depends on practical wisdom, which is an attribute not of the ruled but of a ruler. Here he clearly takes a passive state, that of being governed, to be characteristic of civic virtue, while defining citizenship also in terms of an active element, participating in the governing role. Is Aristotle's understanding of civic virtue contradictory to his definition of citizenship? One key to this problem lies in the definition of citizenship itself: he says that a citizen is one who '*is entitled* to share deliberative and judicial office (ᾧ γὰρ ἐξουσία κοινωνεῖν ἀρχῆς βουλευτικῆς καὶ κριτικῆς)' (*Pol.* 3.1.1275b18–19, my italics, already quoted). Here he defines a citizen in terms of membership of bodies that exercise political authority and leaves open the possibility that a citizen is governed in some cases, while governing in others. For example, in a democracy, a citizen may play an active role in the council this year, but be governed by other citizens next year when he leaves the council, since a defining characteristic of a political system of government is to take turns in public office. Aristotle's definition of civic virtue as the capacity for governing and being governed is therefore not contradictory to his definition of citizenship after all.

It is a harder task for Aristotle to acknowledge the importance of being governed than to acknowledge that of governing, since according to his basic understanding, human happiness lies in activity, not in passivity (*EN* 1.8.1098b31–1099a7, 9.9.1169b10–13, 10.6.1176a33–b9, *DA* 3.5.430a18–19). How does he justify the passive element of civic virtue within his philosophical framework? On the one hand, as Striker points out,[15] the sharing of governing and being governed comes from the demand of justice. Aristotle repeatedly indicates that it is in accordance with justice for similar people to take turns in political authority (*Pol.* 3.16.1287a10–18, 7.3.1325b7–8,

[15] Striker, 'Comments on T. Irwin', 99–100.

7.14.1332b25–9). Furthermore, in *Politics* 1.7 (1255b16–20) he states that political rule is governance among free and equal citizens, and in *Politics* 1.12 (1259b4–6) that in political rule the ruler and the ruled switch their roles in turn, since they try to be equal in nature and avoid differentiations. The necessity of being governed in political rule is therefore justified by the fact that all citizens are equal and similar in quality.

On the other hand, Aristotle does have another way of explaining the necessity of being governed, best illustrated in the following passage: 'a ruler must learn [political governance] by being governed, as one learns to command cavalry by serving under a cavalry-commander and to be a general by serving under a general and by commanding a battalion and a company. Hence, the following saying is also true, namely that it is not possible to govern well without having been governed' (*Pol.* 3.4.1277b9–13, cf. 7.14.1333a2–3). By the analogy of leadership by a general, Aristotle identifies the importance of being governed from an educational perspective. In other words, he includes a passive element in the definition of political governance, because passivity crucially includes being taught by experience, which is important for the acquisition of the art of political governance.

The significance of being governed can be made clearer if we draw attention to the concept of 'governance'. In Greek, as mentioned in Chapter 1, the word 'governance [or rule] (ἀρχή)' originally meant a beginning from which activity starts. In this respect, governance is the starting-point for activity that affects other people, whether it is political or despotic. Those who govern therefore need to be aware of how their own governance affects people by viewing it from the perspective of being governed, and considering how other people feel about being governed and affected by the actions of government. One might, however, argue that from this argument it also follows that a despotic master needs to understand how his own despotic rule affects his slave by becoming a slave and submitting to the rule of another master. How can we acknowledge the educational importance of being governed in political rule but not in despotic rule? A key distinction between them is helpful: in

Politics 3.6 (1278b32–1279a16), Aristotle argues that a master rules a slave to further his own benefit, while a political ruler seeks to advance the common benefit of citizens. A crucial difference between despotic rule and political rule lies in whether the respective types of ruler need take the benefit of the ruled into account. In this respect, the experience of being governed is necessary for a political ruler to understand the meaning of his governance for the governed and thereby effectively exercise political authority for the benefit of others. More specifically, a free person needs to become a citizen by being ruled not only in a household, but also in a polis by other equal citizens, so that he can look after their benefit when he in turn becomes a ruler. Aristotle's distinctions among various types of rule suggest that a political ruler must have passive experiences in a polis in order to cultivate his civic virtue.[16]

Furthermore, Aristotle's emphasis on the importance of habituation in developing virtue generally implies the significance of civic activity, as well as passivity for cultivating civic virtue. As is well known, Aristotle asserts that a human being acquires a virtue (for example, courage) through performing its associated activities (courageous activities) repeatedly. To put it in his terms, the same disposition arises from the same actions (*EN* 2.1.1103b21–2). Given that this argument can be applied to the cultivation of civic virtue in the same way, a human being can cultivate civic virtue only by performing civic activities repeatedly in the judicial and political processes. The basis for becoming a citizen resides neither in patriarchal rule as a household manager nor in despotic rule as a master, but rather in political rule as a ruler. The knowledge of despotic rule or patriarchal rule does not provide a citizen with an insight into how to govern a polis as a citizen. To be sure, Aristotle's emphasis on habituation means that people need to be passively controlled by laws to cultivate virtue, since they tend to yield to compulsion rather than argument, as expressed famously in

[16] Robert Mayhew offers a brief account of political rule in comparison with other types of rule in his 'Rulers and ruled', 526–39.

the last chapter of *EN* (10.9.1179a33–1180a24). However, it also means that citizens acquire civic virtue by being actively engaged with political and judicial practices. Thus, elements of both governing and being governed properly belong within Aristotle's framework for the education of a free person as a citizen.[17]

4.3 The scale of rationality

For our consideration of the characteristics of civic virtue, it is useful to examine the distinction Aristotle makes between the virtue of a ruler and that of the ruled in *Politics* 1.13, because this distinction makes it possible to see that the scale of rationality is essential to identifying differentiations in virtue. Accordingly, I shall explore why Aristotle prioritises public life in the polis over private life in the family by comparing the rationality of citizens with that of family members.

The following passage best illustrates Aristotle's attempt to explain the difference between the virtue of a ruler and that of the ruled in relation to the scale of rationality:

> In a soul, one thing is by nature the ruler and another is by nature the ruled. We say that their virtue is different, as one is the virtue of the rational part and the other is that of the non-rational part. It is then clear that the same is true in other cases as well, and so many things are by nature a ruler or a subject. For a free man rules a slave, a male rules a female, and a man rules a child in different ways. The parts of a soul belong to everyone, but differently. For a slave does not have deliberative ability [τὸ βουλευτικόν] at all, a female has it, but without authority [ἄκυρον], and a child has it, but undeveloped [ἀτελές]. We should therefore suppose that the same conditions are necessarily true also of the ethical virtues. All must partake of virtue, not in the same way, but as much as needed for the work of each. Therefore, a ruler should have complete [τελέαν] ethical virtue, since his task is unqualifiedly that of a master craftsman and his reason [λόγος] is a master craftsman. Other members should have such an amount of virtue as is appropriate

[17] In *Politics* 4.11, Aristotle argues that the rich know only how to rule other people, whereas the poor know only how to be ruled like slaves, and acknowledges the importance of the experiences of both governing and being governed for civic activity. See Chapter 6 for the implications of this argument in Aristotle's distributive theory.

to themselves. It is therefore apparent that ethical virtue belongs to everyone mentioned, and the same temperance does not belong to a woman and a man, neither do the same courage and justice, as Socrates thought, but one is master courage and the other is servant courage and likewise with the other virtues. (*Pol.* 1.13.1260a5–24)

In the context of this passage, Aristotle addresses the question whether a slave needs ethical virtues, such as temperance, courage and justice, beyond instrumental and servile virtue. If a slave does have ethical virtue, on the one hand, how different is he from a free person? It would be strange for him to be a slave in spite of being a human and possessing virtue. If he does not have ethical virtue, on the other hand, how can he be ruled well? He would not be able to work well without virtue. This question comes from the dialogue between Socrates and Meno in Plato's *Meno*. When Socrates asks Meno to define what virtue is, Meno first answers with reference to a wide variety of virtues: the virtue of a man is the ability to manage political affairs, that is, to help friends and harm enemies; the virtue of a woman is the ability to manage a household well, that is, to maintain the household economy and obey her husband. Meno argues that virtue is different as between a child and an elderly man, between a female and a male, and between a free person and a slave, and thereby draws attention to the differences in virtue that correspond to action, age and task (*Meno* 71e–72a). Socrates casts doubt on this answer, stating that although there are various kinds of virtue, all of them must have one and the same form that makes them virtue, just as the health of a woman and that of a man have the same form (*Meno* 72c–73a). Socrates again asks Meno to define what virtue is, and, on second thoughts, Meno answers that virtue is the ability to rule people (*Meno* 73c–d). Socrates immediately raises a problem with this definition: it does not describe the virtue of a child or that of a servant, because children and servants never rule their parents or master. Although Socrates proposes adding 'justly, not unjustly' to Meno's definition, he points out that justice is merely one kind of virtue, not virtue itself, and finally puts the task of defining virtue aside (*Meno* 73d–74a). What he is asking for is a universal definition of virtue that can apply equally in the same form without regard to gender, age or task.[18]

From Aristotle's viewpoint, Socrates' pursuit of a universal definition of virtue makes it difficult to recognise the difference between the virtue of a ruler and that of the ruled, and to see the wide variety in human relationships. Soon after the quoted passage, Aristotle criticises Socrates and instead praises Gorgias (because Meno is a follower of Gorgias)[19] for differentiating the virtue of a man from that of a woman (*Pol.* 1.13.1260a20–8). Aristotle then focuses not only on the work or function (ἔργον) of a human being in general, as he does in the human-function argument in *EN* 1.7, but also on the function of specific positions in various human relationships. His attention to specific functions makes it possible for him to raise the question of how a ruler's virtue is different from a subject's virtue. Furthermore, in the quoted passage (*Pol.* 1.13.1260a5–24), Aristotle makes this difference clear by relating it to difference in deliberative ability (τὸ βουλευτικόν): a slave does not have his own deliberative ability by himself at all, and only partakes of reason as communicated by his master. A woman possesses it by herself, but without authority. In other words, she is considered not to control her natural disposition, or the emotional part of her soul, by her own understanding.[20] Children have not yet developed the deliberative capacity, but are expected to possess it when they grow up. In sum, in Aristotle's view, family members, except for the household manager, have a limited degree of rationality, and their ethical virtue varies with their form of deliberative ability. Family relationships, such as those

[18] For the characteristics of Socrates' question of 'what it is', see Bluck (ed.), *Plato's Meno*, 4–7, 209–13. For the background of Socrates' pursuit of a single determinate feature of virtue, see Scott, *Plato's Meno*, 23–30.

[19] See Bluck (ed.), *Plato's Meno*, 124, Saunders (trans.), Aristotle, *Politics*, 100–1, Scott, *Plato's Meno*, 24–5, and Sharples (ed.), Plato, *Meno*, 18.

[20] As mentioned above, I aim here to illustrate Aristotle's ideas about the relationship between virtue and practical wisdom among various types of humans, and ultimately identify what he has in mind when he refers to the rationality of a citizen. Contravening his idea, we simply need to attribute perfect rationality to women, and thereby ignore the difference between man and woman. For Aristotle's view of women, see Lange, 'Woman is not a rational animal', 1–15, and Mulgan, 'Aristotle and the political role of women', 179–202.

between wife and husband, child and parent, and slave and master, are therefore unequal and are controlled by a household manager.

How then can we clearly recognise the difference between the virtue of a ruler and that of the ruled within Aristotle's theory of ethical virtue? Are there any arguments about the difference between the master virtue and the subordinate forms of virtue? These points can be clarified in light of Aristotle's distinction between 'in accord with correct reason (κατὰ τὸν ὀρθὸν λόγον)' and 'with correct reason (μετὰ τοῦ ὀρθοῦ λόγου)' in *EN* 6.13 (1144b26–7). This distinction is useful for distinguishing a ruler's use of reason from the following of the ruler's reason on the part of the ruled. According to this distinction, for example, it can be said that a slave behaves appropriately 'in accord with correct reason' by following the order of his master. Such a slave, however, does not work by using his own reason, or, in Aristotle's terminology, 'with his correct reason'. In the same way, children do not use their own reason when they follow the instructions of their parents. Aristotle therefore asserts that the virtue of a child does not exist on its own but in relation to someone who guides it (*Pol.* 1.13.1260a31–3), and that the source of servile virtue for a slave is the master, not the instructor who teaches him the tasks (*Pol.* 1.13.1260b3–5).[21] This distinction between 'with correct reason' and 'in accord with correct reason' corresponds to the difference between the master virtue and the subordinate forms of virtue. The

[21] I do not draw a distinction here between husband–wife and father–child relationships, but in *Politics* 1.12 (1259a39–b1) Aristotle opines that a husband rules his wife in a political manner, whereas a father rules his child in the manner of a king. Furthermore, in *EN* 8.10 (1160b24–1161a1, cf. *EE* 7.9.1241b30–2) he holds that a father rules his child in the manner of a king while a husband rules his wife in an aristocratic way, handing over to her the jobs appropriate for a woman. From these remarks it would seem that Aristotle supposes that women have a more developed form of deliberative capacity for their job, whereas children need to be guided completely by their father until they grow up fully. Concerning the rational capacity of a slave, Aristotle argues that a slave needs only a modicum of virtue so that he does not fail to perform his job (*Pol.* 1.13.1260a33–6). He then criticises the view that slaves have no reason at all and need only to be commanded (*Pol.* 1.13.1260b5–7). To illustrate the point, the slave can understand it when one says 'Close the door, *because* it's getting cold in here'; but he is not smart enough to think that out for himself.

differences among the virtues exhibited by the various human relationships can therefore be identified through attention to what form of rationality they incorporate.[22]

How, then, can we identify the rationality of a citizen in the political sphere? As discussed above, Aristotle relates the virtue of a ruler closely to practical wisdom (*Pol.* 3.4.1277a13–20). A good ruler is expected to acquire perfect rationality, through which he can be considered to be a good person as well as a good ruler. In addition, Aristotle classifies kingship as one of the correct constitutions and notoriously argues that if there is a pre-eminently virtuous person in a society, people should appoint him king and follow his instruction (*Pol.* 3.13.1284b25–34). Does Aristotle attribute such complete rationality to an ordinary citizen? First of all, his definition of political justice sheds light on this problem: 'political justice was in accord with the law and belongs to those who are naturally suited for the law; and these were people sharing equally in governing and being governed' (*EN* 5.6.1134b13–15). Here Aristotle asserts that political justice is applicable only to those who are suited for the law – free and equal citizens. This concept of the law provides a clear contrast between an ordinary citizen and the pre-eminent king in *Politics* 3.13: in Aristotle's view, to endorse equality is an injustice to a pre-eminent king, and there is no law for such a pre-eminent king, since he himself *is* the law (1284a9–14). This idea implies that those who are suited for the law do not have so complete a measure of rationality as does a pre-eminent king.

Here is the relevance for the rule of law. In *Politics* 3.15, Aristotle raises the question whether it is more useful to be governed by the best person than by the best laws (1286a7–9). On the one hand, he explores the reason for favouring governance by the best person: laws operate only by general principles and

[22] Although this distinction between 'with correct reason' and 'in accord with correct reason' in *EN* 6.13 is useful for acknowledging a difference between the master virtue and the subordinate forms of virtue, there is a crucial difference between the subordinate forms of virtue in *Politics* 1.13 and natural virtue (φυσικὴ ἀρετή) in *EN* 6.13: the former enable a subject to follow the instruction of a ruler, while the latter is simply a disposition given to a person from birth and does not necessarily enable a person to follow the instruction of practical wisdom.

do not give any instructions about what happens every day. Thus, it is absurd to be guided by written rules in any field where skill is required, such as a medical operation (*Pol.* 3.15.1286a9–16). To put it briefly, the objection to the rule of law focuses on the generality of law. On the other hand, Aristotle explores the reasons for the rule of law in the following passage, where he best illustrates what he has in mind when he refers to the rationality of an ordinary human being:

> In the matters about which the law appears to be unable to make a judgement, a human being would also be unable to find an answer. The law, having educated the rulers properly, appoints them to decide and manage the matters that are left undecided by it, 'to the best of their judgement [τῇ δικαιοτάτῃ γνώμῃ]'.[23] Furthermore, the law allows them to make corrections by introducing anything found by experience to be an improvement on the existing laws. Therefore those who ask law to rule seem to be asking God and intelligence alone to rule, whereas those who ask a human being to rule are asking a wild beast also to rule. For appetite is like a wild beast, and anger perverts rulers and the best men. Law is thus intelligence without desire. (*Pol.* 3.16.1287a24–32)[24]

Here Aristotle argues that the rule of law is more desirable – first, because the law educates rulers so that they can work out a particular problem about which the law cannot give an instruction, and, second, because the law is intelligence without desire, while a human being has desires that pervert good governance. Having asserted that a human being is halfway between a god and a beast in *Politics* 1.2 (1253a25–9), Aristotle here, as elsewhere, assumes that a human being has irrational parts as well as a rational part. In contrast, the law is expected to educate such a human being to enable him to follow its instructions. The law is thus considered to be essentially the product of intellect without desire.[25]

23 This expression comes from the oath taken by Athenian jurors. See Newman, *The Politics of Aristotle*, vol. III, 294.
24 The same idea is found in Plato's *Laws* 4.713e–714a.
25 For Aristotle's theory of the rule of law, see Kraut, *Aristotle*, 451–7, Miller, *Nature, Justice, and Rights in Aristotle's Politics*, 79–84, and Swanson, *The Public and the Private in Aristotle's Political Philosophy*, 97–101. For the ordinary Athenian views of the rule of law, see Ober, *Mass and Elite in Democratic Athens*, 299–304.

This treatment of law is at first glance problematic: given that the law is also established by humans, it must surely reflect human desires. What conception of the law makes it possible for Aristotle to regard law as intelligence without desire? His subsequent argument (*Pol.* 3.16.1287a32–b5) is helpful: refuting the idea that no skill should follow written instructions, Aristotle draws a distinction between a medical operation and politics. While a doctor does not contravene medical principles on account of affection, politicians are susceptible to being corrupted based on personal likes and dislikes. This is because it is impossible for people to judge correctly when it comes to their own affairs. In this respect, the generality, or universality, of the law is a positive advantage, to the extent that the law can keep a distance from a particular situation and the personal affairs of legislators.[26] In contrast, Aristotle does not expect a human being to detach his own emotion from any political decisions he faces. Rather, he maintains that an ordinary citizen is able to behave with complete rationality only within the constraints of laws. In fact, he repeatedly points out that there is no pre-eminently virtuous person who can be an absolute king (*Pol.* 5.10.1313a3–10, 7.14.1332b23–5). In his view, thus, ordinary citizens can achieve full rationality only by exchanging political authority between themselves within the law. Interestingly, Aristotle regards the relationship of governing and being governed in turn as a legal matter (*Pol.* 3.16.1287a17–18). The rationality of a citizen is therefore dependent on his relationship with other citizens, or on the law of governing and being governed in turn.

The scale of rationality is the key to privileging public life in a polis. As discussed above, Aristotle does not assert that family members possess full rationality, although they have a subordinate form of virtue necessary to accomplish their work. In his view, there are no equal relationships in a household. The rationality in a household is limited to that of the

[26] The same argument is found in *Rhet.* 1.1.1354b5–11. As discussed in the previous chapter, Aristotle also draws a distinction between law (νόμος) and decree (ψήφισμα) (*Pol.* 4.4.1292a4–13). In this view, law essentially means a general principle, not a particular judgement.

household manager, who is at best a being halfway between intellect and desire. In a household, therefore, there is no system through which the household manager is governed and educated to achieve full rationality. Furthermore, in despotic rule, a master is allowed to rule a slave as he wants. In this type of rule, there are no regulations or restrictions controlling the master's desire. In contrast, the polis establishes a system for regulating the desires of citizens through their relationships of governing and being governed in turn. Furthermore, the polis creates the opportunity for citizens to listen to the opinions of other citizens who have a more developed rationality, and to share their views of good and justice in the deliberative and judicial processes, just as Aristotle points out in his arguments for the wisdom of the multitude. In this respect, the polis is a community of free and equal persons for the achievement of full rationality, while the household is a smaller community of unequal persons concerned with daily needs. Given that human happiness depends solely on what level of rationality an individual achieves, the polis rather than the household plays the leading role in enabling citizens to acquire full rationality and thereby achieve human happiness. Aristotle therefore does not privilege any sense of belonging to communities from which an individual finds his own identity, as communitarians do, but rather the civic relationship in which citizens can achieve perfect rationality. The priority of political activity over other types of activity comes from its potential to give citizens, as halfway beings, the appropriate context for developing full rationality.

This view of human rationality refutes Mulgan's treatment of Aristotle as a predecessor of the Hellenistic moral philosophers who propose retreating from politics, rather than as a spokesman for civic republicanism.[27] To be sure, the contexts in which Aristotle and 'Aristotelian' republican theorists develop their positions are somewhat different, in that Aristotle sometimes feels compelled to persuade those who are eager to rule other people to play the role of being governed

[27] Mulgan, 'Aristotle and the value of political participation', 195–215.

(*Pol.* 3.6.1279a8–16), while modern republican theorists are motivated by the need to encourage those who feel apathy towards politics to engage in politics. However, Mulgan's arguments are not sufficient to prove that Aristotle considers it more important for fostering human happiness to exercise intellectual and ethical virtues for the benefit of family or personal friends than for the benefit of other citizens. With respect to Aristotle's argument for human happiness independent of luck in *EN* 1.10, as mentioned in Chapter 1, Mulgan argues that the loss of political authority does not rule out the possibility of achieving human happiness, since political success is simply dependent on luck. It would, however, seem that Aristotle's argument about happiness and luck shows that if political activity is considered to be one forum for exercising practical wisdom and virtue, political activity is not dependent on luck at least so far as the achievement of happiness is concerned – since Aristotle clearly maintains that one can exercise virtue independently of luck under any circumstances (*EN* 1.10.1100b35–1101a5). What is problematic in Mulgan is his view of politics, namely, the idea that political success means receiving an offer of political office.

Later in his work, Mulgan argues that by calling human beings political animals Aristotle means only that 'human beings should live in a polis, not that they should necessarily engage in politics'.[28] Mulgan then advances a liberal, Lockean idea that the role of the polis is to make it possible for citizens to protect their lives and property so that they can enjoy their private lives, and emphasises life with family and personal friends, not with other citizens, as essential for an individual's happiness. First of all, however, Aristotle clearly prioritises the good of the polis over the good of the individual in *EN* 1.2.1094b7–10, where, as we discussed in Chapter 2, he regards the cultivation of citizens' virtue as the purpose of a polis. Second, in *EN* 9.9, where Aristotle argues that a happy, self-sufficient person still needs friends, he introduces the idea of a political animal, stating that 'perhaps it is also absurd to make the blessed person

[28] Mulgan, 'Was Aristotle an "Aristotelian social democrat"?', 98.

solitary, since no one would choose to have all goods for himself. For a human being is political and by nature shares lives with others' (1169b16–19). At the end of this chapter, Aristotle argues that for humans, sharing lives (συζῆν) means to share conversation and thought (κοινωνεῖν λόγων καὶ διανοίας), not simply to feed in the same place as grazing animals do (1170b10–14). This argument about the political animal fits perfectly with the famous argument in *Politics* 1.2 (1253a7–18), in which Aristotle defines humans as political in the sense that they share a view of justice and good with the help of language.[29] By calling humans political animals, therefore, Aristotle stresses that it is crucial for human beings to live in a polis not simply to ensure safety, but to share the common view of ethical values in order to lead a good life. As discussed in the previous section, in Aristotle's framework, for humans to cultivate civic virtue it is essential not only to live in a polis, be governed by other citizens and be instilled with the common view of the good, but also to be engaged with public activity and exercise civic virtue regularly in a polis. In addition, Mulgan's distinction between living in a polis and engaging in politics is arbitrary, since republican theorists argue not that humans should *necessarily* engage in politics, but rather that to exercise intellectual and ethical virtue on behalf of other citizens is one type of human happiness. In this respect, Aristotle's politicised conceptions of virtue and rationality support the civic republican idea that sharing one's view of good and justice with other citizens is one essential element for human happiness.[30]

Striker criticises Aristotle's narrow idea of practical wisdom as a capacity for ruling, but in *EN* 6.12 Aristotle himself offers a reason for drawing a distinction between practical wisdom

[29] For Aristotle's view of the differences between humans and other animals, see Irwin, 'The metaphysical and psychological basis of Aristotle's ethics', 44, where Irwin summarises Aristotle's several points that distinguish other animals from humans, such as the lack of universal apprehension in *EN* 7.3.1147b3–5 or the lack of deliberative ability in *DA* 3.11.434a5–10, and regards the most basic point as 'lack of reason'.

[30] In the next section, I shall consider further a hierarchical relation between polis and household with regard to the role of education, in comparison with Arendt's view.

and other skills. He raises a problem about the significance of practical wisdom, suggesting that, if one assumes that practical wisdom is useful for becoming good,

> it will be useless for those who are already good. Neither will it be useful for those who do not have practical wisdom, since it will make no difference whether they have it in themselves or follow others who have it. The advice of others will suffice for us, as with health. For we wish to be healthy, but do not study medical science. (1143b29–33)

Aristotle asks here whether practical wisdom is necessary only for particular experts, such as those in medical science, or for everyone. He then draws a distinction between practical wisdom and medical science, noting that practical wisdom is indispensable for human happiness even if an individual is ethically good (*EN* 6.12.1144a1–9), while medical science is not necessary when people are healthy. In Aristotle's framework, given that human happiness means the activity of a soul in accordance with virtue, the exercise of virtue cannot be entrusted to another person. In this view, to follow another person's guidance about one's own happiness because of one's own lack of practical wisdom is the defining feature of a slave. Political activity also cannot be entrusted to others, because it is also the exercise of practical wisdom for their own and their friends' happiness. In contrast, we can rely on a professional, such as a doctor, a general or an architect, to deal with a specific problem, such as health, war or building. The division of labour is meaningful in these fields. How to integrate such a specific type of good into one's own happiness is, however, not the business of an expert, but one's own job. Given that, in Aristotle's view, politics is also concerned with how to integrate many types of good into the good life and shape the collective lives of citizens as well as individuals, it should not be entrusted completely to the expert. Aristotle's distinction between a particular skill and practical wisdom therefore casts doubt on any political system where the activities of governance are distributed solely to the experts, finding it insufficient to promote the good life of citizens.[31]

[31] In her *Ethics with Aristotle*, 257–60, Sarah Broadie illustrates 'Aristotle's egalitarian conception of practical wisdom' in comparison with Plato's view in the

4.4 Differences between Aristotle and 'Aristotelian' republican theorists

In the preceding sections, I argued that Aristotle regards public life in the polis more highly than private life in the household, since people can achieve full rationality in the polis, where they exchange the roles of governing and being governed in turn. This argument would seem to provide a basis for republican views of politics in terms of the significance of political participation and the priority of political activity over domestic activity. Does Aristotle's political philosophy fully support the views of civic republicanism? Are there any differences between Aristotle and 'Aristotelian' republican theorists? In this section, I am going to address these questions in order to clarify Aristotle's own approach to the issue of how to acknowledge the significance of political life. Although Aristotle, Arendt, Pocock and Sandel all recognise that public life plays a very important role in human life, they differ in their conceptual backgrounds. I shall therefore draw attention to the differences between them (though they have many similarities) and explore the distinctive characteristics of Aristotle's own political thought.[32]

First, Arendt draws a very sharp contrast between the polis and the household in order to acknowledge the importance of public life. In her view, as explained in Chapter 1, the political community is the sphere of freedom, while the household is the sphere of necessity. People can achieve their good life only by having mastered the physical and economic maintenance of life, being freed from labour and work, and participating in the public sphere. In Arendt's view, the polis and the household are completely distinct with regard to their characteristics or purposes.[33] Arguably, this view partially fits with Aristotle's narrative of the development of human communities: Aristotle sees the household as formed to fulfil daily needs, while the

Republic, where practical wisdom is considered to be the 'craft' of specialists who govern a community.

32 For the outline of 'Aristotelian' republican theorists, see Section 1.1.3.

33 See Arendt, *The Human Condition*, esp. 28–37.

polis exists to further the good life (*Pol.* 1.2.1252b12–14, 27–30). Arendt's view, however, needs to be qualified, at least concerning the identification of the household simply as a sphere of necessity, where there is no concern for the good life. In Aristotle's arguments about man as a political animal, he clearly states that 'the sharing of these [i.e. what is just and unjust, what is good and bad, and other things] forms *a household* and a polis' (*Pol.* 1.2.1253a18, my italics). He clearly maintains that the household as well as the polis is a community sharing the sense of good and bad.

The following passage also casts doubt on Arendt's complete distinction between the household and the polis:

> In as much as every household is a part of a polis, these relationships [i.e. the husband–wife and father–child relationships] are the parts of a household, and one must look at the virtue of the part in relation to the virtue of the whole, then one must educate children and wives with a view to the constitution, if the excellences of children and those of wives make any difference in the excellences of a polis. (*Pol.* 1.13.1260b13–18)

The household is considered to be the private sphere where family members not only fulfil daily needs, but also cultivate their virtue. Aristotle thus does not completely separate the household from the polis, but rather integrates it into the whole polis in accord with the principle of its constitution. This idea corresponds to the passage in which Aristotle maintains that education should be of public concern (*Pol.* 8.1.1337a21–32): he opines there that the individual is a part of the polis and thus the individual needs to be educated with an eye towards its constitution. In Aristotle's view, the polis is the highest form of community, in which any smaller community is organised in accordance with its constitution. Arendt's sharp contrast between the household and the polis loses sight of this hierarchical relationship between them.[34]

Furthermore, in order to emphasise the priority of political activity, Arendt develops an oversimplified picture of the

[34] Judith Swanson sheds light on the educational role of the household in challenging Arendt's view (see Swanson, *The Public and the Private in Aristotle's Political Philosophy*, 9–30).

household. She holds that there is neither justice nor law in the household, and implies that a household manager can rule his family members despotically.[35] Aristotle, however, draws a distinction between the rule of a household manager and that of a master in relation to the beneficiary of the rule: despotic rule is for the benefit of the master and only incidentally for the benefit of the slave, while the household's rule is primarily for the ruled, i.e. the wife and child (*Pol.* 3.6.1278b32–1279a8). Here Aristotle compares household management with the arts of medicine and gymnastics: just as a trainer cares for the benefit of a trainee, so does a household manager care for the benefit of the members of the household. The rule of the household is therefore different from despotic rule, in that it is concerned with the benefit of the ruled, while despotic rule is not particularly concerned with the benefit of the slave, who is not a free person, but rather the private property of the master.

In addition, Aristotle asserts that there is justice even in the household, although it is not political justice. In the passage where Aristotle describes various types of justice (*EN* 5.6.1134b8–18), he also distinguishes domestic justice from despotic justice, and implies that the relationship between husband and wife is more egalitarian than the relationship between master and slave. In Aristotle's view, thus, there are distinctions between a husband, a father and a master, even though those roles are performed by one and the same head of the household. In contrast to Arendt's simplified picture, even in the household there are various types of justice according to the scale of rationality. By focusing on the despotic relationship Arendt does not describe the various roles of family relationships and diminishes the value of household management.

To make matters worse, Arendt regards the polis as a sphere of 'no-rule', where no citizen rules any another:

> The *polis* was distinguished from the household in that it knew only "equals", whereas the household was the center of strictest inequality… [To be free]

[35] Arendt says, 'the feudal lord could render justice within the limits of his rule, whereas the ancient household head, while he might exert a milder or harsher rule, knew neither of laws nor justice outside the political realm'; Arendt, *The Human Condition*, 34.

meant neither to rule nor to be ruled... To be free meant to be free from inequality present in rulership and to move in a sphere where neither rule nor being ruled existed. (Arendt, *The Human Condition*, 32–3)[36]

Aristotle, however, sees the distinctive feature of a civic relationship in the polis as the exchange of ruling and being ruled in turn. This is because this relationship makes it possible for citizens to cultivate virtue and achieve full rationality. As I have been stressing, the Greek term 'public office (ἀρχή)' originally means 'beginning'. From this original meaning, the term also signifies 'ruling' or 'governing' in a political sphere, and derivatively means public office.[37] 'Governing' and 'being governed' are thus simply the active and passive aspects of action.[38] When someone acts for the sake of other people, it follows that they are affected by that action. The exchange of ruling and being ruled is therefore another way of articulating the relationship between citizens who act for the sake of one another. Given that Arendt's main thesis is to distinguish 'action' from 'labour' and 'work', it is very bizarre that she regards the civic relationship as one of 'no-rule'. Arendt's view of the civic relationship as 'no-rule' does not recognise this inescapable ingredient of 'action'.

Pocock's version of civic republicanism is partly consistent with Aristotle, especially in his attention to the exchange of governing and being governed as a civic relationship – but his use of terminology, especially 'the universal good', is problematic. According to Pocock's treatment of Aristotle, the defining characteristic of the polis is its universality: in a polis, citizens are engaged in the universal activity of pursuing the common good and become 'the universal being', while an individual's good perishes as time goes by. In Pocock's Aristotle, the polis provides a locus where citizens can enjoy the kind of good that is enduring. In Aristotle's political philosophy, however, there are no arguments about the concept of 'the universal good'. To be sure, as was examined in Chapter 2, Aristotle gives

36 See also Arendt, *On Revolution*, 30.

37 See Aristotle's *Metaphysics* 5.1, esp. 1013a10–13.

38 To look at both the active and passive element in nature reflects Aristotle's principal method for analysing not only human action, but also the structure of the world. See *Pol.* 1.5.1254a28–33 and *DA* 3.4.429b25–6.

priority to the good of the polis over the good of the individual in *EN* 1.2.1094b7–10. However, he does not argue here that the importance of the good of the polis comes from the fact that a polis persists for a longer time than an individual. Presumably, Pocock introduces the concept of 'the universal good' in connection with Aristotle's arguments that the polis is the 'supreme (κυριωτάτη)' community in *Politics* 1.1 and that the art of politics is the most 'strategic (ἀρχιτεκτονική)' art in *EN* 1.2. The polis is, however, the supreme community, not because it enables citizens to become 'the universal being' beyond the perishable individual good, but because it aims at the highest good, namely, the good life (*Pol.* 1.2.1252a1–7). Furthermore, the art of politics is the most strategic art because it is concerned not with an instrumental good such as wealth or victory, but with the highest good, human happiness, for the sake of which it organises other kinds of skill (*EN* 1.2.1094a26–b7). Hence, whether the good of a polis is less perishable is not the central issue with regard to the supremacy of a political community.

Pocock's account of the interpretation of Aristotle's political philosophy in European political thought is somewhat misleading. According to Pocock, there are two ways of reading Aristotle's *Politics*. The first reading is concerned with the themes of 'natural law' and 'the rational direction of politics'. In this view, human beings are supposed to perceive the values inherent in nature and pursue them in society. This reading is the approach found in the tradition of Augustinian and medieval Christianity.[39] Another way of reading Aristotle's *Politics* is concerned with the relation of citizens to their republic. This reading is 'the approach which reveals its importance to humanists and Italian thinkers in search of means of vindicating the universality and stability of the *vivere civile*'.[40] In

39 Concerning the problem of whether in Aristotle we find the origins of 'natural law', developed by the Stoics, Bernard Yack makes a negative comment, since 'natural justice' in Aristotle's *EN* 5.7 is not a 'superior' law by which positive laws are judged. Although Aristotle refers to 'natural law (τὸν νόμον κατὰ φύσιν)' in *Rhet.* 1.13.1373b6, Yack does not regard this reference as Aristotle's own view of law. See Yack, *The Problems of a Political Animal*, 140–9.

40 Pocock, *The Machiavellian Moment*, 66–7.

short, Pocock offers two ways to interpret the main theme of Aristotle's *Politics*: as 'the rational direction of politics' and as 'the relation of citizens to their republic'. He sheds light on the latter subject in order to clarify its significance for Italian humanist thinkers. As I have been stressing, however, Aristotle gives priority to the civic relationship because it enables citizens to achieve full rationality and fully develop their natural capacity for virtue. In this respect, although Aristotle's philosophy influences both medieval Christian philosophers and Italian Renaissance civic humanists, in his theory itself the account of citizens' relation to their polis is intelligible only within the framework for the rational direction of politics. Since Pocock intends to examine Aristotle's influence on Italian civic republicanism and introduces the concept of 'the universal good', which we cannot find anywhere in Aristotle's work, he does not fully illuminate Aristotle's theory of the civic relationship based on human rationality. Unlike Pocock's reading, I think that Aristotle regards an equal civic relationship as the way to achieve full rationality, even if the relationship is perishable with time.

Sandel's treatment of Aristotle's attitude towards liberty is also problematic. As was explained in Chapter 1, Sandel calls his republicanism 'Aristotelian': he treats self-governance as the essential, not instrumental, feature of liberty and thinks that we are free only in so far as we participate in the decision-making process of a free republic.[41] It would, however, seem necessary to consider more carefully how Aristotle treats liberty, and whether he really supports the idea of self-governance, 'positive liberty'. It is useful here to examine the following passage, where Aristotle formulates democratic conceptions of liberty:

> One component of liberty is to rule and be ruled in turn. For democratic justice is based on numerical equality, not on merit. But if this is what justice is, then the multitude must be supreme, and whatever seems right to the majority, this is what is final and this is what is just, since they say that every citizen must have equality. The result is that in democracies the poor have

[41] Sandel, *Democracy's Discontent*, 5, 26, and Sandel, 'Reply to critics', 323–7.

more supreme power than the rich, because there are more of them, and the opinion of the majority is supreme. This is then one characteristic of liberty that all democrats set as the principle of their polis. Another component of liberty is to live as one likes. They say that this is the mark of liberty, since that of slavery is not to live as one likes. This is the second principle of democracy, from which has come out the claim of not being ruled, in particular not by anyone at all, and if impossible, the claim of ruling and being ruled in turn. In this way the second principle contributes to the liberty based upon equality. (*Pol.* 6.2.1317b2–17, cf. 5.9.1310a28–36)

The first component of liberty in this passage is similar to the idea of 'positive liberty', in that here 'liberty' means the sharing of rule in the form of exchanging political authority, although Aristotle also points out here that this conception of liberty ultimately results in simple majority rule. By contrast, the second component of liberty in the passage expresses what is defined as 'negative liberty', since it describes living as one wishes, implying the absence of impediment to the pursuit of one's own ends. Moreover, Aristotle asserts that this conception is also a democratic version of liberty, because it involves seeking not to be ruled by anyone in order to live as one likes, and as a compromise of admitting the same liberty for other people, it allows the exchange of ruling, which forms the basis for democratic justice or the first component of liberty.[42]

This formulation of liberty, however, does not perfectly match what Aristotle considers good for the polis. As we discussed in Chapter 2, Aristotle embraces not a democratic version of justice that seeks equality regardless of merit, but rather an aristocratic version of justice that requires us to distribute political authority according to virtue. In the quoted passage, however, he sees the first component of liberty as conducive to 'numerical equality'. In addition, he notes that this type of liberty creates a situation in which the opinions of the majority prevail over those of the few. This means that Aristotle does not necessarily regard positively what is called 'positive liberty', or

[42] Compare Berlin, 'Two concepts of liberty', 129–30, where Isaiah Berlin maintains that negative liberty is not concerned with the form of government, so that it is not logically connected to democracy. In this view, even a liberal-minded despot can preserve negative liberty, if he allows his subjects a large area of personal freedom.

the ideology of collective control, if it actually results in numerical equality and simple majority rule. According to his distinction between political and despotic rule, this upshot of positive liberty can be seen as an application of despotic rule to the governance of a city, or mastery over the whole city for the benefit of the majority only.

As examined in the previous sections, Aristotle takes a positive attitude towards citizens' sharing of political authority only in so far as it contributes to the cultivation of their character and the sharing of the sense of good. In supporting the sharing of political authority, thus, Aristotle emphasises the political process of being governed by other citizens, as well as governing, as important for the cultivation of virtue. By contrast, when Sandel espouses the sharing of self-governance, he draws attention to the process of governing as crucial for public deliberation about the common good. This is because Sandel is anxious to consider how to empower people who are politically apathetic and to recover a sense of self-governance, since in his view modern liberalism erodes individuals' sense of agency in politics.[43] What is problematic in the doctrine of positive liberty is, then, to regard self-governance as only encompassing the activity of governing, not the process of being governed by other people, although the passive aspect actually provides us with the opportunity to listen to the opinions of wise persons and be concerned with the character of other citizens, on account of the fact that other ordinary citizens affect our own lives through their governance. Aristotle would therefore argue that 'Aristotelian' republican theorists, such as Sandel and Crick, could develop more useful arguments for the cultivation of civic virtue if, in discussing the idea of collective control, they drew more attention to the process of being governed by other citizens, since the concept of reciprocal equality enables us to see the condition necessary for the cultivation of civic virtue more clearly than does the doctrine of positive liberty.

43 Sandel, *Democracy's Discontent*, 4–7, 25–8, and Sandel, 'Reply to critics', 323–7.

4.5 Conclusion

I have examined Aristotle's conception of civic virtue as a capacity for governing and being governed in turn and demonstrated the significance of the elements of both governing and being governed from an educational perspective. Aristotle's framework for the cultivation of civic virtue implies the following two points. First, the experience of being governed is necessary for people to cultivate their capacity for governing and consider the meaning of political governance from the perspective of the governed. Unlike the civic republican theorists, Aristotle acknowledges the importance of being a passive subject for acquiring the skill of political governance. His argument about the cultivation of virtue, however, also implies that people need to engage with politics actively and exercise political authority on their own in order to cultivate the virtue of a citizen. This is because they acquire a virtue through performing its associated activities repeatedly. Unlike Mulgan, therefore, Aristotle does not hold that people simply need to live in a polis and be indoctrinated with the common view of justice and good. Rather, he implies that the relationship of governing and being governed is indispensable for people to cultivate and exercise virtue for the common benefit in the political sphere.

To conclude the chapter, I shall now illustrate this characteristic of Aristotle's theory of educating citizens in comparison with Socrates' and Protagoras' equivalents. It would seem that Aristotle offers a more sensible view of education than Socrates and Protagoras in acknowledging the proper role of citizens' reciprocal relationship in the cultivation of virtue. As is well known, in Plato's *Protagoras* Socrates and Protagoras discuss whether virtue is teachable. On the one hand, Socrates points out that in the Athenian assembly people receive advice from experts when they discuss a technical problem such as building or shipbuilding, since these matters can be learned and taught (*Protagoras* 319b–c). By contrast, when it comes to the governance of a polis, anyone may stand up and give an opinion, whether he is a carpenter, a smith or a merchant, rich or poor, noble or low-born. Nobody criticises him even if he has not learned about it from a teacher. Based on this fact, Socrates concludes that people do not regard this kind of subject as teachable (*Protagoras* 319c–d). In addition, he points out that pre-eminent individuals like Pericles could not teach virtue to their children (*Protagoras* 319d–320b). They have never succeeded in handing over the virtue that makes them good at governing a polis. Socrates therefore concludes that virtue is not teachable.

On the basis of the same fact, Protagoras tells Socrates in reply that in the Athenian assembly when it comes to a matter of civic virtue such as justice (δικαιοσύνη) or temperance (σωφροσύνη),[44] people take anyone's opinions into account because they think that everyone shares justice and civic virtue (*Protagoras* 322d–323a). Protagoras then cites the common practice of correcting and punishing a wrongdoer to argue that it is possible to teach virtue (*Protagoras* 323c–324d): on the one hand, when it comes to undesirable characteristics attributable to nature or chance, nobody tries to correct them or punishes those who have them; rather, people have pity on those possessing them. On the other hand, when it comes to bad qualities of character due to deliberate choice, people become irritated by those who have them, and try to correct them. In fact, people punish a wrongdoer not simply for purposes of retribution, but for deterrence, so that the wrongdoer and those who see him punished will not commit the crime in the future. In Protagoras' view, this clearly shows that Athenians think that virtue can be taught and cultivated.[45]

44 At 323a, Protagoras changes the words αἰδώς and δίκη (used in the myth) to δικαιοσύνη and σωφροσύνη. According to Christopher Taylor, αἰδώς has connotations of self-respect, shame, modesty and respect for others, and is virtually synonymous with σωφροσύνη, which can mean the soundness of mind that makes a man accept a proper role in society and respect others. The choice of the words αἰδώς and δίκη is therefore based on a stylistic rather than semantic concern, since they are appropriate for poetic language. Douglas Cairns offers the same view of Protagoras' use of αἰδώς as Taylor; Taylor (trans.), Plato, *Protagoras*, 85–6, and Cairns, *Aidōs*, 356–60.

45 According to Farrar, Protagoras' trust in individual experience makes it possible for him to support the political participation of citizens in the Athenian assembly. Based on this epistemic difference between Protagoras and Socrates, Farrar

Concerning the possibility of teaching virtue, Aristotle no doubt takes a position close to Protagoras'. This is not only because Aristotle refers to the same fact about praise and blame at the beginning of his enquiry about voluntary and involuntary action in *EN* 3.1 (1109b30–5), but also because, as already discussed, he points out that a citizen must acquire the virtue of governance by being governed in a polis and actively engaged with the associated activities. In his view, the citizens' governance or the relationship of governing and being governed in turn makes it possible for them to cultivate their civic virtue. In this framework, even if a great politician such as Pericles could not teach virtue to his sons, this fact does not necessarily imply that virtue is not teachable, since people need to be educated not only in a household, but also in a polis. Rather, this fact means that in Athens people do not develop a proper relationship for cultivating virtue outside private families. Socrates assumes that political virtue can be taught by a father to his son inside the family, but from Aristotle's perspective Socrates fails to recognise that there must be an educational process outside the family.[46]

Unlike Protagoras, however, Aristotle does not entirely trust Athenian social relationships with an educational role. In his well-known arguments in *Politics* 8.1, he maintains that education should be organised not privately but publicly, since the good character of a citizen preserves the characteristics of a constitution, in the same way that the democratic character preserves a democracy and the oligarchic character preserves an oligarchy (1337a11–18). Aristotle praises Spartans for being eager to educate their children, while Athenians are not particularly concerned with the education of

classifies Protagoras as one of the first democratic theorists in her *The Origins of Democratic Thinking*, esp. 80–7.

[46] In his *Histoire de l'éducation dans l'Antiquité*, 102–3, Henri-Irénée Marrou treats Socrates as the mouthpiece of the old aristocratic tradition. At this time, sophists claim that they can teach knowledge, especially political skill, to anyone, but Socrates casts doubt on this claim in terms of whether on earth political skill can be taught, and points out that education is primarily a matter of gifts, and its role is to develop them.

citizens (*EN* 10.9.1180a24–30).[47] He does not recommend that an individual should individually study whatever he wants to, or feel compelled to, for example, by joining the circle of a sophist, but rather argues that education should be a public concern (*Pol.* 8.1.1337a21–32), presumably because citizens need to cultivate the virtue necessary for the preservation of their constitution by developing civic relationships and engaging in social practices.[48] Unlike Protagoras, thus, Aristotle considers it important for the cultivation of civic virtue that people participate in the reciprocal relationship of governing and being governed in turn, not in the circle of sophists.

I have been considering what conceptual framework makes it possible for Aristotle to develop a political theory somewhat sympathetic towards democracy, and in this chapter have demonstrated that Aristotle's conception of civic virtue implies the significance of the reciprocal relationship of governing and being governed in turn for leading the virtuous life. In order to make clearer the characteristics of this civic relationship, in the next chapter I shall examine Aristotle's arguments about civic friendship through the lens of his conception of friendship in general. How does Aristotle argue that citizens relate to one another, and what kind of friendship do they develop in taking turns in exercising political authority for the common benefit? The conceptual framework for civic friendship will illuminate the characteristics of civic relationships in contrast with other

47 No decrees of the Athenian assembly have been found about educational issues. Those surviving are mainly concerned with foreign policy and the award of honour. See Hansen, *The Athenian Democracy in the Age of Demosthenes*, 155–6. Concerning education in ancient Greece, Richard Kraut notes that although wealthy citizens would have 'their son taught to read and write, no cities of the fifth or fourth century made such an education compulsory or provided funds for it'; Kraut (trans.), Aristotle, *Politics*, 169. Josiah Ober argues that political and judicial processes in ancient Athens were considered to be 'educational systems' for instilling democratic values, in his *Mass and Elite in Democratic Athens*, 156–63.

48 Compare Kraut (trans.), Aristotle, *Politics*, 169–74, where Kraut argues that the necessity of public, not private, education comes simply from Aristotle's view that an individual is part of a polis.

social or familial relationships, especially the necessary conditions for people to develop a friendly relationship in the political sphere without the psychological, emotional and intimate bond that a family has.

CHAPTER 5

CIVIC FRIENDSHIP

5.1 Arguments about civic friendship

I have been considering what conceptual framework makes it possible for Aristotle to develop a political theory somewhat sympathetic towards democracy. In this chapter, I shall examine his view of civic friendship to illustrate the characteristics of citizens' reciprocal relationship of governing and being governed in turn. As is well known, Aristotle treats friendship as important for citizens to build good relationships in the political sphere as well as in the private sphere. For example, in *Politics* 3.9, where he defines the essence or purpose of a polis, he illustrates the significance of friendship as follows:

> A polis is a sharing in living well among families or tribes, for the sake of a complete and self-sufficient life. But this will not be possible unless they inhabit one and the same location and practise intermarriage. That is why marriage connections, fraternities, sacrificial ceremonies and the leisured pursuits of sharing lives came about in each polis. Things of this sort are the work of friendship, because the choice of sharing lives is friendship. (1280b33–9)

Here, Aristotle indicates that friendship makes it possible for people to share their lives and form a polis, and regards friendship as indispensable to the community achieving the good life. He also refers to the importance of friendship at the beginning of *EN* 8. Strikingly, he indicates that legislators are more concerned about friendship than justice, and that justice is not necessary when people are friends, whereas friendship is indispensable even if people are just (*EN* 8.1.1155a22–8, cf. *EE* 7.1.1234b22–5). Although this passage is, as is usually the case when Aristotle begins a fresh enquiry, based on what ordinary people think, he does take into consideration the significance of friendship for uniting a polis.[1]

What form of friendship does Aristotle have in mind when he is suggesting the importance of friendship in the political sphere? In fact, the debates about Aristotle's civic (political) friendship (πολιτική φιλία) in the past few decades have focused on this issue. These debates are crucial for the purposes of the present book, because they are concerned with the problem of what conditions Aristotle thinks are necessary for citizens to develop friendly relationships in a polis. In particular, by examining these debates, I shall consider what the essential elements in civic friendship are as distinct from other types of friendship, such as family love. In this chapter, I am going to argue that reciprocity in political authority makes it possible for citizens to share their lives without the psychological bond of family love, and that on the basis of this idea Aristotle develops a political theory relatively sympathetic towards democracy.

In the scholarly literature on Aristotle's *Politics*, there are two main positions on this issue. On the one hand, John Cooper maintains that Aristotle's conception of citizenship is applicable to all free-born native residents and that each citizen is concerned for the happiness of every other just through being a citizen.[2] Moreover, mainly through passages from *Politics* 3.9, Cooper emphasises the difference between the polis and a commercial transaction, and argues that civic friendship involves mutual goodwill, trust and well-wishing for the moral character of fellow citizens just like virtue-friendship does.[3] In Cooper's view, therefore, 'civic friendship is just an extension to a whole city of the kinds of psychological bonds that tie together a family', and a polis is like a large extended family.[4]

In following Cooper's reading, a recent study also tries to clarify the condition of citizens' concern for one another's

[1] For the outline of Aristotle's concept of friendship in general, see Nehamas, 'Aristotelian *philia*, modern friendship?', Pangle, *Aristotle and the Philosophy of Friendship*, and Price, *Love and Friendship in Plato and Aristotle*.

[2] Cooper, 'Political animals and civic friendship', 228.

[3] Ibid., 234–5.

[4] Ibid., 236. MacIntyre also thinks that Aristotle's civic friendship involves the concern for other citizens' virtue (see MacIntyre, *After Virtue*, 155–9, and Section 1.1.1).

character. From a feminist point of view, Sibyl Schwarzenbach argues that we can find a model for virtue-friendship in a mother's love for her child, which entails bringing up another person to be an independent, ethical being. In her view, this type of activity can be extended to other citizens: according to her interpretation of Aristotle's civic friendship, both civic and personal friendship aim not at the production of things or services, but at the good of beneficiaries (children or fellow citizens). Civic friendship is different from personal friendship only in that it does not involve close emotional ties and intimate knowledge of the friend; rather it retains mutual awareness of, goodwill towards and activity for the good of others in the political and judicial processes. Although her distinction between 'ethical reproduction' and 'productive work' derives from Hannah Arendt's distinction between 'action' and 'work', Schwarzenbach maintains that political science is, as Cooper argues, an extension of household management, as opposed to Arendt's clear separation between household and polis.[5]

Julia Annas, however, casts serious doubt on Cooper's reading concerning the bonds of civic friendship. Although she admits that a citizen has concern for the character and virtue of other citizens, she does not think that this concern can be understood as the bonds of civic friendship. This is because one of the most prominent characteristics of Aristotle's theory of friendship is his idea that friendship is a personal relation, that friends must be known to one another and aware of mutual liking. However, she believes there is 'no way that one could have this kind of relationship with everyone in the city'.[6] Annas is sceptical about the possibility of extending the notion of friendship to all fellow citizens, and thinks rather that to do so is to destroy the nature of friendship.[7] She therefore maintains that there is no 'single special friendly interest that

5 Schwarzenbach, *On Civic Friendship*, 41–58. Jill Frank treats civic friendship as advantage-friendship, but argues that virtue is needed to build friendly relationships among citizens (see *A Democracy of Distinction*, 147–63). Another recent study also follows Cooper's reading; Irrera, 'Between advantage and virtue', 565–85.

6 Annas, 'Comments on J. Cooper', 243. 7 Ibid., 244.

everyone feels for everyone else',[8] and that the friendship Aristotle envisages in the *Politics* is, at most, a matter of personal friendship between a few particular citizens. She concludes that the conception of friendship plays no important role in the *Politics*.[9]

All of these arguments considered, one of the main issues relating to Aristotle's conception of civic friendship is whether citizens have a friendly concern for each other's character. Annas is highly sceptical about this point, stressing the element of a personal relationship in Aristotle's theory of friendship. In her view, the essential elements of friendship are mutual acquaintance, intimacy and shared activity. Cooper, on the other hand, downplays the importance of a personal relationship and draws attention to the element of 'goodwill' as a sufficient condition for forming civic friendship.[10] I think, however, that both readings are somewhat problematic, in that Annas lays very strong emphasis on the importance of personal relations in civic friendship, while Cooper does not recognise that there are other requirements for developing friendship besides goodwill.

In the next section, I shall examine Cooper's and Schwarzenbach's readings, and clarify the characteristics of Aristotle's conception of friendship by focusing on 'reciprocity' and 'sharing', to which Cooper and Schwarzenbach do not draw sufficient attention. I shall address these tasks mainly through passages in *EN*, because the arguments about friendship in *EN* are more elaborate than those in *EE*, especially regarding sharing

8 Ibid., 246.

9 Ibid., 248. In his 'Political friendship and the ideology of reciprocity', 82–99, Malcolm Schofield also shows a sceptical attitude towards Cooper's argument, pointing out that the idea of political friendship presupposes a commercial relationship based on agreement rather than personal trust. Schofield builds his argument with respect to *EE* 7.10. His attention to political friendship as an economic tie comes from Michael Pakaluk, 'The egalitarianism of the *Eudemian Ethics*'. Bernard Yack also regards civic friendship as advantage-friendship in *The Problems of a Political Animal*, 109–27. Bradley Bryan's study in 'Approaching others' also suggests that we should not advance Aristotle's concept of friendship in a modern liberal democracy.

10 See Cooper, 'Political animals and civic friendship', 235, esp. n. 18, and Cooper, 'Aristotle on the forms of friendship', 641–3.

and reciprocity.[11] One point to emerge will be that Cooper and Schwarzenbach's attempts to awaken the concern for other fellow citizens' virtue by analogy with family relationships do not fully recognise the egalitarian implications of Aristotle's civic friendship. I shall therefore argue that extending family love to the sphere of politics is not only impractical, but also not desirable, when we consider how to maintain relationships among citizens and identify the causes of deterioration in those relationships. In Section 5.3, I shall argue that although Annas's criticism of Cooper's reading is mostly correct, she fails to see that civic friendship does play an important role in Aristotle's political philosophy. I shall then define Aristotle's use of civic friendship, which links every citizen to every other citizen, and examine how the conceptual framework for civic friendship serves as a basis for Aristotle's analysis of the civic relationship as it figures in the various constitutions. In light of these arguments, I shall argue in Section 5.4 that what Aristotle describes as civic friendship is basically advantage-friendship, as opposed to the communitarian treatment of civic friendship as virtue-friendship, although in the *Politics* this issue is not clearly addressed. Finally, in Section 5.5, I shall examine Aristotle's criticism of Plato's *Republic* in *Politics* 2 in light of his conception of civic friendship, and illuminate some useful points in this criticism, although sometimes he does not provide an accurate account of Socrates' arguments about the unity of a polis. Overall in this chapter, I shall explore what conditions Aristotle considers necessary in order for citizens to be

[11] Concerning the authorship of *EE*, as mentioned in Chapter 1, I take the standard view that *EE* is an earlier work than *EN* written by Aristotle himself. However, in Anthony Kenny's classic work, *The Aristotelian Ethics*, it is argued that *EN* is earlier than *EE*, which represents a 'mature' version of Aristotle's view of ethics. By contrast, Schofield and Pakaluk cast doubt on the authorship of *EE*. I think that the conception of reciprocity gives us a clue as to this issue. Surprisingly, there is no reference to the word ἀντιπεπονθός in *EE*. This fact implies that Aristotle had not yet fully developed a theory of reciprocity in *EE*, but in *EN* was able to do so using the term ἀντιπεπονθός. It is highly unlikely that (according to Kenny's position) Aristotle dropped the crucial term (ἀντιπεπονθός) from his later theory of friendship in *EE*, or that (according to Schofield and Pakaluk's position) the author of *EE* could not comprehend the role of reciprocity in Aristotle's theory of friendship.

united, although they are not expected to have as close, intimate and emotional a tie with one another as family members do.

5.2 Sharing and reciprocity in friendship

I am going to examine Aristotle's conception of friendship based on his use of 'reciprocity' and 'sharing'. The following passage clearly defines his conception of friendship:

> Love for inanimate objects is not called friendship, since there is no mutual loving, nor wishing for their good . . . People rather say that one should wish a friend good things for his sake. However, those who wish good things in this way, if the same wish is not returned by the other, they call men of goodwill. For friendship is goodwill in reciprocal relationship [εὔνοιαν ἐν ἀντιπεπονθόσι]. Or should we add that friends are aware of the reciprocal goodwill? For many people are men of goodwill to those whom they have not seen yet suppose to be decent or useful, and one of them might feel the same towards him. These people then seem to have goodwill towards each other. But how could one call them friends, given that they are unaware of their attitude to each other? Therefore, they must have goodwill towards each other, wish good things and be aware of it, from one of the causes mentioned above. (*EN* 8.2.1155b27–1156a5)

After identifying three causes of friendship – virtue, pleasure and advantage – here Aristotle points out three necessary conditions for forming friendship: (1) goodwill (εὔνοια), (2) reciprocity and (3) recognition of a friend's attitude towards oneself. Contrary to Cooper's treatment of civic friendship, goodwill is considered to be only one of these necessary conditions. Aristotle distinguishes friendship from goodwill by acknowledging that one can expect a friend to entertain the same wish for oneself.[12] In *EN* 9.5 he draws a clearer contrast between goodwill and friendship in terms of whether people

12 Concerning the relationship of this passage (1155b27–1156a5) to Plato's *Lysis*, see Gauthier and Jolif (trans.), Aristote, *L'Éthique à Nicomaque*, vol. II, 670–2, and Annas, 'Plato and Aristotle on friendship and altruism', 532–5, where she points out that Aristotle makes 'mutual liking' central to the Greek usage of the term 'friend (φίλος)', as opposed to Socrates' non-mutual sense of φίλος, which means that A is 'a friend' to B, when A likes B even if B does not like A, and vice versa. Compare Bryan, 'Approaching others', 762–3, where he quotes the same passage, but does not recognise the element of reciprocity.

shoulder the burden of helping friends: he asserts that goodwill lacks a sense of responsibility for treating friends well, just as one who supports a competitor in a contest does nothing for him (1166b32–1167a3). Aristotle then ironically calls goodwill 'idle friendship (ἀργὴν φιλίαν)' (1167a8–12), since a person of goodwill superficially, sometimes suddenly, professes to love those whom he supports, and yet takes no pains concerning them. By contrast, friends take an active part in supporting their friends, and goodwill can become friendship only through habitual intercourse (συνήθεια).[13]

Furthermore, the concept of 'sharing' is of especial importance for identifying the characteristics of various kinds of friendship. The following passage draws distinctions between many types of friendship and shows that the extent to which people share is the extent of their friendship:

> Friendship and justice seem, as we have said at the beginning, to be concerned with the same objects and to be found among the same persons. For in every community there seems to be some form of justice, and friendship as well. At least people call their fellow-voyagers and fellow-soldiers friends, and so do members in any other kinds of community. And the extent to which they share is the extent of their friendship, as it is also the extent of justice. And the proverb 'what friends have is common property' tells the truth, since friendship exists in a community. Now brothers and comrades have all things in common, but others have limited things in common, some have more and others have less, because some types of friendship are closer and other types are less close. And the claims of justice differ as well. (*EN* 8.9.1159b25–35)

This passage explains how different the many types of human relationship are from one another. Although I have so far translated φιλία as 'friendship', the Greek term has a wider meaning than the English equivalent: it is also applicable to 'love' between parent and child, husband and wife, elder and younger. Aristotle distinguishes these kinds of love based (as he puts it) on superiority from friendship between comrades based

[13] Compare Cooper, 'Aristotle on the forms of friendship', 642, where he refers to a particular passage in the chapter (*EN* 9.5.1167a10–14) to emphasise the element of goodwill, but the key point in this passage is not that goodwill becomes friendship just through habitual intercourse, as Cooper argues, but that goodwill is idle friendship, since it lacks reciprocity. See also *EE* 7.7.1241a2–14.

on equality. Moreover, even among friendships of equality, he indicates that the friendship among brothers or close friends is different from other types of friendship such as the friendship of citizens, and considers their differences in terms of the extent to which they have things in common. In a household, for example, family members share many activities and goods, while citizens do not share as broad a range of things. Therefore, Aristotle argues, family members love one another more deeply than citizens. In the passage quoted above, he uses the etymological connection between 'community (κοινωνία)' and 'to have in common, or share (κοινωνεῖν)', to show that friendship exists in a community and that accordingly friends have something in common.

In the context of the quoted passage (1159b25–35) Aristotle also notes the close relationship between friendship and justice. He maintains that the deeper the friendship or love is, the more demanding the requirements of justice are. For example, stealing the property of a close friend is more unjust than stealing from a citizen, and failing to help fellow citizens is more unjust than failing to help foreigners. Furthermore, injuring one's own father is more unjust than injuring other people. In this respect, as Schofield argues, the Greek conceptual scheme of friendship and justice is different from its modern equivalent, since from a modern perspective, friendship and justice are irrelevant: friendship is considered relevant to private relationships, while justice relates to public relationships. That is, people are likely, and allowed, to treat their friends well, differently from the way they treat others. In contrast, justice is impartial, and, accordingly, people are required to treat each other equally without any distinctions based on personal relationships.[14] As an example of this view of justice, a special article on the murder of one's own parents (parricide) would nowadays be considered to be against the concept of human rights in the legal code, which holds that every individual shall be treated equally. Aristotle, however, asserts that injustice to a father is greater than injustice to other humans. While Socrates seeks one and the

[14] Schofield, 'Political friendship and the ideology of reciprocity', 82–3.

same definition of justice in any human relationship,[15] Aristotle argues that justice differs from relationship to relationship.

This is one of the clearest pieces of evidence that Aristotle draws a distinction between civic friendship and family love, as opposed to assimilating them, as Cooper and Schwarzenbach do. In Aristotle's view, the requirements of civic friendship are not so severe as those of family love, because the extent of sharing between citizens is not so broad as it is within a family. Although the flexibility of the Greek vocabulary for friendship makes it possible to use the terminology of the family to describe a civic relationship in a polis, Aristotle fully acknowledges the difference between various kinds of human relationship. Cooper's argument is not sensitive to this distinction when he argues that civic friendship involves the psychological bond of a family being extended to a state level.[16]

There are two additional problems with Schwarzenbach's interpretation of Aristotle's civic friendship. First, presumably because of Rawlsian or Kantian influence, Schwarzenbach supposes that civic friendship is impartial and distinguishes it from what she calls 'political patronage', which means the ordinary Greek view of justice: 'helping friends and harming enemies'.[17] Aristotle's position on this Greek view of justice is, however, not so simple as Schwarzenbach envisages. This is because Aristotle holds that one of the necessary conditions for forming friendship is, as examined through the quoted passage (*EN* 8.2.1155b27–1156a5), 'reciprocity (ἀντιπεπονθός)', which

[15] See Plato's *Meno* 72a–73c.

[16] Cooper, 'Political animals and civic friendship', 236.

[17] Schwarzenbach, *On Civic Friendship*, 53. In Plato's *Republic* 1 (332d), for example, Socrates' interlocutor, Polemarchus, puts forward this idea, and argues that it is just for a person to return the same benefits to those who benefit him and the same disadvantages to those who harm him. Additionally, in Plato's *Meno* 71e, Meno says that the virtue of man is to be able to manage public affairs, in so doing to benefit his friends and harm his enemies, and to be careful not to cause harm to himself. For Aristotle's remarks on this view, see *Top.* 2.7.113a1–19 and *Rhet.* 1.9.1367a20–3. For the Greek view on helping friends and harming enemies, see Dover, *Greek Popular Morality in the Time of Plato and Aristotle*, 180–4, and Blundell, *Helping Friends and Harming Enemies*, 26–59. Carl Schmitt defines 'the political' with reference to the friend–enemy antithesis, although he draws a distinction between public and private enemies, and leaves room in the private sphere for the Christian idea 'love your enemy' (see Schmitt, *The Concept of the Political*, esp. 27–9).

means not only returning good for good (helping friends), but also bad for bad (harming enemies). Aristotle's understanding of this concept is best illustrated in *EN* 5.5. On the one hand, he admits that any unqualified idea of reciprocity is not exactly identical with justice, because it does not fit with either of the types of particular justice, distributive and corrective justice (1132b23–31). In relation to distributive justice, since people need to distribute profits according to how much work each person contributes to common business, it is not in accordance with justice that a person should return equal benefit or harm to those who benefit or harm him. In relation to corrective justice, what kind of punishment a criminal receives should be different depending on the status of the person and the voluntariness of the action. Aristotle therefore argues that it is not in accordance with corrective justice to impose a punishment commensurate to the injury that a criminal inflicted, like 'an eye for an eye and a tooth for a tooth'.[18]

On the other hand, Aristotle recognises the importance of reciprocity for the bond of a polis in the following passage:

> In communities for exchange, however, this way of being just, reciprocity that is proportionate rather than equal, holds people together; for a polis is maintained by proportionate reciprocity. People seek to return either evil for evil, since otherwise their condition seems to be slavery, or good for good, since otherwise there is no mutual giving, and it is mutual giving that holds them together. (*EN* 5.5.1132b33–1133a2)

[18] For Socrates' criticism of this view of justice, see Plato, *Republic* 1 (335b–e), where Socrates argues that a man of justice never makes other people bad by harming them. See also *Crito* 49a–d, and, for its details, Vlastos, *Socrates*, 194–9. Concerning this argument, James Adam says, 'it was by means of this Socratic weapon that Plato achieved this noble anticipation of Christian ethical theory' (*The Republic of Plato*, vol. 1, 21). It would, however, seem that Plato does not dismiss this view of justice completely, since in *Republic* 2 (375a–376c), he compares the role of a guardian in the polis with that of a hound which is gentle to those whom it knows while aggressive against those whom it does not know. Furthermore, while Socrates criticises the idea of harming enemies, he leaves room for the other side of the idea, 'helping friends', in recognising the characteristics of a civic relationship. Plato's ethics cannot be thus easily assimilated to Christian ethics. For a discussion of how reciprocity works in Plato's *Republic*, especially in the arguments about going back into the cave, see Gill, 'Altruism or reciprocity in Greek ethical philosophy', 313–17.

Here Aristotle admits that to return good for good maintains a civic relationship in the polis, although he slightly modifies the concept of reciprocity by saying 'proportionate reciprocity (τὸ ἀντιπεπονθὸς κατ' ἀναλογίαν)', which is different from unqualified reciprocity insofar as it does not necessarily return the same benefit or the same harm. The point of proportionate reciprocity is to return not the same object but a benefit that is commensurate with the object received.[19] Aristotle therefore uses the concept of reciprocity, first, as has been explored above, to draw a distinction between friendship and goodwill and shed light on the element of action in friendship, and, second, to develop a conceptual framework for analysing the civic relationship. 'Political patronage', taking the form of reciprocity, is thus the most crucial element in understanding not only the characteristics of a civic relationship in ancient Greece in general, but also Aristotle's conception of civic friendship.

For seeing how reciprocity plays a very important role in Aristotle's friendship, it is useful to compare Aristotle's conception of friendship and a Christian conception of 'charity', which does not usually take a reciprocal response from others into account. Although there are many minor differences among Christian notions of 'charity', their most important common element is the rejection of 'the reciprocity principle': for example, Timothy Jackson argues that a Christian conception of 'charity' goes beyond the reciprocal principle and requires care for others without qualification, regardless of their merit, while Aristotelian 'friendship' is based on the egalitarian principle of getting and giving the same.[20] According

[19] For the role of proportionate reciprocity in Aristotle's economic theory, see Chapter 6.

[20] See T. P. Jackson, *Love Disconsoled*, 54–91. For a slightly different account of 'charity', see Porter, '*De ordine caritatis*', 197–213, where he argues that Aquinas regards 'charity' as true friendship 'based on mutual communication between God and the justified', although in Aquinas' view charity is independent 'both of the neighbor's attractiveness and of the presence of a response from him or her'. René Gauthier and Jean Jolif also offer an account of the difference between Aristotle's and Aquinas's conceptions of friendship in their *L'Éthique à*

to this conception of 'charity', even if other people do not benefit us, we need to be friendly to them and look after their benefit. Moreover, even if enemies do great harm to us, we need to put enmities aside and instead love our enemies for God's sake. In contrast, Aristotle does not expect that people will develop friendship when they do not give each other some benefit, whether it is virtuous behaviour, advantage or pleasure. Arguably, he does not promote the idea of retribution, returning evil for evil, but his conception of friendship or love is deeply rooted in reciprocity. Concerning the love between parent and child, he also maintains that there must be some reciprocity, in that children treat their parents with great respect, since their parents gave them nurture, education and birth, the greatest good (*EN* 8.7.1158b21–8, 8.11.1161a15–21). When political philosophers do not take the concept of reciprocity seriously, as in Schwarzenbach's argument about a mother's love for her child, therefore, their arguments tend to be based on the concept of 'charity' rather than 'friendship'.

Second, Schwarzenbach's modification of friendship loses sight of an egalitarian implication for politics contained in Aristotle's definition of friendship: in order to accommodate the educational concern for other citizens' virtue, using the model of a mother's love, Schwarzenbach regards as central to friendship the reciprocal *goal* to *establish* the equality of morality, as opposed to Aristotle's conception of friendship between already mature, independent, autonomous, similar citizens.[21] This modification, based on an unequal family relationship, obscures the treatment of equality in friendship that we see in the following passage:

Nicomaque, vol. II, 691–3. By contrast, the classical Greek conception of χάρις is inextricably related to the conception of reciprocity. For this point, see a passage in *EN* 5.5 (1132b34–1133a5), which I shall examine in Chapter 6, and Blundell, *Helping Friends and Harming Enemies*, 33–4. Unfortunately, Aquinas does not comment on this point in comparison with the Christian ideal, but instead reformulates Aristotle's conception of friendship for his arguments about charity in his *Summa Theologiae*, II–III, q. 23, a. 1. See also his *Commentary on Aristotle's Nicomachean Ethics*, 309–10, 480–1.

[21] Schwarzenbach, *On Civic Friendship*, 49–50.

Equality does not seem to be the same in justice and in friendship. For in justice, equality is primarily in merit, and secondarily in quantity. But in friendship, equality is primarily in quantity and secondarily in merit. This is clear when great difference occurs in virtue, vice, wealth or something else. For they are no longer friends and do not even expect to be. (*EN* 8.7.1158b29–35)

Although Aristotle generally reinforces the typical Greek connection between justice and friendship, here he illustrates a difference between them in terms of equality. In particular, he seems to have distributive justice in mind, because when it comes to distributing political authority, the defining characteristic of a constitution is dependent on what value its system aims at, whether virtue, wealth or freedom. In this respect, what counts as valuable primarily determines the method of distributing political authority (*EN* 5.3.1131a25–9). And in any system there can be legitimate claims to very different treatment from one person to another; for example, when one person contributes to the community a hundred times more than another person, the benefits should be distributed in a ratio of one hundred to one. It is thus in accordance with justice to distribute different amounts of resources. When it comes to corrective justice, however, merit is not essential; rather, people need to look only at the amount of damage, loss or harm, not at a criminal's or a victim's merits, such as whether they are rich or poor (*EN* 5.4.1131b32–1132a6). Nonetheless, concerning distributive justice, as the quoted passage argues, equality in merit is primary, and equality in quantity is secondary.

In contrast, when it comes to friendship, Aristotle expects friends to be equal primarily in terms of quantity. Soon after the quoted passage, he also argues that people cannot be friends with a god-like person, such as a great king or a perfectly good person (*EN* 8.7.1158b35–1159a5). This is because friendship is deeply dependent on reciprocity, which requires friends to return proportionate benefits to each other, whether friendship is based on virtue, advantage or pleasure. In this respect, equality in terms of quantity is primary in friendship. This view of friendship means that when Aristotle stresses the importance of friendship for politics, he implies that citizens need to be quantitatively equal in terms of virtue, wealth and anything else in order to preserve their relationships. Friendship thus carries a significant implication for egalitarian politics.[22] Schwarzenbach's attempts to awaken interest in other citizens' virtue on the basis of family ties do not recognise this egalitarian element necessary for friendship, but rather entail the risk of incorporating unequal relationships into civic friendship.

Schwarzenbach's view of civic friendship is actually more appropriate to a monarchical regime than to the sorts of constitution that most concern Aristotle. She does not acknowledge the close relationship between a father's love for his children and a king's love for his subjects: in *EN* 8.11 (1161a10–22), Aristotle compares the rule of a king with the rule of a father over his child in the sense that a king looks after the happiness of people by exercising his capacity for virtue, just as a father does with his child. In Aristotle's view, such relationships are based on superiority, and accordingly friendship and justice exist in proportion to merit. Kingship is political governance in so far as it cares for the benefits of the governed, but it is not political governance, in that it lacks an exchange of political authority between the king and his subjects. In particular, in the absolute kingship (παμβασιλεία) wherein a king governs a polis for life, there is no reciprocal equality between the king and other free individuals. Aristotle therefore sometimes distinguishes kingship from political governance.[23] Even though Schwarzenbach replaces a father with a mother, the logical structure of her account of where the concern for other

[22] Pakaluk also points out the egalitarian implication that Aristotle's conception of friendship holds for politics: 'the tendency of friendship, rather, is to close differences and equalize, since its aim is some kind of strict reciprocation or equality – which typically requires rough equality in the powers, virtues, and abilities of the persons involved' (Pakaluk (trans.), Aristotle, *Nicomachean Ethics*, 96). For the implications that Aristotle's friendship holds for the distribution of resources, see Chapter 6.

[23] At the very beginning of the *Politics*, Aristotle distinguishes political governance from kingship, domestic rule and despotic rule, as opposed to Plato's idea that they are one and the same (*Pol.* 1.1.1252a7–16). Concerning people's complaint about the lack of reciprocity of political authority in the absolute kingship, see *Pol.* 3.16.1287a8–18.

people's virtue come from is tantamount to this 'paternal' idea, in the sense that it relies on the superiority of parents over their children in terms of virtue. Thus, the analogy between civic friendship and family love needs to be more circumspect, given that the superiority of virtue traditionally fostered the ideology of monarchic government.[24]

5.3 Sharing and reciprocity of political authority

In light of Aristotle's conceptual framework for friendship, especially 'sharing' and 'reciprocity', I shall next examine what characteristics he ascribes to the civic relationship in *Politics* 2 and 3, and see whether that way we get a better sense of the concept of civic friendship, which links every citizen to every other citizen (something of course ruled out as impossible by Annas). My strategy is to explore the concept of civic friendship by considering what citizens share and what reciprocal relationships they have in the polis, since Aristotle maintains that the extent to which people share is the extent of their friendship.

To begin with, in *Politics* 3.3, Aristotle clearly defines a polis as a community, or a sharing, of a constitution by citizens (κοινωνία πολιτῶν πολιτείας) (1276b1–4). In his view, a polis no longer retains its identity when its constitution or the ordering of its political authority changes, even though its inhabitants and territory do not change. This understanding corresponds to his definition of citizenship in *Politics* 3.1, where, as we explored in Chapter 4, he defines a citizen as one who is entitled to *share* deliberative and judicial office (κοινωνεῖν ἀρχῆς βουλευτικῆς καὶ κριτικῆς) (1275b18–20, my italics). As opposed to a definition based on ethnicity or territory, he uses the

[24] In *On Civic Friendship*, 138–9, Schwarzenbach acknowledges that the conception of a father's love for his son has historically justified a feudal-like paternalism, but she does not take seriously the risk of introducing unequal relationships based on a mother's love into a civic relationship. Concerning how the governance of a king is traditionally justified by the image of a father's rule over his child, see Pateman, *The Disorder of Women*, 33–57. From a feminist viewpoint Pateman points out that modern social contract theory dispensed with this image of patriarchal governance, but what she calls 'the fraternal social contract' still relies on the dominance of men and the exclusion of women from a political society.

terminology of 'sharing' to identify what is characteristic of the civic relationship and to show that citizens have political authority in common.

Aristotle also uses 'reciprocity' as a principle of enabling citizens to share political authority in his criticism of Plato's common ownership system in *Politics* 2:

> As mentioned before in the *Ethics*, it is reciprocal equality that maintains a polis. This principle is necessary even among citizens who are free and equal. For they cannot all hold office simultaneously, but each can hold office for a year or for some other appointed period. In this way, then, it results that all govern, as if shoemakers and carpenters changed their jobs and did not always keep the same kind of work. (*Pol.* 2.2.1261a30–7)

Here Aristotle argues that reciprocal equality makes it possible for citizens to exchange not only goods or commodities, as discussed in *EN* 5.5, but also political authority. In this view, reciprocal equality means that various kinds of people are to perform public service in turn. The reciprocal exchange of the roles of governing and being governed is thus a practical way of sharing political authority among many citizens. In the context of this passage, however, Aristotle is not necessarily eager to refer to the concept of reciprocity, since he states that 'it is evidently better, if possible, that the same persons govern a polis' (*Pol.* 2.2.1261a38–9). Just as Plato asserted, Aristotle too maintains that it is better that each person concentrates on his own work, and that experts should work on the administration of politics without exchanging political authority among citizens. At the same time, Aristotle takes into account the fact that people are by nature equal, and in this case, he argues, it is in accordance with justice that a polis is managed by equal citizens in turn.

Is there, then, any passage where Aristotle evaluates the reciprocal exchange of political authority more positively? The following passage in *Politics* 3.6 provides a positive account of the principle of reciprocal equality:

> Whenever political authority is organised on the basis of equality and similarity among citizens, they claim to take turns in exercising it. In earlier times as far as people were by nature equal and similar, they claimed the entitlement

to take turns at public service, and expected someone else to look after their own good, as they did the same for somebody else before. But nowadays people want to rule continuously because of the profits from public money and from public office, as if they were sick and would be cured by being always in office. (1279a8–16)

Here Aristotle does not explicitly use the term ἀντιπεπονθός, but expresses the idea of reciprocity that ordinary people hold concerning the exchange of political authority: according to reciprocal equality, a person can expect other people to work for his own benefit since he works for their benefit. In this view, people are expected to take turns in public service and exercise political authority for the common interest. At the same time, Aristotle complains about the lack of reciprocity in contemporary politics and makes an ironical remark about people's attitude towards staying in public office.

It would seem that this view of the reciprocal equality of political authority resolves the problem of sharing goods, which was raised in Aristotle's criticism of Plato's common ownership: people are not concerned with common property (*Pol.* 2.3.1261b33–40), and the sharing of property itself does not necessarily promote friendship (*Pol.* 2.5.1263b15–25). In Aristotle's view, people are concerned with, and take great care of, their own private property. The sharing of goods thus needs a principle on the basis of which people feel responsible for looking after them, just as parents do for their own children and not for many children who are communally parented. At the same time, there must be a principle to prevent people from tyrannically making use of common goods for their own private interests. In particular, when it comes to political authority, people are likely to make private use of it. Aristotle thus introduces the concept of reciprocity in the quoted passage (*Pol.* 3.6.1279a8–16) to prevent 'corruption' or the private use of political authority,[25] and to enable citizens to be concerned with the common benefit in such a way as to look after the good of other citizens when they exercise political authority precisely because other citizens look after their own good on other

25 See Euben, 'Corruption', 220–46.

occasions. In this view, therefore, the reciprocal equality of political authority plays a key role in distributing political authority in such a way that citizens feel an appropriate sense of responsibility for exercising it.

Although in Book 3 of the *Politics* Aristotle does not explicitly refer to the concept of civic friendship, this concept of reciprocity with regard to political authority is the defining characteristic of civic friendship. In *EE* 7.10, there is a similar passage where he defines the characteristic of civic friendship: 'Here too there is the relationship of governing and governed that is neither by nature nor monarchical, but occurs in rotation, and not for the purpose of benefactions, like a god, but to create an equality in the good and in public service. Civic friendship in fact tends to be based on equality' (1242b27–31). In this passage, Aristotle posits that the civic relationship is based on equality while family and king–subject relationships are based on superiority, and regards the element of taking turns based on equality as the essential characteristic of civic friendship. Civic friendship is thus one kind of friendship that citizens promote when they mutually look after the good of other persons through the exercise of political authority or public service. Although Annas argues that there is no single special type of civic friendship that links every citizen to every other citizen,[26] Aristotle clearly defines civic friendship as one that relates to the exchange of political authority or public service based on equality.

The problem with Annas's treatment of friendship lies in the fact that she places very strong emphasis on, or misunderstands the point of, a 'personal relation' in Aristotle's conception of friendship. According to Annas, 'friendship is a relation that requires intimacy and shared activity', but '[o]ne cannot "live with" or share one's life and activities with every other citizen just as such'.[27] She attributes the impracticability of civic friendship to the lack of intimacy and shared activity between citizens. First, however, Aristotle does not require 'intimacy'

[26] Annas, 'Comments on J. Cooper', 246. [27] Ibid., 243.

or an emotional bond between citizens as Plato does. Although he points out the recognition of other people's attitude towards oneself as one necessary condition for forming friendship (*EN* 8.2.1155b27–1156a5, already quoted), this recognition simply means the awareness that other people also have a favourable attitude towards oneself.[28] Citizens can thus fully develop this awareness if they hold each other accountable for their use of political authority. It would seem that if we apply Annas's criteria, we cannot regard advantage-friendship between merchants under commercial agreement as 'friendship', since it does not presuppose 'intimacy' between them. Given that both Aristotle's and the ancient Greek conceptions of friendship in general include a wide variety of social relationships, Aristotle would be likely to consider Annas's concept of friendship highly modernised because of her attention to personal, intimate relationships.

Second, Annas does not grasp 'the shared activity' between citizens: in her view, mutual well-wishing is never applicable to the relationship of ruler and ruled, since 'one does not live with one's rulers or know anything about their tastes'.[29] To be sure, Aristotle argues that in tyranny there is nothing in common between a tyrant and his subjects. For this reason, he adds, there is little or no friendship in tyranny, just as there is no friendship between craftsman and tool, soul and body, or master and slave (*EN* 8.11.1161a31–b5, cf. *EE* 7.9.1241b17–19). As explained above, however, the defining characteristic of a civic relationship is the sharing of political authority. Reciprocal well-wishing for the good of other citizens through political authority makes it possible for citizens to have political authority in common. That being so, from Aristotle's

[28] Annas refers to a passage in *EN* 9.4 (1166a2–10) as evidence for the requirement of intimacy. It would, however, seem that this passage does not express Aristotle's general definition of friendship, but simply refers rather to what ordinary people think about the characteristics of friendship, in order to explain that a good person has those characteristics in relation to himself. See Annas, 'Comments on J. Cooper', 243. Concerning the issue of intimacy in friendship, see also Konstan, 'Reciprocity and friendship', 283–6.

[29] Annas, 'Plato and Aristotle on friendship and altruism', 553.

viewpoint, Annas's distorted view of political authority can be made intelligible only on condition that we consider no constitutions other than tyrannical rule.

Concerning the relation between friendship and political authority, we can fully understand Aristotle's position if we look at his analysis of friendship in a democracy; interestingly, his conceptual framework for friendship implies a rather positive evaluation of democracy. On the one hand, he asserts that in deviant constitutions, there is friendship as well as justice only to a slight degree (*EN* 8.11.1161a30–1). This is because deviant constitutions are concerned with the benefit of rulers only, thereby lacking reciprocity between the rulers and the ruled. In this respect, in a democracy people do not fully develop friendship, since, according to Aristotle's typology of constitutions, people in a democracy govern their polis for the benefit of the majority only, and lack reciprocity between the few and the many. On the other hand, Aristotle argues that among deviant constitutions friendship is most fully developed in a democracy, because citizens therein are more or less equal and have many things, such as political authority and honour, in common (*EN* 8.11.1161b9–10). In his view, as I have been stressing, the extent to which people share is the extent to which friendship can develop. In a democracy, the extent of sharing among equal citizens is broad, and accordingly civic friendship is developed fully, although among the majority only. In this respect, Aristotle's conception of civic friendship fits with a democracy better than with a kingship, in spite of the fact that a democracy is a deviant constitution. As opposed to Annas's implicitly undemocratic understanding of political authority, therefore, 'the sharing of political authority' and 'the mutual well-wishing of citizens through political authority' are perfectly feasible conceptions if we adopt a more egalitarian view of political authority.

5.4 Advantage- or virtue-friendship?

In the previous section, I clarified that civic friendship is defined as a kind of friendship that citizens develop when they look after the good of others mainly through the exercise of political authority. Which kind of friendship, then, advantage- or virtue-friendship, does Aristotle have in mind as civic friendship, when he analyses the civic relationship and draws attention to the importance of friendship for politics? In order to address this problem, I shall examine three arguments to support the claim that he considers civic friendship to be advantage-friendship, as opposed to the communitarian interpretation of civic friendship as virtue-friendship. However, I shall also argue that this issue is not clearly addressed in the *Politics* and that the conceptions of sharing and reciprocity come to the fore in describing citizens' relationships.

First, in *EE* 7.10, Aristotle identifies what form of equality is characteristic of civic friendship and clearly defines civic friendship as advantage-friendship (1242a6–9). Here he suggests that people form civic friendship because they are not self-sufficient, and he considers the diversity of people's abilities to be advantageous for mutual help and sharing their lives. Moreover, although in discussing the equality of civic friendship he refers to the equality of political authority (1242b27–31), in most parts of *EE* 7.10 he takes the exchange of goods between citizens to be a typical manifestation of civic friendship. He assimilates civic friendship to legal friendship, which is based on agreement, and distinguishes it from ethical friendship, which is based on trust (1242b32–7, 1243a31–3); when people need to repay the provider of goods, those in a relationship of civic friendship have an eye to both the agreement and the thing, while ethical friendship takes into account only the intention of the provider (1243a31–3). Civic friendship, therefore, presupposes the exchange of goods as equally measured by the value of goods, which is fixed in advance through agreement, and this exchange is supposed to be based on advantage-friendship.[30]

[30] For Aristotle's theory of how to measure the value of products, see Chapter 6. Schofield focuses on the difference between 'contract' and 'trust' in transaction as a key difference between political and ethical friendship (see 'Political friendship and the ideology of reciprocity', 91–4).

Second, Aristotle's argument about concord (ὁμόνοια) also suggests that he regards civic friendship as advantage-friendship. In *EN* 9.6 and *EE* 7.7 he treats concord as one kind of friendship, on the ground that it is not just sameness of opinion (ὁμοδοξία), such as about an astronomical issue, which might be held by those who do not know one another. He argues rather that a polis is in concord when citizens come to agreement about what is advantageous and act on their common resolution. Concord is concerned with practical issues, for example, that public officials should be chosen by election, that the alliance with Sparta is definitely necessary and that somebody else must take over government. Aristotle indicates that concord seems to be civic friendship, because it is concerned with advantage and with what affects life (*EN* 9.6.1167b2–4). Here he apparently presupposes that civic friendship is concerned primarily with advantage, not necessarily with citizens' character.[31]

Third, Aristotle's argument about the proper number of friends in *EN* 9.10 and *EE* 7.12.1245b19–25 also refutes the idea that civic friendship is virtue-friendship. Concerning the issue of whether we should have as many virtuous friends as possible, he argues that the number of friends a person has should be limited to how many people can feasibly share their lives. He suggests that it is hard to share one's life with many people, first because many people cannot all be friends with one another, and second because people cannot share the pleasure of one friend and the grief of another friend at the same time. He therefore maintains that friends should be a few in the case of virtue-friendship. By contrast, he mentions that people can have many friends only in a political manner (πολιτικῶς) (*EN* 9.10.1171a15–20). Here he contrasts virtue-friendship and civic friendship by saying that people can be friends with many people in a political manner without being obsequious, while

[31] In *EE* 7.7.1241a32–3, Aristotle defines concord as civic friendship, but in this passage it is not clear whether he presupposes that civic friendship is advantage-friendship. Richard Bodéüs offers a detailed account of Aristotle's conception of concord in his *Le Véritable politique et ses vertus selon Aristote*, 157–67.

it is impossible to be friends with many people on the basis of virtue-friendship.

The above three arguments show that both ethical treatises presuppose the idea that civic friendship is advantage-friendship. Are there any strong arguments to support the position that civic friendship is virtue-friendship? For this position, Cooper refers to the arguments in *Politics* 3.9,[32] where Aristotle distinguishes a polis from a military alliance and commercial exchange in that it is concerned with the virtue of other citizens (1280a34–b5). Certainly, this understanding of a polis is greatly different from that in the ethical treatises, especially in *EE*, where he identifies a civic relationship with the exchange of goods. In *Politics* 3.9 he repeatedly notes the difference between commercial transactions and the polis (1280b17–23, 29–31), because in a commercial association people are not concerned with one another's virtue and vice, but only with how to avoid being harmed by one another. Aristotle therefore does not have the exchange of goods in mind when he is considering civic relationships in *Politics* 3, but rather examines the equality of citizens in terms of the exchange of political authority.

As explained in Section 5.2, however, mutual concern or mutual goodwill does not fulfil all of the necessary conditions for Aristotle's conception of friendship, since friends need to be aware of other people's attitude towards themselves. There is, however, one passage in *Politics* 7.4, where he regards acquaintance with other citizens' character as important for politics:

> the activities of a polis are those of the rulers and those of the ruled, and the tasks of the rulers are decision and judgement. In order to make decisions on matters of justice and to assign public office on the basis of merit, citizens must know what character each citizen has. In a country where this condition does not exist, the business of electing officials and deciding lawsuits must go badly. (1326b12–18)

In this context, Aristotle considers the proper size of an ideal polis, and clarifies that citizens must know one another's character in order to manage public affairs well. One of the characteristics of Aristotle's ideal polis is that he does not have a

[32] Cooper, 'Political animals and civic friendship', esp. 234–5.

modern, large nation-state in mind as the best political community, but a small city in which citizens can have the whole polis within their own sight (*Pol.* 7.4.1326b22–4). Although it might be rare for citizens to have a friendly concern for one another, in the arguments about an ideal polis in Book 7 Aristotle at least maintains that citizens' mutual acquaintance makes it possible for citizens to govern their polis well.[33]

However, how can we reconcile Aristotle's requirement of acquaintance with other citizens with his other assertion that one cannot have many virtuous friends? MacIntyre suggests that it is 'by being composed of a network of small groups of friends' that friendship enables citizens to bond together, even though the number of citizens in ancient Athens reached some tens of thousands. In his view, we need to think of friendship in a polis as 'a sharing incorporated in the immediacy of an individual's particular friendships'.[34] Arguably, MacIntyre's suggestion is loosely based on Aristotle's own view of friendship in a polis: in *Politics* 3.9 (1280b33–9, already quoted), Aristotle argues that some social activities, such as marriage, fraternities and sacrificial ceremonies, enable citizens to share their lives in the polis. 'A network of small groups of citizens' promotes their connection to society at large. It would, however, seem dubious that what Aristotle has in mind as the unit of friendship is 'the immediacy of an individual's particular friendships', since he states that 'a polis is a sharing in living well among *families or tribes*' (1280b33–4, my italics), and that 'a polis is the community of *tribes and villages* for the sake of a complete and sufficient life' (1280b40–1281a1, my italics). Here Aristotle seems to have villages, tribes and families in mind as the units of friendship, and argues that there should be social activities enabling the formation of friendly relationships between those units. It is therefore not plausible to give a communitarian interpretation of these texts or argue that Aristotle regards civic friendship as virtue-friendship between particular individuals.

33 See also *Pol.* 5.11.1313a41–b6, where Aristotle points out that it is better for the preservation of a tyranny that citizens do not know one another.

34 MacIntyre, *After Virtue*, 156.

There is a more plausible communitarian interpretation, namely, the importance of a shared recognition of good. As explained in connection with the passage in *Politics* 3.9 (1280b33–9), the element of 'sharing lives (συζῆν)' is crucial for developing friendship, and it plays an important role also in distinguishing friendship from goodwill in *EN* 8.5 (1157b17–19). In this view, a friend takes up burdens and finds pleasure in 'sharing lives' with friends, while a person of goodwill supports others from the outside. In another passage, examined in Chapter 4, Aristotle more clearly defines the essential characteristic of 'sharing lives' not as staying in the same place, like cattle, but as the sharing of reasoning and thought (κοινωνεῖν λόγων καὶ διανοίας) (*EN* 9.9.1170b10–14). This idea corresponds to the notion of a political animal in *Politics* 1.2, where Aristotle defines human beings as political animals in the sense that only humans have language (λόγος) through which they can deliberate and communicate what is just and unjust and what is good and bad (1253a7–18). As we explored above, he identifies the essential characteristic of a polis, as well as that of citizenship, as the sharing of political authority rather than ethnicity or territory. These arguments seem to imply the importance of a shared understanding of good, mainly in assembly or judicial court, and sometimes in the context of personal relations. Furthermore, in the argument about concord in *EN* 9.6, Aristotle argues that concord is found among decent people, because they are generally speaking of the same mind, while base people cannot be in concord, because they seek more than their fair share of benefits and shirk their share of labours and public service (1167b4–16, cf. *EE* 7.7.1241a21–30).[35] Although concord, or civic friendship, is not 'virtue-friendship', since it does not rely on acquaintance with other citizens' personal character, here Aristotle implies that only virtuous people can lead a communal, political life for their own common advantage.

[35] In *EE* 7.7.1241a25–30, however, Aristotle points out the possibility that even base people can be in concord, when they choose and desire the same thing.

This treatment of Aristotle would not seem to support Yack's criticism of communitarians. Based on the same passage (*Pol.* 1.2.1253a7–18), Yack regards the characteristic of a political animal as reasoned speech and argument, and emphasises the element of conflict and competition in the civic relationship.[36] This is because if we focused on devotion to the common good as the meaning of 'political', bees and ants would be more political than human beings, since they seem to subordinate themselves much more completely to the common good of their respective communities.[37] In Yack's view, human language gives us the potential to have conflict with each other. For this reason, unlike communitarians, he argues that we do not need a moral consensus in order to participate in a political community, but need only share in the practice of holding each other accountable to standards of mutual obligation that Aristotle associates with political justice. It would, however, seem that Yack places very strong emphasis on the element of conflict and competition in Aristotle's theory. Aristotle asserts that the sharing of goodness and justice makes a household and a polis (*Pol.* 1.2.1253a18). This suggests that a certain kind of agreement about goodness and justice is necessary for people to live in a polis. Even if a serious conflict of opinion arises in a political community, he expects that members of a polis will resolve that conflict through conversation and finally come to a consensus about goodness and justice. This treatment of Aristotle is not markedly different from a certain form of communitarianism, which expects that people from different backgrounds will resolve political issues in a dialectical way or through public deliberation.[38]

[36] Yack, *The Problems of a Political Animal*, 51–87. [37] Ibid., 51–2.

[38] In *HA* 1.1.488a7–13, Aristotle defines political animals as those that have some common activity, and by this definition, classifies men, bees, wasps, ants and cranes as political animals. In this context, the defining characteristic of political animals is simply the fact that members of a group perform common or shared activities. In *Politics* 1.2, however, Aristotle regards humans as more political than any other gregarious animal. This is because only humans can have a common view of justice and good, more than simply holding each other accountable to the standard of moral obligations. Yack's treatment of communitarianism represents

All of these things considered, how does Aristotle's *Politics* characterise civic friendship? Unfortunately, there are no conclusive assertions within the *Politics* about whether civic friendship is virtue- or advantage-friendship. Certainly Aristotle does not explicitly say that civic friendship is virtue-friendship in the *Politics*, nor indeed anywhere in his extant corpus. Given that one of the essential arguments about friendship in *EE* and *EN* is the division of friendship into three types, it is fairly strange that the *Politics* is completely silent about what kind of friendship is involved in the civic relationship. One possible reason is that Aristotle had deviant as well as correct constitutions in mind when he was writing the *Politics*, and accordingly could not describe the civic relationship in general as based on some specific form of friendship. In addition, in a passage about the reciprocal equality of political authority, he complains about the lack of reciprocity in contemporary politics (*Pol.* 3.6.1279a13–15, already quoted). This analysis suggests that one thing preventing him from considering what sort of friendship citizens actually have is that the lack of reciprocity makes it impossible for citizens to develop friendship, regardless of whether it is virtue- or advantage-friendship. To sum up: when Aristotle describes the civic relationship, the terminology of 'sharing' and 'reciprocity' comes to the fore, rather than 'friendship'. Where he does refer to friendship in the *Politics*, he regards it as a prerequisite for getting a polis to function well. However, before considering whether the civic relationship is actually based on virtue- or advantage-friendship, he considers it more important to explore a general framework for civic relationships through the conceptions of sharing and reciprocity. This framework, as I shall examine in detail in the next chapter, provides useful insights into the problem of how to establish a friendly relationship between citizens.

only one extreme position, which has a totalitarian conception of the relationship between individual and state, namely, the idea that an individual shapes his identify by submitting completely to his city. Many communitarian theorists, however, consider 'reasoned speech and discussion' indispensable to politics. As explained in Chapter 1, MacIntyre is not reluctant to acknowledge the role of conflict in ethics; MacIntyre, *After Virtue*, 163–4.

5.5 Aristotle's criticisms of Plato's *Republic*

Finally, I shall examine Aristotle's criticism of Plato's *Republic* in *Politics* 2.2–5 in order to compare his political philosophy with Plato's and summarise the implications of his arguments about friendship for politics. Although this criticism is problematic in many respects and sometimes does not demonstrate an accurate understanding of Socrates' views,[39] Aristotle's arguments about friendship do illuminate his criticism, because he begins his enquiry by considering what citizens should share, and the extent to which they share is, as was explored above, the extent of their friendship. Book 2 is dedicated to the investigation of the constitutions of other poleis that are said to be well governed and those described by other people that are held to be good. He regards the issue of sharing as the natural starting-point of this investigation, because it is impossible for citizens to share nothing (*Pol.* 2.1.1260b36–1261a9). In Chapters 2–5, he examines the well-governed polis that Plato's Socrates hopes to establish in speech, or 'Callipolis', and particularly takes issue with Socrates' common ownership system of wives, children and property. It would seem then that Aristotle's conception of friendship is one of the underlying assumptions of *Politics* 2.2–5.

Although Aristotle offers many criticisms of Plato's *Republic*, the most essential point involves the unity of Callipolis. Plato's Socrates fears that if citizens are allowed to have their own wives, children and assets, different citizens will feel pleasure and sorrow about different things, and become concerned with their own property only, and on that account he attempts to unite the polis through the common ownership system (3.417a–b, 5.457d–465d). Aristotle argues that Socrates' idea likens a polis to a household or an individual, and repeatedly maintains that a polis should not try to be as united as possible (*Pol.* 2.2.1261a16–22, 1261b6–15, 2.5.1263b29–1264a1). This criticism is not exactly fair to Socrates' view. Aristotle points

[39] For an examination of the problems of Aristotle's criticism of Plato's *Republic*, Saunders (trans.), Aristotle, *Politics*, 106–26 is the most useful critical commentary.

out that a polis consists not only of many people, but also of many different types of people. He draws a distinction between a polis and a military alliance in such a way as to argue that it is more useful for a military alliance to have a larger number of people, even if they are all of the same kind, while this would not necessarily be useful for a polis (*Pol.* 2.2.1261a22–30). At the end of Chapter 2, he suggests that a wide variety of people contributes to the self-sufficiency of a polis, and, accordingly, that what is less unified is more self-sufficient and more desirable than what is more unified (1261b10–15). This argument does not identify the problem of Socrates' Callipolis, because Socrates also argues that a polis comes about because each of us is not self-sufficient, and that people of different kinds share their lives to provide goods and services for one another (*Republic* 2.369b–c). Aristotle draws a contrast between unity and variety in a polis in terms of whether it is composed of people of a single kind or different kinds, but Plato's Socrates does not argue that a polis is united when it is composed of people of a single, homogenous kind only. Rather, Socrates maintains that a polis is united, just and happy when people of different kinds do their own work and develop harmonious relationships among themselves (cf. *Republic* 4.423d, 434c).[40]

However, there are two useful points in Aristotle's criticism of the unity of Callipolis: the elimination of private concern for family members and assets, and the complete separation between the guardians (including the auxiliary class) and the productive workers. As to the first point, the following passage in *Politics* 2.3 best illustrates the problem with Socrates' 'common ownership':

> What is held in common by the largest number of people receives the least care. For people give most attention to their own property, less to what is communal, or only as much as falls to each individually. For apart from other things, the thought that someone else is attending to it makes them neglect it all the more (just as a large number of household servants sometimes give worse service than a few). Each of the citizens comes to have a thousand sons,

[40] In his 'Aristotle's criticism of Plato's *Republic*', 187–91, Richard Stalley follows Aristotle's mistaken criticism of the *Republic*.

and they do not belong to him as an individual. Any of them is equally the son of any citizen, and so will be equally neglected by them all. (1261b33–40)

In the wider context of this passage, Aristotle points out the impracticality of communising children and wives, and argues that people lose interest in the nurture and education of children who are not their own. In the same way, in *Politics* 2.4, he argues that a father's love for his child becomes watery under Socrates' common ownership system of children, and that people will take little care of 'their' communal fathers or children (1262b15–24). In Aristotle's view, people are concerned with 'their own property and what is beloved (τό τε ἴδιον καὶ τὸ ἀγαπητόν)', but Socrates' common ownership system does not allow citizens to have such feelings towards their children.[41]

In *EN* 10.9 Aristotle acknowledges the positive characteristics of both public and private education. On the one hand, as explained in Chapter 4, he praises the Spartans for the fact that their legislators are concerned with the education of their youth, and maintains that it is best if education is the object of public concern in a community (1180a24–30, cf. *Pol.* 8.1.1337a21–32). On the other hand, he also recognises the importance of private education, using the analogy of medical treatment (1180b7–13): he argues that 'education adapted to an individual is actually better than a common education for everyone, just as individualised medical treatment is better'. This is because 'treatment in particular cases seems to be more precise when each person receives special attention, since he is then more likely to get the suitable treatment'. In Aristotle's view, thus, individualised education can be more responsive to the needs and characteristics of each individual person. This argument would seem to provide the basis

[41] For a detailed account of Aristotle's theory of private and common property, see Frank, 'Integrating public good and private right', 258–77, and Frank, *A Democracy of Distinction*, 54–80. Aristotle's argument casts serious doubt on the idea of sharing political authority, since from this argument it follows that a greater number of citizens lose interest in the governance of a state, because citizens do not seriously care for common property – the state (*res publica*). I have argued this point in Section 5.3 with reference to reciprocity.

for Aristotle's criticism of Socrates' common ownership system of family members in *Politics* 2; Socrates' abolition of private family relationships loses the advantage of private education, which Aristotle identifies with providing good care for family members through adaptation according to each individual's needs.

Aristotle's arguments about friendship also illuminate this criticism from a slightly different angle. As explained above, he asserts that people develop friendship to the extent that they have things in common. Socrates' attempt to communise as much property as possible bears a close resemblance to equating a polis with a family, since family love involves sharing a wide range of things and experiences. In this respect, it is possible to say that Socrates' common ownership system does not necessarily intend to abolish the existence of the private, intimate relationship among family members, but rather to expand it to apply to all citizens.[42] According to Aristotle, however, a common ownership system in a large community such as a polis does not achieve what Socrates hopes it will, because a large number of people cannot be as seriously concerned with common property as are a small number of family members. As argued in the previous section, Aristotle expects that only a few people will develop virtue-friendships, while a large number of citizens can form advantage-friendship. Socrates hopes that the same psychological bond that makes family members share their concerns will motivate citizens likewise to care about what happens in their polis, but in Aristotle's view there cannot be such an emotional tie among many citizens. In this respect, Aristotle's criticism of Socrates' common ownership system can be better understood with reference to his argument about the proper number of virtue-friends.[43]

42 In this respect, Cooper's civic friendship is described as 'a Stoicised version of Plato's vision of the community of the guards in Book v of the *Republic*', since Cooper and Plato both expect that the civic relationship will achieve unity through something like the psychological bond of a family. See Schofield, 'Political friendship and the ideology of reciprocity', 87.

43 In his *Aristotle's Criticism of Plato's* Republic, 73–6, Robert Mayhew also points out the relevance of Aristotle's argument about the proper number of virtue-friends for his criticism of Socrates' common ownership system.

The second point Aristotle makes about the so-called unity in Callipolis is that there is little friendship between the guardians and the productive workers there:

> There will inevitably be two poleis in one, each in opposition to the other. For [Socrates] makes the guardians into a sort of garrison, and the farmers, craftsmen and the others into the citizens. Hence the indictments, lawsuits and such other bad things as he says exist in other poleis will all exist among them too. And yet Socrates claims that because of their education they will not need many regulations, such as town or market ordinances and others of that sort, although he assigns this education only to the guardians. (*Pol.* 2.5.1264a24–32)

Here Aristotle argues that if the productive workers have private property while the guardians do not, Callipolis will have conflict between these two social groups. He raises the problem of the unity of Callipolis, although Plato's Socrates assumes that the common ownership system among the guardians makes it possible for them to be the allies, not enemies, of their fellow citizens (*Republic* 3.417a–b). As has been stressed, people form friendships to the extent that they have things in common, but in Callipolis the guardians and the productive workers have different property systems.[44] Moreover, the productive workers are not allowed to share political authority in Callipolis, but are instead required to concentrate exclusively on their own jobs. To make matters worse, Aristotle argues, they are not expected to receive the same education that the guardians do, even though education is what enables people to cultivate their virtue and share ethical views. In Socrates' theory, if people do not have the faculty of reason in their own soul, it is better for them to follow the instruction of those who do possess reason. This is because they will be close friends if they are instructed by the same thing, namely, reason (*Republic* 9.590d). In the *Republic*, however, Socrates does not address how to develop an appropriate level of understanding among

44 Along with many scholars, I think that the productive workers in Callipolis have private property, but in his *Aristotle's Criticism of Plato's* Republic, 129–37, Mayhew argues that it is unclear whether they have private property, just as Aristotle points out in *Pol.* 2.5.1264a13–18. For a similar discussion, see also Stalley, 'Aristotle's criticism of Plato's *Republic*', 185–7.

the productive workers. As Aristotle points out, Socrates' arguments about moral education in Books 2 and 3, as well as mathematical education in Book 7, involve the education of the guardians only (*Republic* 2.376c).[45]

Aristotle's argument about the importance of action uncovers a serious problem with Socrates' exclusion of ordinary citizens from the political process. Although friendship does involve mutual liking, in Aristotle's view the essential element of friendship lies in its active side, namely, loving, rather than its passive side (*EN* 8.8.1159a27–b1, 9.9.1169b10–11, 9.11.1171b20–5). The following passage illuminates the importance of the active side of friendship:

> Every craftsman likes his own product more than it likes him if it becomes animated. Presumably, this holds true of poets most of all, since they love their own poems exceedingly and are fond of them like children. This is then similar to the case of benefactors. For the beneficiary is their product, and so they like their beneficiary more than the product [i.e. beneficiary] likes its producer. The reason for this is that existence is choiceworthy and lovable for all, and we exist by being in actuality (since we do so by living and acting). The product is in some sense the producer in actuality. He is thus fond of the product, because he is fond of his being too. This is natural, since the product in actuality indicates what the producer is in potentiality. (*EN* 9.7.1167b34–1168a9, cf. *EE* 7.8.1241a35–b9)

It is argued here that a producer or benefactor likes his product or beneficiary more than the latter likes the former, since the product is the result of the activity of its producer. In this respect, the product indicates the essence, or existence, of its producer, just as a house indicates what the carpenter is in potentiality (the capacity for, or art of, house-building). In contrast, soon after the quoted passage, Aristotle argues that a beneficiary finds nothing in a benefactor other than some advantage, which soon passes away, and that accordingly he

45 In her 'Shame, separateness, and political unity', Nussbaum argues that Plato and Aristotle differ sharply on the issue of whether autonomy of choice is necessary for self-respect. It is, however, not precise to say that '[Plato] stresses the need for control and order; the other [i.e. Aristotle] is willing to tolerate a certain amount of disorder for the sake of autonomy' ('Shame, separateness, and political unity', 422). Rather, Aristotle criticises Plato's Socrates in such a way as to point out that Socrates' ideal polis is not properly designed for control and order.

does not love the benefactor as persistently as the benefactor loves him. Actually, this argument is originally expressed in the conversation between Socrates and Cephalus in the *Republic* (1.330b–c), and Aristotle frames Socrates' argument in his own metaphysical terms.

This argument implies the significance of people's participation in the political process for persistently looking after their polis. The importance of action for politics is that by their own activity, people become benefactors in politics and thereby can regard themselves as truly living in their society. If they are not allowed to take action concerning the governance of their polis, they will do nothing but passively expect the government to do things for them and eventually lose interest in caring for their society. In this respect, Aristotle's conception of friendship underlies participatory politics. By contrast, Socrates' complete separation between the guardians and the productive workers deprives the latter of the opportunity to take responsible action for managing their whole polis. To be sure, the productive workers are also expected to be benefactors in the polis by providing their products or services for one another, but they are not allowed to shape the lives of people at large through the exercise of political authority. In this respect, they cannot regard their polis as their own product and do not love it as persistently as the guardians do. Rather, they will be hostile to their own polis, just as in *Politics* 3.11 (1281b28–30) Aristotle considers it dangerous to exclude ordinary citizens from public office. From Aristotle's perspective, therefore, Plato's Socrates divides the polis into two hostile groups and fails to see how the productive workers can develop a sense of love for their own polis.

5.6 Conclusion

Thus far, I have been examining what kind of relationship Aristotle envisages as desirable for citizens and what conditions he considers are necessary for citizens to develop it in a polis. To this end, I have argued that he characterises the civic relationship according to the sharing or exchange of political authority for the common benefit. He defines civic friendship as one that citizens develop when they look after one another's good by exercising political authority in turn. Clearly, he recognises the difference between relationships among family members and among citizens. He does not expect citizens to share as broad a range of possessions, life-experiences and emotional ties as family members do, and thus asserts that civic friendship is not so deep as family love, because the extent to which people share is the extent of their friendship. In this respect, although Plato, as well as some 'Aristotelian' scholars, considers it desirable to unite a polis through something like the psychological bond of family members, Aristotle does not consider this possible, because people cannot have many virtue-friends. Basically, he regards civic friendship as advantage-friendship, although he also maintains that a polis needs to be concerned with citizens' virtue and that only virtuous people can form advantage-friendship, because they can be of the same mind. In other words, a legislator should design the constitution, educational system and other social arrangements in a polis so that they cultivate citizens' virtue to develop friendly relationships among them, but such relationships are not necessarily based on virtue-friendship, but on advantage-friendship. In the *Politics*, Aristotle uses the concepts of sharing and reciprocity to describe the nature of the civic relationship under ordinary circumstances, and deems it in accordance with justice that people take turns in holding public office and exercising political authority for one another's good.

It would seem that this perspective provides a realistic account of the kind of civic relationships necessary for managing a polis. In the next chapter, I shall examine how Aristotle uses the concept of reciprocity for formulating 'commutative justice' and develops his argument about the distribution of property in a polis for fostering the middle class. Since Chapter 4, I have been considering what conceptual framework makes it possible for Aristotle to develop a political theory somewhat sympathetic towards democracy, and have clarified that the reciprocal relationship of governing and being governed is crucial for people to cultivate civic virtue and develop a friendly relationship among themselves. I have also pointed out that this reciprocal relationship in exercising political authority is the essential characteristic of the civic relationship, in contrast with other social and familial relationships. In what follows, I shall illustrate the economic condition of this civic relationship. The concept of reciprocity also elucidates the characteristics of Aristotle's economic analysis.

CHAPTER 6

RECIPROCITY IN THE POLITICAL ECONOMY

6.1 Problems of the economy in Aristotle's political philosophy

I have examined Aristotle's conceptions of civic virtue and civic friendship to argue that the idea of reciprocal equality enables his political philosophy to appear somewhat democratic. In this chapter, I shall examine how the concept of reciprocity is operative in his economic analysis. His view of the economy is, however, the least intelligible aspect of his ethical and political writings for modern democratic theorists, and is sometimes regarded as notoriously unsatisfactory. Aristotle repeatedly underestimates those who work on economic activities: in *Politics* 3.5, for example, he maintains that we do not need to regard as citizens those who engage in 'necessary tasks'. Here he asserts that the best polis does not permit a craftsman to be a citizen, since the virtue of a citizen can be cultivated only by those who are relieved of such necessary work (1278a8–13, cf. *Pol.* 6.4.1319a24–30). Similarly, in *Politics* 7.9, he argues that in the best polis a citizen should not lead the life of craftsmen or merchants, since such life is contrary to virtuous life (1328b37–1329a2). In addition, it is well known that in *Politics* 1.9 and 10, he criticises the art of retail because its purpose is not the use of goods, but the acquisition of money. Throughout his *Politics*, he does not have a favourable attitude towards economic activity for sustaining life or increasing wealth. Given that a democracy is a constitution in which any free person is permitted to participate in the political process regardless of their job, Aristotle's exclusion of those who engage in economic activity is an undemocratic element in his ideas of politics.

Hannah Arendt's view follows this undemocratic understanding of the economy and politics. As explained in

Chapter 1, she excludes the economy from politics completely: in her view, the management of the economy is the business of a household, not of a polis. A polis is a sphere of freedom, in which people participate only after they have managed the household economy and mastered the necessities of life. Until the rise of the sphere of 'society', politics had never been concerned with social and economic policies. In Arendt's view, therefore, 'political economy' is a contradiction in terms.[1] In contrast, Martha Nussbaum explores her 'social' democratic theory through Aristotle's ideas of human happiness. In her view, a government needs to pursue social-economic policies, such as 'the division of land, the arrangement for forms of ownership, the structure of labor relations, institutional support for forms of family and social affiliation, ecological policy ... with a view to good human functioning'.[2] She argues that social and economic policies are essential for achieving her ideal of society, where every person is equally able to develop human functional capabilities. Although this idea appears totally inconsistent with Aristotle's exclusion of day-labourers, merchants and craftsmen from citizenship, she extracts the principle of social and economic policies from Aristotle's ideas of human happiness.[3]

These completely opposite views on the place of the economy in politics arise from the difficulty of defining 'the economy' in Aristotle. There are long-standing controversies concerning how to map his economic analysis onto his framework for politics. His economic analysis has been severely criticised by neo-classical economists, such as Joseph Schumpeter, for being 'decorous, pedestrian, slightly mediocre, and more than slightly pompous common sense'.[4] In Schumpeter's view, Aristotle tries to analyse actual market mechanisms, but fails to do so because he imposes his value judgements on reality. He considers the business of a trader, a ship-owner, a shopkeeper and a money-lender only in moral and political terms.

[1] Arendt, *The Human Condition*, 28–37.
[2] Nussbaum, 'Aristotelian social democracy', 76.
[3] For Nussbaum's capabilities approach, see Section 1.1.2.
[4] Schumpeter, *History of Economic Analysis*, 57.

Although he is motivated to explore economic theory, economic problems from the viewpoint of modern economics escape his notice because of what Schumpeter considers to be pre-scientific common sense.[5]

Against this type of criticism, there are two ways of reading Aristotle that acknowledge the importance of his economic analysis. One reading maps his economic analysis onto his conceptual framework for ethics and politics. For example, Moses Finley proposes that we should draw attention to the background of Aristotle's economic analysis, namely, justice in Book 5 of the *Nicomachean Ethics* and self-sufficiency in Book 1 of the *Politics*. In Finley's view, although Aristotle's arguments in these books cannot be classified as 'economic analysis' according to Schumpeter's definition, it does not make any sense to examine whether they give us useful insights into the problems of modern economics or not, since Aristotle intends not to analyse market mechanisms, but to evaluate economic activity within his ethical and political framework.[6]

The other reading aims to acknowledge Aristotle's contribution to modern economics. In following Karl Marx's reading, Scott Meikle evaluates Aristotle positively as the first theorist who draws a distinction between use-value and exchange-value, and addresses the question of why different products are commensurable in exchange, although he thinks Aristotle could not resolve this problem.[7] Meikle stresses the significance of Aristotle's distinction between use-value and exchange-value for economics, since which of these two values predominates in a society determines whether that society has a capitalist or pre-capitalist economy. By Meikle's definition, 'economics is the study of the developed forms of exchange-value and of regularities in its movement', that is, 'actual market mechanism'.[8] Aristotle's analysis of exchange value therefore shows that what he attempts to analyse is an early form of capitalist economy.

5 Ibid., 57–8, 64–5.
6 Finley, 'Aristotle and economic analysis', 140–58. Karl Polanyi offers a similar type of reading in his 'Aristotle discovers the economy', 64–94.
7 Meikle, 'Aristotle and exchange value', 157–63. See also Marx, *Capital*, vol. 1, Book I, Part 1, Chapter 1, 3, (a), (2), (iii) 'The equivalent form', 147–52.
8 Meikle, 'Aristotle and exchange value', 178.

In what follows, I shall opt for the former of these two readings and make a stronger case along the lines of Finley's position, although not without important qualifications. The above controversies show that we should not discuss what Aristotle considers the problems of the economy in politics without any theoretical reflection on the meaning of 'the economy'. It would be a mistake simply to insist, on the one hand, that Aristotle assigns the business of the economy not to politics but solely to household management, since he does not consider how to control a market economy in the *Politics*, or, on the other hand, that Aristotle's political theory is concerned with the social and economic conditions of citizens, although he occasionally excludes from citizenship those who engage in economic activity. There is a need to illustrate the conceptual background of his 'economic' analysis in order to examine his insistence that a citizen should not engage in economic activity. After examining his framework for the economy, we can understand where his concern for social-economic policy comes from. In the next section, therefore, I shall examine the role of the concept of reciprocity in Aristotle's theory of exchange in *EN* 5.5, and argue that there he does not analyse the mechanism of a market economy, but instead establishes the standard of justice in exchange between citizens. In particular, I shall offer an account of how to equalise the value of different products in a way different both from Meikle's Marxian economics, which formulates the concept of 'human labour' as the standard of value, and from Schumpeter's neo-classical economics, which assumes that the value of products is determined by the relationship between their supply and demand. In Section 6.3, I shall examine the concept of reciprocity as one type of 'particular justice', and make clearer the distinctions between distributive, corrective and commutative justice in *EN* 5. In Section 6.4, I shall examine Aristotle's criticisms of commercial activity in *Politics* 1.8–11 through attention to the concept of 'nature', and illustrate a crucial difference between what he regards as problematic in *EN* 5.5 and in *Politics* 1.8–11. In Section 6.5, finally, I shall point out that the concept of reciprocity plays an important role also in his distributive theory of property in a polis, and shed light on his insights into the problem of the 'political economy' in a way different from both Arendt's and Nussbaum's views of social-economic policies.

6.2 Reciprocity in the exchange of goods

I shall first address the problem of whether Aristotle analyses the mechanism of a market economy. The following passage is of especial importance for specifying the context of *EN* 5.5 and considering what he has in mind as 'exchange (ἀλλαγή)':

> People seek to return either evil for evil, since otherwise their condition seems to be slavery, or good for good, since otherwise there is no mutual giving [μετάδοσις] and it is mutual giving that holds them together. Indeed, that is why they make a temple of the Graces prominent, so that there will be repayment [ἀνταπόδοσις]. For this is what is special to graciousness. When someone has been gracious to us, we must do service for him in return, and also ourselves take the initiative in being gracious again. (1132b34–1133a5)

In the context of this passage, as discussed in Chapter 5, Aristotle is considering the ordinary Greek view of justice: helping friends (good for good) and harming enemies (bad for bad). Just as Socrates does, he denies that this view is exactly identical with justice, but admits that proportionate reciprocity (τὸ ἀντιπεπονθὸς κατ' ἀναλογίαν) holds a polis together with regard to the exchange of goods. He then begins to examine this view of justice, especially reciprocity (good for good), as 'commutative justice' or 'justice in exchange'. In the quoted passage, he clarifies the condition in which citizens are able to give goods mutually. His careful use of the terms 'mutual giving (μετάδοσις)' and 'repayment (ἀνταπόδοσις)' shows that here he does not intend to explore the structure of a market economy, but the condition of mutual giving between citizens. This is because the Greek word μετάδοσις primarily means the process of giving goods to one another, and the related word ἀνταπόδοσις or ἀντίδοσις signifies repayment in return for giving. In this passage, Aristotle mentions by way of illustration the case in which one gives a gift to others and now expects them to make a repayment for the gift.[9] Furthermore, in the last sentence quoted, he points out the necessity of taking the initiative in giving goods next time. When another person takes the initiative in giving, one should not only make repayment, but also take the initiative in being gracious again. This passage therefore shows that the context of *EN* 5.5 is not necessarily a commercial transaction in a market economy, but mutual giving, on the basis of which Aristotle considers the concept of commutative justice that covers a wide variety of exchange, from barter to transaction in a market.[10]

This context continues in the next argument, since Aristotle now considers how to make 'repayment (ἀντίδοσις)' between two people (*EN* 5.5.1133a5–10).[11] Here he considers the case, between a carpenter and a shoemaker, of exchanging a house for shoes, and addresses the problem of how to equalise a house and shoes, since these have different values: in his view, we first need to make their products proportional, such that one house equates to a few hundred pairs of shoes, and, next, how they will receive the products of each other proportionately. How, then, can we assess the value of various kinds of product so that they become commensurable one with another? There is an enigmatic passage that has confused many scholars:

> Reciprocity will then be secured when things are equalised, so that the product of a shoemaker is to that of a farmer as the farmer is to the shoemaker. However, they must be introduced into the figure of proportion, not when they have already exchanged, since in this case one of the extremes has both excesses, but when they still have their own products. (*EN* 5.5.1133a31–b3)

Here Aristotle seems to argue that the value of a product needs to be determined in proportion to its producer. However, what

9 Polanyi argues that the Greek word μετάδοσις signifies '"giving a share", especially to the common pool of food, whether a religious festivity, a ceremonial meal, or other public venture was in question'; Polanyi, 'Aristotle discovers the economy', 93.

10 Concerning the Athenian practice of lending free of interest, based on friendship, and in particular its relevance to Aristotle's texts, see Millett, *Lending and Borrowing in Ancient Athens*, 109–26.

11 Compare Meikle, 'Aristotle and exchange value', 179–81, where he thinks that the context changes.

is puzzling is the method of equalising products 'as the farmer is to the shoemaker'. What elements in a farmer or a shoemaker should we look at when we estimate the value of products?[12] Neo-classical economists such as Schumpeter think that the value of products is determined by the relationship of their supply and demand,[13] while Marxian theorists maintain that the standard of value must be the 'labour cost' necessary to make the product.[14] By contrast, Karl Polanyi suggests that what needs to be introduced here is the 'status' of a producer in society. In his view, the performance of each person should be exchanged at a rate proportionate to the status of each, so as to maintain the community.[15] These interpretations, however, do not have strong textual support in Aristotle. Polanyi grounds his interpretation in his conception of the historical nature of an archaic economy, but Finley and Meikle argue that Aristotle is not attempting to theorise an archaic economy, because,

[12] The author of the *Magna Moralia* makes an oversimplified comment about this relation in saying that 'just as a farmer is to a household-maker, a household-maker is to a farmer' (*MM* 1.33.1194a13–14). This is one of the facts to support Rowe's view of the author as 'a mind of relatively limited capacity', refuting Cooper's defence of Aristotle's authenticity of *MM*. See Rowe, 'A reply to John Cooper on the *Magna Moralia*', 172, and Cooper, 'The *Magna Moralia* and Aristotle's moral philosophy', 195–211. It would seem that in 1193b37–1194a25 the author of *MM* develops the idea that one who works harder should receive more goods, but we might do better not to rely on this author to interpret Aristotle's own thought.

[13] Schumpeter, *History of Economic Analysis*, 61, where he says that 'Aristotle may have taken normal competitive prices as standards of commutative justice or ... he was prepared to accept as "just" any transaction between individuals that was carried out at such prices'. Schumpeter, however, points out that what Aristotle has in mind may be 'labour cost' as in Marxian economics. See Schumpeter, *History of Economic Analysis*, 60–2, esp. n. 1. Sally Humphreys also argues that the just price is a market price, especially the normal market price for the place and the season, although she is not a neo-classical economist, but a historian influenced by Polanyi. See Humphreys, *Anthropology and the Greeks*, 52.

[14] See Marx, *Capital*, Book I, Part 1, Chapter 1, 3, (a), (2), (iii), 'The equivalent form', 147–52. John Stewart also presents the labour-cost theory when he says: 'As the labour required for the production of the more valuable unit stands to the labour required for the production of the less valuable, so must the number of the less valuable units stand to unity'; Stewart, *Notes on the Nicomachean Ethics of Aristotle*, vol. I, 464. See also Grant, *The Ethics of Aristotle*, vol. II, 120–1, where he introduces the idea of 'labour cost'. René Gauthier and Jean Jolif also suggest that 'labour [*travail*]' is the measure of value through reference to *MM* 1.33.1194a7–25 (see their *L'Éthique à Nicomaque*, vol. II, 377).

[15] Polanyi, 'Aristotle discovers the economy', 88.

at the time of Aristotle, the market economy had already begun to thrive.[16]

In *EN* 9.1 there is a passage that sheds light on this problem. Aristotle raises the problem of whether a giver or a recipient should fix the price, and considers the method of entrusting a recipient to estimate the value, just as Protagoras tells his students that they should evaluate how much they think his knowledge is worth.[17] In the case of virtue-friendship, such as the teaching of philosophy, Aristotle argues that there will be no complaints, since a giver or a teacher gives their service simply because of and for the sake of friends, and the repayment should be made in return for the intent of a giver. When the exchange is not of this type, however, Aristotle proposes the following procedure for repayment:

> If the giving is not like this, but on some condition, presumably the repayment must be ideally what each of them thinks accords with the worth of the gift. If they do not agree on this, however, it would seem not merely necessary, but also just [δίκαιον], for the recipient to fix the repayment. For if the other receives in return as much benefit as the recipient received, or as much as the recipient would have paid for the pleasure, the giver will have got from him the return that is deserved. Indeed this is also how it appears in buying and selling . . . Presumably, however, he [i.e. a recipient] must evaluate not how much it seems to be worth after he has got it, but how much he evaluated it before he got it. (*EN* 9.1.1164b6–21, cf. 8.13.1163a9–23)

In this passage, first of all, Aristotle admits that a recipient needs to repay what both a recipient and a provider consider to be proportionate. If they do not come to an agreement on

[16] Finley and Meikle undertake detailed research on the wide variety of interpretations concerning this text. See Finley, 'Aristotle and economic analysis', 145–50, and Meikle, *Aristotle's Economic Thought*, 132–5. This passage seems to be unintelligible to Finley, when he says, 'I must confess that like Joachim, I do not understand what the ratios between the producers can mean.' See Finley, 'Aristotle and economic analysis', 148, and also Gauthier and Jolif (intro.), Aristote, *L'Éthique à Nicomaque*, vol. II, 383. Meikle attributed this unintelligibility to Aristotle himself, as mentioned in Section 6.1, in suggesting that Aristotle could not formulate the concept of 'abstract human labour' as the measure of value. Dimitris Kyrtatas argues that Aristotle has no understanding of labour as a general concept, and that for this reason the value of labour is not the criterion for reciprocal exchange; Kyrtatas, 'Domination and exploitation', 150–2.

[17] For the method of Protagoras, see Plato's *Protagoras* 328b–c, and, for its details and reasonableness, see Denyer (ed.), Plato, *Protagoras*, 120.

the value of the product, however, he suggests that the recipient, not the provider, should fix the value of the product or service, because the standard of repayment must be the benefit or pleasure of the recipient. In addition, in the last sentence quoted, he adds that a recipient needs to evaluate the product before receiving it. This point precisely corresponds to the enigmatic passage in *EN* 5.5 (1133a31–b3, already quoted), where he maintains that people need to equalise different products before exchanging them. If this passage in *EN* 9.1 makes a clearer statement of how to equalise different products, then the enigmatic phrase 'as the farmer is to the shoemaker' in *EN* 5.5 means 'as the benefit or pleasure of a farmer is to that of a shoemaker before exchanging their products'. Aristotle thus proposes that we should look at the benefit or pleasure that a recipient will have, when we estimate the value of a product. He does not have the status or labour cost of a producer, but the benefit or pleasure of a recipient in mind as the criterion for equalising the values of products.[18]

This theory of value-setting is the clearest evidence that Aristotle does not analyse the mechanism of a market economy, but rather considers the just price for exchanging goods in general, particularly by way of giving and repayment. His theory of fixing the value of goods is completely different from its

[18] Henry Jackson's point, 'haggling', can also be one type of the agreement that Aristotle has in mind, because Aristotle regards a transaction in a market 'from hand to hand' as a type of legal friendship in *EN* 8.13.1162b26. See H. Jackson (ed.), *The Fifth Book of the Nicomachean Ethics of Aristotle*, 98. Lindsay Judson argues that the criterion for estimating the value of goods should be 'need (χρεία)' and says 'the ratio "as builder is to shoemaker" is the ratio of the strength of their needs for the goods in question' in his 'Aristotle on fair exchange', 168–9. Certainly, Aristotle argues that people exchange their products only when they *need* the product of each other, but this interpretation does not properly explain why he maintains that people must estimate the values of goods *before* they exchange the goods, since once they exchange products they do not have any need for products, and accordingly it is pointless for him to claim the necessity of estimating the value before exchanging products. Judson thinks that, after the exchange, 'the builder's need for shoes will be his need . . . for a *second* pair' in his 'Aristotle on fair exchange', 171–2, but it also seems bizarre that Aristotle makes a trivial point of calculating the value of shoes based on the need for the first pair rather than the second pair of shoes. I think that although Aristotle argues that 'need' is what presses people to engage with the exchange of goods, he formulates the criterion for the value of a product more specifically by taking the element of benefit or pleasure into account.

equivalent in modern economics: in a market, as is well known, the price of goods is determined by the relationship between supply and demand. The more a product is in demand and the less a product is in supply, the higher its price becomes, and vice versa. The price of a product is fixed in such a way that the supply of and demand for a product are in balance.[19] Although Polanyi thinks that Aristotle has no knowledge of the self-regulating price-setting of supply and demand,[20] it would seem that Aristotle notices this principle of price-setting when he talks about the monopoly of olive-presses and iron in *Politics* 1.11.[21] There he understands that the price of a product rises when its demand increases. Even though this argument from the *Politics* shows that he knows the structure of price-setting in a market economy, he considers how to equalise the value of products in *EN* 5.5. This contrast clearly proves that Aristotle does not give a scientific account of the mechanism of price-setting in a market economy, but considers the condition of giving and its repayment between citizens in order to maintain their relationships. This condition is involved with reciprocal equality between citizens concerning their respective benefit.

Aristotle's theory of a just price-setting, however, does not mean that he criticises a transaction in a market according to commutative justice, but rather that he regards it as one type of 'just' or fair exchange. In the quoted passage (*EN* 9.1 .1164b6–21), he says that price-setting with a view to the benefits of recipients is exactly the way price-setting is conducted in a market. Here a transaction in a market is a piece of evidence for Aristotle to argue that people can maintain their relationships

19 In his *Elements of Pure Economics*, 83–207, esp. 180, Léon Walras offers the original, detailed account of 'general equilibrium', and formulates the law of supply and demand fully. As Walras argues, modern economists no longer believe in the labour-cost theory, but instead think that value depends on 'scarcity' in relation to demand. In this view, things other than labour also have value and are exchangeable, if they are scarce and useful, but things that are not scarce, such as sun, air and water, do not have value, even though they are useful. See Walras, *Elements of Pure Economics*, 201–7.

20 Polanyi, 'Aristotle discovers the economy', 87.

21 Finley shows that the principle of price-setting was already common knowledge in ancient Greece, in his 'Aristotle and economic analysis', 141, n. 29.

in the exchange of goods when they agree on the values that they gain from one another's products. In his view, thus, agreement between those who exchange goods in a market fulfils the condition for them to develop a reciprocal relationship. As I shall argue in Section 6.4, Aristotle's criticism of commercial activity in *Politics* 1 is based on his conception of 'nature', not on his conception of commutative justice. In fact, there is no criticism of commercial activity in *EN* 5.5. The exchange of goods in a market is therefore in accordance with Aristotle's conception of commutative justice.

Marx and Meikle's reading is thus misleading for understanding Aristotle's intent in *EN* 5.5. They suppose that Aristotle was insightful in posing the question of how different things are equalised, but that he could not identify the crucial element, namely, the abstract concept of labour, which determines the price of goods. In their view, Aristotle could not develop the Marxian value theory, which assumes that how much labour people spend on making a product determines the price of the product. As evidence for this interpretation, Meikle refers to Aristotle's saying that 'it is in truth impossible for such different things to become commensurable' (*EN* 5.5.1133b18–19) and argues that Aristotle does not find in products the element that makes products commensurable.[22] This criticism, however, arises from a misunderstanding of the context of Aristotle's theory. As I have been stressing, Aristotle does not intend to offer a scientific account of the structure of a market economy. He explores justice in the exchange of goods, and accordingly he attributes the principle of price-setting to agreement between the parties concerned. It may be true that Aristotle does not shed light on anything like labour, but it is better to say that he does not need to involve any such concept, because the purpose of his analysis is to identify the reciprocal condition that holds citizens together. His price-setting theory based on agreement is thus sufficient to identify this condition.

[22] Meikle, *Aristotle's Economic Thought*, 28–42, and his 'Aristotle and exchange value', 160–3.

Moreover, on account of the fact that Aristotle draws attention to exchange-value, Meikle introduces the misunderstanding that what Aristotle was trying to analyse is the early form of a capitalist economy. Meikle supposes that the distinction between exchange-value and use-value corresponds to the difference between a capitalist and pre-capitalist economy.[23] The exchange of goods, however, has various forms, from barter to mutual giving to retail and trade. Even when friends offer gifts to each other, those gifts have exchange-value. The analysis of exchange-value therefore does not necessarily imply the study of a capitalist economy. In addition, in *EN* 5.5, when Aristotle refers to 'exchange', he uses two words, mutual giving (μετάδοσις) and exchange (ἀλλαγή). These terms are neutral as to whether it is the exchange of goods in a market or not.[24] If Aristotle had exchange in a market specifically in mind, he should have referred to the art of retail (καπηλική) or the art of foreign trade (ἐμπορική). There is, however, no reference to these words in *EN* 5.5. His careful use of terminology also implies that he aims to consider not simply how to make things commensurable as Meikle interprets him, but how to set a just price between citizens. Meikle's approach seems to encourage people to study not Aristotle's economic analysis but Marxian economics, because Aristotle was, in his view, eventually surpassed by Marx. It would, however, seem that Aristotle provides more useful insights not into how to analyse the mechanism of a market, but into how to reciprocate citizens' relationships in the exchange of goods.

6.3 Particular justice

Before moving on to explore the conceptual background to Aristotle's criticism of commercial activity, I shall examine the concept of reciprocity in comparison with other types of 'particular justice': distributive and corrective justice. Usually, the

[23] Meikle, 'Aristotle and exchange value', 178–9.

[24] A passage in *Politics* 1.9 (1257a16–28) draws a clear contrast between these words and καπηλική, which means 'the art of retail'; I shall examine it in Section 6.4.

concept of reciprocity is considered to be one of *three* forms of 'particular justice'.[25] In Aristotle's texts, however, there are several points that cast doubt on this view. First, at the end of *EN* 5.2 (1130b30–1131a9), he gives notice that there are *two* types of particular justice, one of which is concerned with the distribution of goods, and the other of which is concerned with correction in transactions, but here he does not refer to justice in exchange at all. He refers rather to selling (πρᾶσις) and buying (ὠνή) as examples of voluntary transactions that corrective justice is concerned with (*EN* 5.2.1131a3). He thus seems to assume that the exchange of goods is what corrective justice deals with and does not propose that there is justice in exchange as one type of particular justice. In addition, in the very first sentence of *EN* 5.4 (1131b25), after his investigation into distributive justice, he mentions that 'the one which is left is corrective justice', and thereby implies that there is no further type of particular justice which he is going to explore other than corrective justice.[26] Second, Aristotle defines corrective justice in general as the mean between 'gain' and 'loss', and notes that these terms, 'gain (κέρδος)' and 'loss (ζημία)', originally came from voluntary exchange, and meant respectively 'having more than one should' and 'having less than one originally had' in buying and selling (*EN* 5.4.1132b11–16). Here he does not make clearer what 'having more' means in exchange, as he does in *EN* 5.5, but instead takes it as part of corrective justice. Third, as discussed already, the concept of reciprocity has something to do with the exchange not only of goods, but also of political authority. Aristotle treats the concept of reciprocity as a principle of exercising political authority for the common benefit of citizens, and asserts that it is in accordance with

[25] H. Jackson (ed.), *The Fifth Book of the Nicomachean Ethics of Aristotle*, 87–8. See also Irwin (trans.), Aristotle, *Nicomachean Ethics*, 232–3, Rowe (trans.), Aristotle, *Nicomachean Ethics*, 339, 343, and Kraut, *Aristotle*, 103. They classify 'justice in exchange', 'commutative justice' or 'justice as reciprocal exchange' as the third type of justice. By contrast, Charles Young finds the discussion of reciprocity 'harder to connect to the discussion of particular justice' in his 'Aristotle's justice', 187. Gauthier and Jolif also cast doubt on Jackson's view that reciprocity is the third type of particular justice in their *L'Éthique à Nicomaque*, vol. II, 371–2.

[26] On account of this passage, Burnet regards what is called commutative justice as part of corrective justice in his *The Ethics of Aristotle*, 217.

justice for citizens to exchange the roles of governance when they are equal. To return good for good is thus not exclusively concerned with the exchange of goods. 'Commutative justice' in *EN* 5.5 is, rather, just one application of the concept of reciprocity.

All these things considered, it would seem that when Aristotle was writing *EN* 5.1–4 he had not yet developed his theory of commutative justice fully. For this reason, he did not give notice that there are 'three' types of particular justice at the end of *EN* 5.2. Presumably, Aristotle addressed the arguments about commutative justice when he felt it necessary to tackle the common Greek view of justice, τὸ ἀντιπεπονθός. He then admitted that proportionate reciprocity, not unqualified reciprocity, is one kind of particular justice concerning the exchange of goods and formulated its principle, governing both voluntary transactions in the form of giving and its repayment, and transactions of buying and selling in a market.

This interpretation helps to draw a distinction between corrective and commutative justice, even though both are concerned with voluntary exchange in a market. The problem of buying and selling in corrective justice is simply the breach of an agreement. If a carpenter and a shoemaker agree on the exchange of a house for a pair of shoes, but the shoemaker breaks this agreement, or exchanges a defective product, then a judge should order the shoemaker to exchange a pair of sound shoes with the carpenter according to 'corrective justice', even if this agreement seems unreasonable to the carpenter. By contrast, the problem that 'commutative justice' deals with is how to calculate the value of a product so that both parties come to an agreement: what should I repay my friend with when I receive a gift from him? How much should I pay for the knowledge a sophist teaches to me? If one does not repay a proper amount of goods, then one is greedy, or 'has more' than one should.[27] Aristotle thus introduces proportionate reciprocity to define what 'having more (πλεονεξία)' means more specifically

[27] Compare Kraut, *Aristotle*, 154–5, where he obscures the distinction between 'corrective justice' and 'justice as reciprocal exchange'.

concerning the exchange of goods. It is, therefore, possible to draw a distinction between corrective justice concerning voluntary exchange and commutative justice, in so far as the former is concerned with the fulfilment of a contract, while the latter is concerned with the assessment of the value of a product.[28]

A more complicated problem lies in the relationship between distributive justice and the concept of reciprocity. Given that the concept of reciprocity is relevant to the exchange of political authority as well as that of goods, how is it related to distributive justice, which is also relevant to the exchange of political authority? I think that distributive justice is concerned with the allocation of political office, while the concept of reciprocity is primarily concerned with the exercise of political authority. As we explored in Chapter 2, the concept of distributive justice is introduced into the argument of the *Politics* to address the problem of how to distribute political authority according to the merit of the community's members. It is concerned with the distribution of particular political offices to the persons fit for each office. By contrast, the concept of reciprocity is concerned with the problem of how to use political authority. It requires citizens, once they are assigned to political office, to exercise political authority mutually for the benefit of other citizens, or return good for good. There is, however, a passage where Aristotle applies the concept of reciprocity also to the problem of the distribution of political authority: in the criticism of Plato's *Republic*, he introduces the concept of reciprocal equality to set up entitlement to an equal share of political authority (*Pol.* 2.2.1261a30–b6). Only on condition that citizens are equal, Aristotle argues, does this concept require them to take turns in political authority, so that they all participate in the political process. Rotation of public offices among equal citizens is thus in accordance with commutative justice. Furthermore, the idea of reciprocity requires citizens not only to take turns in political authority, but also to exercise political authority for one another's benefits. This idea of reciprocity is best illustrated

[28] In his 'Aristotle on fair exchange', 148–56, Judson also draws a distinction between commutative and corrective justice in terms of whether it is concerned with 'making an equal return' or not.

in the passage where Aristotle formulates the characteristics of political governance in comparison with despotic and domestic rule: as discussed in Chapter 5, Aristotle introduces the concept of reciprocity, although without reference to the term τὸ ἀντιπεπονθός, to formulate citizens' claim to the equal benefit that they look for through the exercise of political authority (*Pol.* 3.6.1279a8–13). He regards political office (and also public service) as a certain kind of burden, and not necessarily as an honour (which distributive justice is concerned with), that is to say, the burden of looking after the benefit of other persons. In this view, an equal share of political authority is a necessary condition for citizens to bear the burdens of returning good for good through the exercise of political authority. By contrast, Aristotle does not apply the concept of distributive justice to the problem of how to use political authority. Hence, one point of applying the concept of reciprocity is to seek equality, once political offices are allocated according to distributive justice, from both sides of political authority, namely, who takes on the burden of exercising it and who receives the benefit of governance. As I shall argue in Section 6.5, Aristotle's applications of the concept of reciprocity to the spheres of both the economy and politics, or the exchange of goods as well as political authority, help us to address the problem of how to consider the place of the economy in politics.

6.4 Criticisms of commercial activity

Next I shall examine Aristotle's criticisms of commercial activity in *Politics* 1.8–11, and illustrate a crucial difference between his conceptual backgrounds in *Politics* 1.8–11 and in *EN* 5.5.[29] The arguments in *Politics* 1.8–11 presuppose his teleological

[29] Compare Meikle's view of 'the integrity of analysis' between *EN* 5.5 and *Politics* 1.8–11, in his *Aristotle's Economic Thought*, 68–86. Meikle underestimates the difference between these books, in considering that *EN* 5.5 addresses a general problem concerning the possibility of exchange of any kind, while *Politics* 1.8–11 deals with 'a derivative type of exchange'. In this section, I shall point out that Aristotle in *Politics* 1.8–11 examines not only 'a derivative type', but also a wide variety of the arts of obtaining wealth and, by introducing the concept of nature, aims to draw distinctions between them.

conception of 'nature': in the context of Book 1 of the *Politics*, the term 'by nature' means 'in accordance with the function or purpose of each thing'. Whether something is natural or unnatural is determined by whether it helps to fulfil its purpose or not. Aristotle's economic analysis in *Politics* 1.8–11 is located in his attempt to integrate smaller parts, such as master–slave, husband–wife and father–child relationships, into a polis according to the hierarchy of purposes. The aim of his economic analysis is thus to identify the significance of economic activity in a polis by clarifying the purpose of economic activity. To this end, he uses the concept of 'nature' so that he can consider what type of economic activity is or is not in accordance with its purpose.[30]

This conceptual background illustrates a slight difference between Aristotle and Arendt on the place of the economy. One of Aristotle's arguments misleads Arendt into thinking that the economy is integrated only into a household. In order to recognise the importance of the wide variety of the art of obtaining wealth, Aristotle first raises the question whether the art of obtaining wealth (χρηματιστική) is identical with the art of household management (οἰκονομική) (*Pol.* 1.8.1256a1–10). He then draws a distinction between them by acknowledging that the role of the art of obtaining wealth is to acquire property, while that of household management is to use the property that the art of obtaining wealth acquires (*Pol.* 1.8.1256a10–13). This question gives us the impression that he attempts to integrate the art of obtaining wealth only into a household, not into a polis as such.

However, Aristotle acknowledges the significance of the art of obtaining wealth by identifying its purpose. As one type of the art of obtaining wealth, he first focuses on methods for obtaining the provision of food, such as agriculture, livestock or hunting. Here he argues that the art of acquiring food is by nature a part of household management, because it must prepare such things as are necessary for life or are useful for a

[30] For Aristotle's conceptions of 'nature', see Lloyd, 'The idea of nature in the *Politics*', 184–204, Miller, 'Naturalism', 322–5, and Reeve, 'The naturalness of the polis in Aristotle', 512–17.

household or *a polis* (*Pol.* 1.8 1256b26–30, my italics). In his view, these means of acquisition are natural, since they are in line with their purpose: to provide food necessary for life. As a result, such acquisition of wealth is not intrinsically boundless, because the art has its end, namely, the provision of goods necessary for life or a good life. Aristotle's main strategy here is thus to integrate economic activity into its purpose, not simply into a household. The reference to 'a polis' in the quoted passage (*Pol.* 1.8.1256b26–30) shows that he aims to integrate the art of obtaining wealth into a polis as well as a household, and leaves room open for the possibility that he will develop an argument for economic concern in a polis.[31]

Aristotle next examines the art of obtaining wealth through exchange. The problem of whether this type is natural is more complicated, because the purpose of property does not seem to reside in exchange. In order to identify the varieties of exchange, he draws a well-known distinction between use-value and exchange-value, and divides various types of exchange, it would seem, into three. Since this division of the types of exchange is useful for considering where Aristotle's criticisms of commercial activity come from in the *Politics*, and for identifying the difference between the conceptual backgrounds in *EN* 5.5 and in *Politics* 1.8–11, I shall illustrate the characteristics of each type of exchange.

The first type of exchange comes from the necessity of acquiring goods, that is, in a Marxian formulation, commodity and commodity (CC') (*Pol.* 1.9.1257a19–30).[32] Regarding why people exchange goods, here Aristotle has 'need' in mind, in the same way as in *EN* 5.5: in his view, people exchange goods when they have a little of some products and much of others.

[31] See also *Pol.* 4.15.1299a23, where Aristotle points out that there are public officials who are concerned with citizens' economic activities.

[32] 'Commodity' is a theoretical term, which Meikle defines as 'the historical social form acquired by the product of labour in a society whose social relations are those of private labour and private exchange', in his 'Aristotle and exchange value', 157. Furthermore, 'commodity' usually means a product sold in a market, but Aristotle does not necessarily have exchange in a market in mind. Here I do not mean to follow the Marxian reading, but in using this Marxian formulation I wish to make it easy to recognise the difference between various types of exchange.

In a household, exchange is not necessary, because household members share their property with one another. When people live apart, they need to exchange goods in order to provide for one another. Aristotle admits that this type of exchange is not contrary to nature, because it satisfies the self-sufficiency of people's lives (*Pol.* 1.9.1257a28–30).

The second type is exchange through currency: commodity, money and commodity (CMC`) (*Pol.* 1.9.1257a30–41). His explanation of the role of currency also follows the general method of *Politics* 1, namely, to identify its purpose through the narrative of development: when people began to import what was in short supply and export what was abundant to foreign countries, currency was created, because goods were not necessarily easy to carry. Here Aristotle points out two positive characteristics of currency: to be easy to carry and to make it possible to measure various goods.[33] If currency facilitates the process of exchange through these characteristics, it is not necessarily contrary to nature. In fact, he has in mind 'each of the necessary things in accordance with nature (ἕκαστον τῶν κατὰ φύσιν ἀναγκαίων)' as what is imported (*Pol.* 1.9.1257a34–5), and calls this type of exchange 'necessary exchange (ἀναγκαίας ἀλλαγῆς)' (*Pol.* 1.9.1257b1). In his view, therefore, the use of currency does not itself necessarily make exchange contrary to nature.

The third type of exchange is the art of retail (καπηλική), or MCM`, which was originally developed from the second type (*Pol.* 1.9.1257a41–b10). The art of retail is concerned with how and from what sources people can make the greatest profit. In Aristotle's view, this art is intrinsically boundless, because its end is the acquisition of property regardless of use. Moreover, it is contrary to nature, because the purpose of this art is to accumulate currency, in spite of the fact that the purpose of currency is not to accumulate itself, but to make it possible for people to exchange goods. In this sense, moneylenders (MM`)

33 Polanyi classifies various functions of money into four types: payment, standard of value, store of wealth and means of exchange. See Polanyi, *The Livelihood of Man*, 102–4, and Schumpeter, *History of Economic Analysis*, 62–3.

are most contrary to nature, since they create money from money by charging interest (*Pol.* 1.10.1258b2–8).

This type of exchange is fundamentally different from the first (CC`) and the second (CMC`). The point of the latter transactions is that C` has the same value as C. The purpose of these transactions is not to acquire M, but to obtain C` and eventually use C`. In these transactions people do not intend to accumulate money, but rather to exchange what is abundant with what is necessary for themselves. In contrast, the point of the third type of transaction (MCM`) is that the amount of M` must be larger than that of M. If M` is equivalent to M, this business does not make any sense. The purpose of this business is to increase the amount of money by repeating this process, as MCM`C`M``. Aristotle criticises this type of economic activity in terms of its principle, 'increasing profit'. He does not necessarily criticise the use of money or transactions in a market as such, since he asserts that CMC` is not contrary to nature. Rather, he criticises the use of money for the wrong purpose. Unlike in *EN* 5.5, therefore, in *Politics* 1.8–11 he considers not whether the exchange of goods between citizens is in accordance with their reciprocal relationships, but whether the exchange of goods is integrated into the purpose of goods, namely, the use of goods for a household or a polis. In other words, the conceptual background in *Politics* 1.8–11 is different from that of *EN* 5.5, in that it relies on the teleological concept of 'nature', through which Aristotle criticises the 'attitude' of retailers towards their exchange, not their relationship with other citizens.

This conceptual background in the *Politics* can be made clearer when we look at Aristotle's criticism of the abuse of people's capacities for money-making (*Pol.* 1.9.1258a8–14): once people are involved with this money-making process, they try to increase their profit by making use of any human ability, such as courage, general leadership or medicine. Although the purpose of courage, general leadership and medicine is brave behaviour, victory and health, respectively, a merchant misuses them for the wrong end, i.e. making money. In Aristotle's view, thus, merchants do not necessarily act without virtue, but they exercise their virtue for the wrong purpose. His criticism of commercial activity in *Politics* 1.8–11 is directed not only at the life of craftsmen who are busy working, but also at the attitude of those who are relieved from necessary work simply on the basis of wealth accumulation.

Ironically, the most basic assumption of modern economics presupposes individuals who try to increase their own profit. Human nature in modern economics does not have any end, but it has an indefinite desire for profit. An individual is supposed effectively and endlessly to pursue their own profit in a competitive market. On the basis of this assumption, modern economics aims to explain any and every economic phenomenon. It would seem that this assumption is understandable, because modern economics analyses the mechanisms of a market economy, in which people are structurally organised to increase their own profit. This idea of a market economy is, however, not the principle of Aristotle's conception of 'the economy', because the purpose of household management is not to obtain profit, but to use property for life or the good life (*Pol.* 1.8.1256a10–13). The principle of household management is thus not indefinite, but instead has an inherent, natural end. Although the etymological origin of 'economy' lies in the Greek word 'household (οἶκος)', the principle of modern economics is completely different from Aristotle's view of household management.[34]

In this respect, Polanyi's approach is more attractive than that of any other scholar. His renowned distinction between the 'embedded' and the 'disembedded' economy in relation to society is useful if we wish to consider Aristotle's integration of economic activity into a community. Polanyi's framework prevents us from falling into the anachronism of applying the conceptual framework of modern economics, which analyses

[34] For example, Walras assumes that in a market 'each party to an exchange seeks the greatest possible satisfaction of his wants'. In this view, competition is the primary force in setting values, even 'of the doctor's and lawyer's consultation, of the musician's and the singer's recitals, etc.'. See Walras, *Elements of Pure Economics*, 83–4, 143. Polanyi examines the assumption of modern economics through his distinction between formal and substantive definitions of economics in his *The Livelihood of Man*, 19–21.

the structure of a market economy 'disembedded' from society, to Aristotle's economic analysis, which examines the economy 'embedded' in a household or a polis.[35] I think, however, that Polanyi's conception of 'society' or 'community' is somewhat misleading, since he assumes that the rate of exchange needs to satisfy the requirement of 'philia (φιλία)' (which he translates as 'goodwill') to maintain the bond of a community.[36] In other words, it must be based not on the interests of individuals but on those of the community.[37] Moreover, based on the well-known distinctions between 'status' and 'contract' and between '*Gemeinschaft*' and '*Gesellschaft*', he regards Aristotle's conception of community (κοινωνία) as '*Gemeinschaft*', in which 'status' plays an important role in social relationships, and intimacy and mutual trust prevail.[38]

I think that Polanyi's above dichotomies, 'status' and 'contract', and '*Gemeinschaft*' and '*Gesellschaft*', do not contribute to an adequate interpretation of Aristotle's conception of 'community'. First, Aristotle integrates economic activity into a household and a polis, but this integration does not mean that the interests of the whole household and the whole polis have priority over those of their individual members. According to his distinction, as was discussed in Chapter 4, both political governance and domestic management look after the benefit of the governed, while despotic rule cares only for the benefit of a master (*Pol.* 3.6.1278b32–1279a21). In the former types of management, therefore, people use their property for the benefit of its members.

[35] Polanyi, 'Aristotle discovers the economy', 67–72.

[36] Ibid., 80. [37] Ibid., 88.

[38] Ibid., 68–71. Polanyi calls Aristotle 'a philosopher of *Gemeinschaft*' in ibid., 88. Meikle criticises Polanyi's approach as 'primitivism', which focuses solely on 'the archaic economy', where gift and counter-gift prevailed more dominantly than exchange in a market economy. Although Meikle's criticism identifies a problem in Polanyi's approach, this criticism is not helpful if we wish to avoid a 'modernistic' interpretation of Aristotle's economic analysis. It is a characteristic of a 'modernist' to draw an arbitrary distinction between 'primitivism' and 'modernism'. See Meikle, 'Aristotle and exchange value', 177–81. For the intellectual background of Karl Polanyi, see Humphreys, *Anthropology and the Greeks*, 31–75.

Second, Aristotle's conception of community includes a wide variety of relationships, from intimate family bonds to individualistic commercial agreements. It does not necessarily entail a single form of mutual relationship reliant simply on trust. In this respect, Polanyi's conception of 'society' is too naive to provide an adequate formulation of Aristotle's conception of 'community'.[39] It would seem that this problem stems from the fact that Polanyi ignores Aristotle's distinction between legal and ethical friendship in *EN* 8.13:

> Legal friendship is based on fixed terms, one of which is a purely commercial type 'from hand to hand', while the other is more generous as to the time of repayment, based on agreement of the exchange of one thing with another. In this type, the debt is clear and not disputable, but its deferral of payment is something friendly... By contrast, ethical friendship is not based on fixed terms. One presents a gift, or whatever else, on the assumption that the recipient is a friend. (1162b25–32)[40]

In legal friendship, Aristotle says, there are fixed terms concerning what to exchange for what. He presupposes a sort of 'contract' of exchange in this type of friendship. By contrast, in ethical friendship, there is no contract concerning what to exchange. In this case, just as Polanyi's interpretation holds, it is possible to assume strong mutual trust in each other's character. This type of transaction is, however, not the standard case of exchange in what Aristotle envisages as exchange between citizens. Concerning the problem of how to reciprocate products in exchange, as was explored in Section 6.2, Aristotle argues that if there is no agreement, then we need to look at the benefit or pleasure of a recipient. Here he clearly has in mind the interest, not of a community, but of an individual. Furthermore, he admits that in this type of friendship there are many disputes and complaints about how to make a repayment

39 Yack's criticism of the communitarian concept of 'communion' could be directed at Polanyi; Yack, *The Problems of a Political Animal*, 61–2.

40 In *EE* 7.10 (1243a31–b14), this distinction is between 'political' and 'ethical', although its content closely corresponds to the distinction between legal and ethical friendship. For this distinction, see Schofield, 'Political friendship and the ideology of reciprocity', 82–99.

(*EN* 8.13.1162b5–9). His theory of value-setting in exchange is therefore dependent not on the concept of an intimate community, in which mutual trust prevails, but rather on a kind of 'association', in which the concept of a contract also plays an important role. Polanyi's idea of the economy as 'embedded' in 'society' is thus useful for defining 'the economy' in Aristotle, but their views of 'society' differ. In the next section, I shall examine Aristotle's view of the civic relationship in a political community – or, in Polanyi's term, 'society' – in which economic activity is embedded and institutionalised by looking at his arguments for distributing property in a polis.

6.5 Distribution of property in a polis

The previous sections showed that Aristotle considered it necessary to integrate economic activity into a polis as well as a household, and that he regarded reciprocity in the exchange of goods as significant for maintaining civic relationships and keeping the bond of a polis together. There is, however, a practical problem of how to preserve this reciprocal relationship among citizens, if some people are wealthy and others are poor. Ideally, it is desirable to give goods to one another in the situation where citizens are totally equal in terms of wealth, but there is actually great difference in wealth among them. Given that egalitarian politics is heavily dependent on the equality of wealth, such a difference is a serious obstacle to keeping the bond of a polis together. Aristotle addresses this problem in *EN* 8.14, and points out the positive role of honour in enabling society to deal with it:

> Someone who provides nothing for the community receives no honour, since what is common is given to the person who does service to the community, and honour is something common. For it is impossible both to make money from the community and to receive honour from it at the same time, since no one endures the smaller share of everything. Hence they allot honour to the person who suffers a monetary loss [by holding office], and money [but not honour] to the person prepared to accept gifts [in office]; for what is in accordance with worth makes them equal and preserves friendship, as we have said. (1163b6–12)

Here Aristotle defines honour that is given to an eminent individual as something common (τὸ κοινόν). In his ethics, honour is not one of the supreme values, because honour depends on the judgement of the people who give it, and it is not necessarily based on the goodness of the individual who receives it (*EN* 1.5.1095b22–30). In the passage above, however, Aristotle points out that honour is useful for preserving a political community if it is bestowed upon the person who greatly, in particular financially, contributes to the community. In fact, in ancient Greece, the wealthy were able to receive honour by engaging in public service (λειτουργία): they supported public activities financially, such as the construction of warships or the performance of plays, and in some cases also actually managed these activities. If the work was successful, the wealthy individual as a benefactor and manager was praised with regard to his generosity. By contrast, taxing a person without in turn offering any reward was considered to be the mark of tyrannical rule, except in time of war.[41] Aristotle's argument in the above passage follows this ancient practice: he proposes that we should give honour, as a reward, to the wealthy so that none of the citizens receives a smaller share of benefit. Moreover, the quoted passage implies that a polis is a community in which people distribute not only profits, but also burdens, or duties, which they must carry out to receive benefits. Someone who holds public office or makes a financial contribution to the polis is considered to be one who takes less benefit. Aristotle then draws attention to the necessity of repaying the loss with honour. In his view, therefore, reciprocity with regard to burdens as well as profits is indispensable in sustaining a political community.

Aristotle does, however, have mixed feelings about any policy of distributing cash to the poor. There is a passage where

[41] See Finley, *The Ancient Economy*, 164. Ober argues that liturgies and war taxes (εἰσφορά) can be viewed as instruments of economic redistribution from the richer citizens to the poorer in his *Mass and Elite in Democratic Athens*, 199–202. Millett argues that public services can be also seen as disruptive of elite cohesion, since they were, according to Millett, 'a weapon that the rich turned against each other' in the judicial court to reveal how the opponent did not contribute to the polis sufficiently by public services. See Millett, 'The rhetoric of reciprocity in classical Athens', 227–53.

he shows an ambivalent attitude towards the distribution of money:

> Where there are public revenues, we should not do what demagogues do now. For they distribute any surplus, but once people get it, they demand the same amount of money again. This kind of assistance to the poor is like a jug with a hole. But a true democrat should be concerned about how the many do not become very poor, because poverty is a cause of a corrupt democracy. We should therefore so engineer things that prosperity is building up over the longer term. Since this is also advantageous to the wealthy, whatever is left over from the revenues should be collected together and distributed in lump sums to the poor, especially if one can collect money enough for the acquisition of a piece of land, or failing that, enough for a start in business or farming. (*Pol.* 6.5.1320a29–b1)

Aristotle criticises contemporary democracy, where demagogues distribute cash to the poor without reserve, and considers this policy to be endless and pointless. In fact, Athenian democracy did frequently impose public service on the wealthy, and the poor were dependent on the welfare provided by the city. In other passages, Aristotle suggests stopping wasteful redistribution policies such as support for a festival (*Pol.* 5.8.1309a14–20),[42] and warns that in a democracy the government should not confiscate and distribute the assets of the wealthy (*Pol.* 3.10.1281a14–19). These two passages describe the problems not only of cash handouts, but also of the redistribution of the land that the wealthy own for sustaining their lives.[43] Aristotle recognises that this kind of redistribution policy does wrong to the wealthy and destroys a polis. On the other hand, in the quoted passage (*Pol.* 6.5.1320a29–b1) he admits the merits of distributing extra revenues to the poor in order to support their business and make them stand on

42 See also *Pol.* 2.7.1267a41–b5, where Aristotle argues that people ask for more and more payment since their desire is insatiable, although it is not certain whether 'payment of two obols' here means payment to jurors, a theoric fund or a subsistence grant after the Peloponnesian War. See *Ath. Resp.* 28.3, Rhodes, *A Commentary on the Aristotelian Athenaion Politeia*, 355–6, and Susemihl, *The Politics of Aristotle*, 268.

43 See also *Ath. Resp.* 10.1, 11.2 and 12.3–4, where the author describes Solon's policy and shows that the abolition of debts and the redistribution of land were crucial issues between the wealthy and the poor.

their own feet.[44] He also argues that a truly democratic politician should recognise the danger of poverty. How, then, does poverty cause democracy a serious problem? Why does Aristotle support a distribution policy in spite of his aversion to the confiscation of property by the poor?

Aristotle offers reasons for avoiding poverty in *Politics* 4.11, and those reasons can be summarised in the following three points. First, the wealthy and the poor have a tendency to be masterful and slavish respectively, and, if this tendency is allowed to develop, the politics of free persons will be lost. According to Aristotle's analysis, the wealthy are inclined to be arrogant and fond of governing, while the poor are inclined to be servile and fond of being governed. The wealthy never wish to be subject to the governance of other people, and nor do they know how to be governed, because they have been unaccustomed to being governed since their childhood at home and do not learn how to be governed even at school. By contrast, the poor do not know how to govern and only know how to be ruled like a slave. To be guided by reason is difficult both for the rich, handsome, strong and well-born, and for the poor, who are weak and lacking in status. Therefore, if the gap in resources widens, the community will be filled with masterful and slavish persons, and the politics of free and equal individuals will disappear (*Pol.* 4.11.1295b1–27).

Interestingly, here again Aristotle analyses human relationships within his own framework for friendship, in saying that the poor feel envy for the wealthy while the wealthy look down on the poor, and accordingly they are short of both friendship and political community, since a community is a mark of friendship (*Pol.* 4.11.1295b22–4). In this view, the economic gap deprives the wealthy and the poor of common concerns and in consequence does not promote friendship between them. This is because, as we explored in Chapter 5, people

44 According to David Keyt, public revenues (πρόσοδοι) here means those that are surplus and not collected from the notables, such as the revenues from the silver mines at Laurium or from customs dues on the trade at the Piraeus. See Keyt (trans.), Aristotle, *Politics*, 218.

develop friendship to the extent that they have things in common, and equality in quantity is an important condition for building friendship. By contrast, the middle class is likely to be open to reason, and neither eager nor reluctant to hold public office. In Aristotle's view, a polis should aim to consist of as many of those who are similar and equal as possible, and this condition is found among the middle class.

Second, when there is considerable disparity in income, the conflict between the wealthy and the poor becomes more severe, and one party will try to monopolise political authority (*Pol.* 4.11.1296a7–13). This analysis is based on the history not only of Athens, but also of ancient Greece in general, where oligarchs and democrats fiercely struggled against each other to impose their own form of government. A large economic difference generally promotes faction, and if citizens are split into factions, the government cannot reconcile conflicts among them. By contrast, the polis in which there are many people of the middling sort, neither too rich nor too poor, is free from faction and division. Aristotle thus expects that this middle class will play an important role in reconciling the rich and the poor, and preventing them from leading a faction.[45]

Third, when some people possess a great deal of property while others have little, the constitution will become either an unmixed oligarchy or an extreme democracy, and both constitutions will have the potential to bring about a tyrant (*Pol.* 4.11.1295b34–1296a5). In the case of an unmixed oligarchy, a magnate excessively accumulates wealth and, like a tyrant, will have powerful leverage over the community. In the case of an extreme democracy, a demagogue fawns upon the mass of the poor against the wealthy and will have great influence on the whole polis. Aristotle points out that most tyrants emerge from this type of demagogue, while only a few tyrants come from

45 For the conflict between the many and the few in ancient Greece, see Fuks, 'Patterns and types of social-economic revolution', 9–39, and Fuks, 'Social revolution in Greece in the hellenistic age', 40–51. See also De Ste Croix, *The Class Struggle in the Ancient Greek World*, 69–80, where he argues that Aristotle regards a man's economic position as the crucial factor in influencing his behaviour in politics.

oligarchic magnates (*Pol.* 5.10.1310b12–16, cf. 5.5.1305a7–10). In his view, the former type of tyrant is created to confiscate the property of the wealthy and distribute it to the poor. The middle class, by contrast, balances both sides and prevents the constitution from becoming inclined to tyranny. They are thus expected to play a role in saving the middle position of a polis against extremism.

In sum, Aristotle advocates his distribution policy not simply because equality of property is the true equality that politics should aim at, but because, with the economic gap widening, social conflicts become more serious, an alternation among citizens in taking up public office does not occur, and, to make matters worse, there is a possibility that a tyrant may be created. He develops his idea of a distribution policy not in terms of the concept of distributive justice, but in terms of the concept of a reciprocal relationship of governing and being governed among citizens. He supports only a policy by which extra revenues are distributed for citizens to acquire their own land or engage in business, and has a negative attitude towards the wholesale confiscation of the property of the wealthy, since the confiscation of property causes enmity between the wealthy and the poor, and deprives them of friendship. He suggests instead that a distribution policy should be designed so that citizens can stand on their own feet economically. The equality Aristotle seeks is thus a reciprocal relationship in political authority.

I shall here illustrate further the characteristics of Aristotle's idea of a distribution policy in comparison with the practices of Pericles on the one hand and Cimon on the other. In the *Constitution of Athens*, the author[46] makes an interesting comment about their distribution policies:

[46] Concerning the authorship of this work, see Rhodes, *A Commentary on the Aristotelian Athenaion Politeia*, 58–63, where Rhodes says, '*A. P.* was originally written towards the end of the 330's and revised in the early 320's, while the latest unambiguous reference in the *Politics* is to the murder of Philip of Macedon in 336', and accordingly '[n]o one would now deny that *A. P.* is the Ἀθηναίων Πολιτεία from the collection of πολιτεῖαι attributed in the ancient world to Aristotle, that it was written in the 330's and 320's when Aristotle was in Athens, and that it is a product of the Aristotelian school', but from the stylistic, historic and practical evidence, Rhodes concludes that 'Aristotle could have written this work himself, but I do not believe he did'. Thus, the authorship of the *Athenian Constitution* is

Moreover, Pericles introduced payment for jury service, as a political measure to counter the enormous wealth of Cimon. Cimon had as much property as a tyrant had: he performed public services magnificently; and he maintained many of his fellow-demesmen: for any man of Laciadae who wished was able to go to him every day and obtain enough supplies. Furthermore, all his land was unfenced, so that anyone who wished was able to enjoy the fruits. Pericles' property was insufficient for this kind of service. He was therefore advised by Damon of Oa (who seems to have been the originator of many of Pericles' measures, and for that reason was ostracised later) that since he was less supplied with private property, he should give the people their own property; and so he devised payment for the jurors. (*Ath. Resp.* 27.3–4)[47]

This passage illuminates the difference between Cimon's and Pericles' policies for the distribution of wealth: in Cimon's policy, the resources of distribution come directly from Cimon's property. Other fellow citizens in his district were able to sustain their basic needs effectively by having recourse to these. Through this policy, however, they were dependent on Cimon's private wealth. In this sense, they became 'household members' of Cimon's family, and lost their independence from, and equality with, Cimon. In Pericles' policy, by contrast, the distribution of property is supported and determined by the polis, although its resources were not actually 'their own property', as the quoted passage says, but other resources, such as the 'public funds' of the Delian League or the poll tax on resident foreigners. In this policy, poor citizens are not dependent personally on some particular wealthy family and are able to augment their family income somewhat by performing such public services as jury duty and participation in the popular assembly.[48]

From Aristotle's perspective, however, neither of these types of lavish distribution is properly in accordance with the principles of a polis. Although in Pericles' policy a citizen remains

not clear, but I refer to this work simply to illustrate the characteristics of Aristotle's arguments for property distribution in the *Politics*, in comparison with what the author of the *Athenian Constitution* describes as Pericles' and Cimon's policies.

47 The translation basically follows Rhodes (trans.), Aristotle, *The Athenian Constitution*, in consultation with Rhodes, *A Commentary on the Aristotelian Athenaion Politeia*, 340–2.

48 Polanyi draws this contrast as 'manorial *oikos*' and 'democratic *polis*', and expresses a favourable attitude towards Pericles' policy in his *The Livelihood of Man*, 178.

independent of a particular wealthy family, he is dependent on a wasteful distribution of the city's budget. Although payment for jury service is useful as a part of citizens' income, they cannot sustain their lives without the expenditure of the city's budget. In this system, the polis itself becomes 'a large household', in which citizens always receive cash for sustaining their life from the government, not from their own property or work. Aristotle does not support this type of dependence and instead proposes that we should devise a distribution policy for citizens to sustain their lives by themselves, by allowing them to have a piece of land or an amount of money sufficient for work in business or agriculture (*Pol.* 6.5.1320a29–b1, already quoted).

I shall here finish this analysis by drawing a contrast between Aristotle's own and 'Aristotelian' distributive theories. First, Aristotle's distribution policy in a polis clearly opposes Arendt's view that the economy is not the business of a polis in his framework for politics. In his view, politics should be concerned with the economic situation of citizens. Given that any economy is an institutionalised process of acquisition and distribution of goods necessary for life or the good life in a community, it is also integrated into a polis. Although Aristotle does not propose that a polis should be like a large household in which citizens can sustain their life through the expenditure of the government's budget, he expresses considerable concern for the economic situation of citizens, and suggests that it is in the interests of a stable democracy to eliminate poverty and its dependence culture, enabling citizens to stand on their own feet. In this respect, Aristotle's political philosophy includes the element of the 'political economy' that Arendt regards as a contradiction in terms.

Furthermore, Arendt draws attention to the concept of 'isonomy', 'the equality of those who form a body of peers', as what is characteristic of Greek political thought.[49] Presumably, it is

49 See Arendt, *On Revolution*, 23. Concerning the use of this word in ancient Greek political works, see Vlastos, 'Isonomia', 337–66, and Vlastos, 'ΙΣΟΝΟΜΙΑ ΠΟΛΙΤΙΚΗ', 164–203, where he explains how this word was related to the ideal of democracy. In his view, *isonomia* means equality of law not in an economic domain but in a political sphere, namely, equal rights in the law-making,

one of the important characteristics of the ancient Greeks that they built a political arena in which citizens had equal rights to decide their public issues, even though they had inequality in terms of wealth, family background and other differences. Aristotle, however, is not satisfied with a formal equality of rights to participate in the political process, but is concerned with how inequality in politics comes from difference in wealth. If all citizens were self-sufficient farmers or aristocrats, then there would be no serious inequalities to cause trouble in politics. However, in a society where people exchange goods and accumulate wealth through money, this may lead to enormous economic inequalities, which result in political conflicts. This is because the principle of a market economy, namely, 'increasing profit', sometimes does not fit harmoniously with the principle of a polis, 'reciprocity', in that there are no restrictions in a market economy on preserving the reciprocal equality of citizens. The role of politics is thus not only to keep the social environment of a market economy thriving, but also to preserve reciprocal relationships between citizens through social and economic policies. When the economy began to take the early form of the capitalist economy in classical Greece, Aristotle was able to recognise the difference between the principle of politics on the one hand, and that of a market economy on the other. In this respect, although there is no argument about how to control a market economy in his political works, he takes seriously equality in an economic sphere as well as in a legal or political sphere for preserving civic relationships.

Second, Polanyi's formulation of 'redistribution' makes it difficult for us to acknowledge the significance of Aristotle's distributive theory. According to Polanyi's well-known categories, as well as 'reciprocity' and 'exchange', 'redistribution' comprises one form of economic integration, which he introduced in order to classify a wide variety of economic activities. By 'integration' he means 'the institutionalized movements

law-administering and law-enforcing power of the state. See also Finley, *Democracy Ancient and Modern*, 73. By contrast, Hansen makes a negative comment about the view that *isonomia* is the central aspect of democratic equality in his *The Athenian Democracy in the Age of Demosthenes*, 81–5.

through which the elements of the economic process – from material resources and labor to the transportation, storage, and distribution of goods – are connected'.[50] In this category, 'redistribution' designates 'the movements towards a center and out of it again', while 'reciprocity' 'describes the movement of goods and services ... between corresponding points of a symmetrical arrangement', and 'exchange' represents a movement 'between any two dispersed or random points in the system'.[51] 'Redistribution' thus captures the practices of a wide variety of communities relating to the storage and distribution of goods and labour, from the primitive hunting tribe to the vast storage systems of ancient Egypt, Sumeria, Babylon or Peru.[52] The taxation system in modern states is also classified as one type of redistribution in the sense that it is the collecting of resources and distributing them from the centre. Polanyi argues that the process of redistribution forms a political system, whether it is 'that of tribe, city-state, despotism or feudalism of cattle or land'.[53] This categorisation is useful in analysing the embedded process of the economy in society, but his neutral attitude towards the moral and philosophical implications of governmental policies makes any more detailed use of the notion of 'redistribution' difficult. In Aristotle's theory, as discussed above, the distribution of property in a polis is closely related to the concept of 'reciprocity'. He advocates a distribution policy only in so far as it develops the reciprocal relationship between citizens. This idea is far more egalitarian than any other type of redistribution, such as the storage system of ancient Egypt. Moreover, as we explored in Section 6.2, Aristotle considers a just price in the exchange of goods from the viewpoint of 'reciprocity'. The ideal type of exchange is also understood as one that promotes the reciprocal relationship between citizens. 'Reciprocity' therefore plays the central role in Aristotle's theory of the economy, as opposed to Polanyi's division of economic activities into three categories.[54]

[50] Polanyi, *The Livelihood of Man*, 35. [51] Ibid., 36.
[52] Ibid., 40. [53] Polanyi, *The Great Transformation*, 52.
[54] For various types of the concept of 'reciprocity' in anthropology, see van Wees, 'The law of gratitude', 13–49.

Third, Nussbaum's capabilities approach relies on a different idea about justifying a distribution policy. In her view, as was explained in Chapters 1 and 2, a government needs to provide the social surroundings where people can 'equally' achieve a set of human capabilities. The distribution policy relating to property is thus justified by the thought that various types of goods are necessary for the achievement of basic human capabilities. As we have explored in this section, however, Aristotle is primarily concerned with how to develop the reciprocal relationship of governing and being governed in turn. He takes other resources such as wealth or honour into account only in so far as they affect political rule. In other words, he acknowledges the importance of the distribution of property not because it promotes the equality of 'capabilities', but because it makes it possible for citizens to build a reciprocal relationship of governing and being governed. Aristotle's conceptual framework for the distribution of property is thus based not primarily on the concept of human happiness, but rather on the reciprocal equality of political authority.

Moreover, Aristotle takes into account not only the distribution of benefits, but also that of duties. He is greatly concerned with the problem of how to distribute burdens without causing complaints from the wealthy, since too many burdens do not promote friendship between the wealthy and the poor. According to his framework for friendship, as I explained in Chapter 5, one should not only express goodwill, but also actively take equal burdens in supporting friends (*EN* 9.5.1166b32–1167a12). Aristotle also proposes that we should offset the losses incurred by the wealthy by giving honour to them (*EN* 8.14.1163b6–12, already quoted). By contrast, Nussbaum's capabilities approach focuses on one side of politics: she does not stress the sources of the budget from which a polis manages the resources necessary to distribute goods to the needy and achieve equality of capabilities. Even if her capabilities approach appeals to a sense of justice, her social-economic policy would be unlikely to be supported by the wealthy, unless she develops the method of rewarding them for their burdens.[55] In this respect, Aristotle's conception of reciprocity is useful if we wish to consider both sides of egalitarian politics.

6.6 Conclusion

Since Chapter 4, I have been arguing that reciprocal equality is a key concept for Aristotle to develop a political philosophy somewhat sympathetic towards democracy within his framework for aristocratic governance. In this chapter, I have considered how the concept of reciprocal equality is operative in his theory of political economy. To conclude the chapter, I shall summarise the arguments about the role of reciprocity in this subject. First, the concept of reciprocity plays a leading role in his economic analysis in *EN* 5.5. Aristotle addresses the problems not only of how to make things commensurable, but also of how to preserve citizens' reciprocal relationship in the exchange of goods. The object of his economic analysis is not to develop the 'scientific' value-theory of commodities, but to formulate the theory of a just price. In *EN* 8.13 and 9.1, Aristotle develops this theory in arguing that the value of goods should be set in accordance with agreement on the benefit or pleasure of a recipient before exchanging them. He therefore proposes making the exchange of products reciprocal in such a way as to ensure that the benefit or pleasure of each recipient is equal.

Second, the difference between *EN* 5.5 and *Politics* 1.8–11 concerning what Aristotle has in mind as 'exchange' enables us to identify the difference between the principle of a polis and that of a market economy: respectively, reciprocity and increasing profit. Reciprocity is the principle of preserving civic relationships in a polis, while increasing profit may result in that great difference of wealth between citizens that undermines their relationships. Although Aristotle does not support a wasteful distribution policy by which a polis becomes like 'a large household', he proposes that politics should be concerned

55 Nussbaum tends to appeal to a sense of justice, a moralised compassion for the needy and altruistic ties between citizens, as the bases of social cooperation in her *Frontiers of Justice*, 156–9.

with the economic conditions of citizens so that they preserve a reciprocal relationship of governing and being governed in turn. He therefore refers to the concept of reciprocity to justify the distribution of property in a polis, and integrates economic activity into politics in order for citizens to develop the relationship that promotes civic friendship and ensures the cultivation of civic virtue.

CONCLUSIONS

To conclude the whole argument, I shall summarise the positive characteristics of Aristotle's political philosophy, especially its useful insights into the problem of how to integrate the multitude into society. In this book, I have been considering what conceptual framework makes it possible for Aristotle to develop a political theory somewhat sympathetic towards democracy even within his aristocratic framework for a good polis. I have argued that Aristotle proposes integrating the multitude into the political process because in his view it is possibly dangerous to exclude them from politics, and that the concept of reciprocal equality then serves as a basis for his conception of the civic relationship as the exchange of the roles of governing and being governed. I have shown how his arguments about civic virtue, civic friendship and economic arrangements are based on this idea of reciprocal equality. Hence, I think that Aristotle's theory of the mixed constitution and his idea of reciprocal equality give us the intellectual resources for developing a theory of integration.

It is useful here to recapitulate Aristotle's distinction between political, domestic and despotic types of rule, because his conception of political governance also presupposes the idea of reciprocal equality. The characteristics of each type of rule can be summarised in the following way (*Pol.* 1.7.1255b16–20, 3.4.1277a33–b16, 3.6.1278b30–1279a21):

Despotic (δεσποτική) rule:

1. by a master over his slave
2. primarily for the benefit of the master himself
3. without the exchange of authority between master and slave.

Domestic (οἰκονομική) rule:

1. by a household manager over his family members
2. primarily for the benefit of the family members
3. without the exchange of authority between members.

Political (πολιτική) rule:

1. by free and equal individuals over themselves
2. for the benefit of one another
3. through the exchange of authority in turn.

At the very beginning of the *Politics*, Aristotle maintains that there is a distinction between political, domestic and despotic rule, as opposed to Plato's assimilation of them (*Pol.* 1.1.1252a7–16). What is important in Aristotle's distinction is that concern for human happiness is not the right standard for distinguishing between political and domestic rule, *pace* Kantian liberal theorists, who assume that it is patriarchal if, in a political society, serious attention is paid to concern for the happiness of its members.[1] The standard is instead concerned with whether there is a reciprocal exchange of political authority among citizens. In Aristotle's view, the characteristic of patriarchal governance is that people do not take turns in governance, although they benefit from that governance.

Aristotle thus draws a clear contrast between political and domestic rule, and places greater intrinsic value on the exchange of authority in a political sphere. This is because the exchange of governing and being governed in turn makes it possible for citizens to look after their common benefit, cultivate civic virtue and promote civic friendship. The *Politics* can be understood as developing a project designed to build and preserve this reciprocal relationship within an aristocratic

[1] See Kant, 'On the common saying', vol. II, 74, where Immanuel Kant regards governance as patriarchal only on the condition that a ruler looks after the happiness of his subjects, because Kant presupposes a monarchy in his arguments about politics, and accordingly the image of patriarchy fits easily with a monarch who looks after the happiness of his subjects on their behalf. This understanding of politics makes Kant find it difficult to incorporate the conception of happiness into politics. By Kant's definition, whether a political system is 'a republic' or not depends on the fact that it is controlled by the law, not on the degree of the political participation of its citizens.

framework, even though citizens are greatly different one from another in terms of virtue and wealth. On the one hand, Aristotle does not hold the modern, egalitarian idea that human beings are created equal, and that their political, civil and social rights are inalienable. On the other hand, he expects citizens to be sufficiently equal that they can exchange political authority in turn to achieve full rationality. This complex attitude towards human equality makes his political theory useful for acknowledging the importance of the exchange of political authority for the development of virtue in a political sphere.

There is a passage where Aristotle expresses a view of the desirable society in which every person is concerned with every other person's virtue:

> Everyone then acknowledges and praises those who are very eager to do the noble thing. If everyone strives for the noble thing and strains to behave most nobly, then everything in public will be as it should be and privately an individual will have the greatest of all goods, if virtue is a thing of that sort. So a good person should be a self-lover, since he will make himself better off by behaving nobly and benefit other people, but a base person should not. (*EN* 9.8.1169a6–13)

This passage is located in the chapter where Aristotle considers whether one should love oneself or not. Basically, he argues that a good person should be a self-lover, since his essential characteristic is reason (*EN* 9.8.1168b35–1169a1, cf. 1168b30, 1169a5, 17–18), which makes it possible for him to do the noble thing and thereby makes both him and other people better off. The concept of virtue that Aristotle assumes here is politicised, in the sense that virtue enables its possessor to achieve noble things in public life and benefit other citizens. Hence, people praise those who are eager to do fine things, since people's shared understanding of the politicised concept of virtue reinforces the custom of giving honour to those who benefit their society. Aristotle thus envisages a good society where people acknowledge each other's virtue that contributes to their common benefit.

For this reason, in Aristotle's political philosophy, both distributive justice and reciprocity play crucial roles in developing a theory of political distribution. Although these two types of particular justice can be seen as expressions of the more basic notion of justice as giving somebody their due, 'a due' is here defined according to people's merit in distributive justice or according to the benefit they contribute to each other in a relation of reciprocity. In particular, Aristotle applies the concept of distributive justice primarily to the problem of distributing political authority. In this view, political authority needs to be distributed to people according to their merit or virtue. This is because those who have virtue make the best use of political authority for the common benefit of citizens. As we examined in Chapter 6, the concept of reciprocity is also applied to the distribution of political authority, but it is primarily concerned with how to exercise political authority: it requires citizens, once they are assigned political office, to exercise political authority mutually for the benefit of other citizens, or return good for good. In this respect, although there is a tension between aristocratic and democratic elements in Aristotle's political philosophy, his basic idea is to allow for the aristocratic governance that looks to the common benefit of citizens. He develops a theory of integration that ensures a relative equality of citizens on the basis of the notion of reciprocity while establishing an aristocratic government in which the majority of ordinary citizens as a group also play a role in the deliberative and judicial processes.

This way of interpreting Aristotle seems to me to suggest not only a helpful approach to his political works in themselves, but also a better account than has hitherto been available of why we need to read them in present-day democratic society. Although present-day democratic theorists have been using Aristotle's political philosophy as an intellectual resource for communitarianism, the capabilities approach and civic republicanism, I have been arguing that the original offers a more interesting vision of politics. In particular, I have been clarifying the characteristics of Aristotle's political philosophy by examining his notions of democracy, civic virtue, friendship and the economy, and considering how his conceptual framework gives fresh insights into the problems of political philosophy. Those insights can be summarised as follows.

First, Aristotle's political philosophy makes it possible for us to acknowledge present-day complacencies or unexamined assumptions in modern democratic theories. As was discussed in Chapter 3, his theory of the mixed constitution enables us to recognise that 'modern democracy' consists not of a democratic government, but rather of a mixed constitution encompassing the elements of democracy, oligarchy, or aristocracy and monarchy. For this reason we need to be wary about the inherent tendency of modern democracy to become an oligarchic or monarchic government. Unlike liberal democratic theory, which draws attention solely to the problem of whether a government secures basic human rights, Aristotle's political philosophy suggests that we should balance various requirements of governance and integrate the element of aristocracy while considering the stability, wealth and freedom of a political society. Paradoxically, his idea of aristocratic governance makes it possible for ordinary citizens to be integrated into the deliberative and judicial processes not individually but collectively. Although 'Aristotelian' political theories have been criticised in that they advocate the political participation of the people without considering an appropriate form of restriction on popular rule,[2] Aristotle himself is, as was examined in Chapter 3, more careful about the problem of how to integrate the majority into the political process. In this respect, he provides us a theory of integration or political participation of ordinary citizens without committing itself to the idea of populism.

Second, Aristotle's theory of reciprocity makes it possible for us to address the questions regarding the distribution of duties or burdens. As discussed in Chapters 2, 3 and 6, some 'Aristotelian' scholars sympathetic towards liberalism, such as Nussbaum, tend to reflect on the meaning of governance from the perspective of beneficiaries and thereby consider what benefit a government should distribute among citizens. By contrast, Aristotle's own political philosophy suggests that we need to think also about the distribution of duties or burdens in light of

[2] Pettit, *Republicanism*, 8, 17–19.

the requirement that all citizens contribute as such in some way to the governance of a city. Given that a democracy is established with a view to seeking equality or fairness between citizens, no democratic system is workable unless there is a certain degree of equality in duties or burdens. From Aristotle's perspective, the distribution of political authority can be also seen as the distribution of duties, in that rulers must exercise political authority for other citizens' benefit. One difficult problem for political distribution is accordingly how to apply both of the two principles of political distribution, 'from each according to their abilities' and 'to each according to their needs', at the same time. Aristotle's political philosophy, therefore, in effect makes the point that the assignment of duties as well as benefits needs to be examined more thoroughly to build a cooperative, friendly relationship between citizens.

Third, Aristotle's political philosophy makes it possible for us to think about ethical and political principles together, as opposed to the situation in modern moral and political sciences. In particular, in contrast to Arendt's clear division between politics and economics, it suggests that we need to examine ethical, political and economic dimensions of reciprocal equality in combination to halt the strong and consistent trend of democracy towards simple majority rule. This is because reciprocal equality is the most important condition needing to be satisfied if citizens are to cultivate civic virtue and develop friendship between them, unlike positive liberty, which, if elevated to the key consideration, would mislead us into treating democracy simply as a system in which people govern a city, not a system in which they are governed by other ordinary citizens. In this respect, extensive modification of the concept of democracy away from majority rule, or the sovereignty of the people, to reciprocal equality in governing and being governed in turn is needed for us to consider how to make a democratic system workable from ethical, political and economic perspectives. Hence, what is now important for democratic political theory is not the ideology of 'no-rule', but a conceptual framework for analysing the relationship of governing and being governed in turn. Aristotle's political philosophy suggests that we should consider the distribution of resources in general for the preservation of the reciprocal relationship between citizens.

Finally, Aristotle's political philosophy offers a more positive account of popular participation even within his aristocratic framework. To be sure, it would not seem that his theory of political participation is easily applicable to a modern democratic state, since it is practically impossible to integrate such a large populace into the political process directly without representatives in the central government. Instead, Aristotle's theory sheds light on the importance of a local community, where citizens can develop reciprocal relationships of governing and being governed in turn between them. What is a fundamental idea in his theory is that citizens can cultivate civic virtue only through social practices of both governing and being governed. Without integrating the majority into social relationships, they will lose a sense of sharing in political authority, become passive in politics and consider the role of governance solely from the perspective of a recipient.[3] The present book has been arguing for the significance of agency in politics, and of the way citizens relate to each other, as against the role of a state as an entity distinct from its citizens. As was discussed in Chapters 4 and 5, Aristotle's conception of the political animal means not simply that people should live in a polis to be indoctrinated with a dominant view of ethical values, but rather that people need to share the views of justice and good, and exercise the faculty of practical reason in the political process. Without this proper understanding, shared between citizens, of the concept of the 'political', the danger is that a political sphere will be organised simply as a place for domination over other citizens or competition for economic prosperity and public office. Aristotle's theory of political participation therefore

[3] In her *On Revolution*, 126, 232–9, Arendt argues that the American founding fathers were concerned about how to preserve 'the revolutionary spirit', or a sense of participation in the constitution-making process, among the general populace even after the actual end of the revolution.

enables us to develop a model for integrating a wide variety of people into the deliberative and judicial process on a local level, and thereby keep up a sense of self-governance, which is a basis for political governance also on a national and international level.

BIBLIOGRAPHY

1 Texts, translations and commentaries of Aristotle's *Politics*

Barker, Ernest (trans.), Aristotle, *Politics*, revised with an introduction and notes by R. F. Stalley, Oxford World's Classics (Oxford University Press, 1995).

Dreizehnter, Alois, *Aristoteles' Politik* (Munich: Wilhelm Fink Verlag, 1970).

Everson, Stephen (ed.), Aristotle, *The Politics and the Constitution of Athens*, Cambridge Texts in the History of Political Thought (Cambridge University Press, 1996).

Jowett, Benjamin (trans.), *Politica*, revised edition, in W. D. Ross (ed.), *The Works of Aristotle*, vol. x (Oxford: Clarendon Press, 1972).

Keyt, David (trans., with a comm.), Aristotle, *Politics: Books V and VI*, Clarendon Aristotle Series (Oxford: Clarendon Press, 1999).

Kraut, Richard (trans., with a comm.), Aristotle, *Politics: Books VII and VIII*, Clarendon Aristotle Series (Oxford: Clarendon Press, 1997).

Lord, Carnes (trans.), Aristotle, *The Politics* (University of Chicago Press, 1984).

Newman, W. L., *The Politics of Aristotle*, with an introduction, two prefatory essays and notes critical and explanatory, vols. I–IV (Oxford: Clarendon Press, 1887, 1902).

Pellegrin, Pierre (trans.), Aristotle, *Les Politiques* (Paris: Flammarion, 1993).

Reeve, C. D. C. (trans.), Aristotle, *Politics* (Indianapolis, IN: Hackett Publishing Company, 1998).

Robinson, Richard (trans., with an intro. and a comm.), Aristotle, *Politics: Books III and IV*, Clarendon Aristotle Series (Oxford: Clarendon Press, 1962).

Ross, W. D. (ed.), *Aristotelis Politica*, Oxford Classical Texts (Oxford: Clarendon Press, 1957).

Saunders, Trevor J. (trans., with a comm.), Aristotle, *Politics: Books I and II*, Clarendon Aristotle Series (Oxford: Clarendon Press, 1995).

Schütrumpf, Eckart (trans., with a comm.), Aristoteles, *Politik*, Bücher I, II–III, IV–VI, VII–VIII (Berlin: Akademie-Verlag, 1991, 1996, 2005).

Simpson, Peter L. Phillips, *A Philosophical Commentary on the Politics of A ristotle* (Chapel Hill, NC: University of North Carolina Press, 1998).

Sinclair, T. A. (trans.), Aristotle, *The Politics*, revised and re-presented by Trevor J. Saunders, Penguin Classics (London: Penguin Books, 1981).

Susemihl, Franz, and R. D. Hicks, *The Politics of Aristotle*, a revised text with an introduction, analysis and commentary (London: Macmillan, 1894).
Tricot, J. (trans.), Aristote, *La Politique*, 7th edn (Paris: Librairie Philosophique J. Vrin, 1995).

2 Texts, translations and commentaries of Aristotle's other works

Barnes, Jonathan (ed.), *The Complete Works of Aristotle: The Revised Oxford Translation*, 2 vols. (Princeton University Press, 1984).
Bekker, Immanuel, *Aristotelis Opera* (Berlin: Walter de Gruyter, 1960).
Burnet, John (ed.), *The Ethics of Aristotle* (London: Methuen, 1900).
Bywater, I. (ed.), *Aristotelis Ethica Nicomachea*, Oxford Classical Texts (Oxford: Clarendon Press, 1894).
Gauthier, René Antoine, et Jean Yves Jolif (trans., with an intro. and a comm.), Aristote, *L'Éthique à Nicomaque*, 2 vols. (Institut Supérieur de Philosophie de l'Université de Louvain, 1970).
Grant, Alexander, *The Ethics of Aristotle*, 2 vols. (London: Longmans, Green, and Co., 1885).
Inwood, Brad, and Raphael Woolf (trans. and eds.), Aristotle, *Eudemian Ethics*, Cambridge Texts in the History of Philosophy (Cambridge University Press, 2013).
Irwin, Terence (trans.), Aristotle, *Nicomachean Ethics*, 2nd edn (Indianapolis, IN: Hackett Publishing Company, 1999).
Jackson, Henry (ed.), *The Fifth Book of the Nicomachean Ethics of Aristotle* (Cambridge University Press, 1879).
Kenyon, F. G. (ed.), *Aristotelis Atheniensium Respublica*, Oxford Classical Texts (Oxford: Clarendon Press, 1920).
Lennox, James G. (trans., with a comm.), Aristotle, *On the Parts of Animals*, Clarendon Aristotle Series (Oxford: Clarendon Press, 2001).
Pakaluk, Michael (trans., with a comm.), Aristotle, *Nicomachean Ethics: Books VIII and IX*, Clarendon Aristotle Series (Oxford: Clarendon Press, 1998).
Rhodes, P. J., *A Commentary on the Aristotelian Athenaion Politeia* (Oxford: Clarendon Press, 1981).
(trans., with an intro. and notes), Aristotle, *The Athenian Constitution*, Penguin Classics (London: Penguin Books, 2002).
Ross, W. D. (ed.), *Aristotelis Ars Rhetorica*, Oxford Classical Texts (Oxford: Clarendon Press, 1959).
(ed.), *Aristotelis De Anima*, Oxford Classical Texts (Oxford: Clarendon Press, 1956).
(ed.), *Aristotelis Topica et Sophistici Elenchi*, Oxford Classical Texts (Oxford: Clarendon Press, 1958).
Aristotle's Metaphysics, a revised text with an introduction and a commentary, 2 vols. (Oxford: Clarendon Press, 1924).

Rowe, Christopher (trans., with an historical intro.), Aristotle, *Nicomachean Ethics*, philosophical introduction and commentary by Sarah Broadie (Oxford University Press, 2002).
Stewart, J. A., *Notes on the Nicomachean Ethics of Aristotle*, 2 vols. (Oxford: Clarendon Press, 1892).
Susemihl, Franz, *Aristotelis Quae Feruntur Magna Moralia* (Leipzig: Teubner, 1883).
Walzer, R. R., and J. M. Mingay (eds.), *Aristotelis Ethica Eudemia*, Oxford Classical Texts (Oxford: Clarendon Press, 1991).

3 Secondary literature

Adam, James (ed., with critical notes, comm. and app.), *The Republic of Plato*, 2 vols. (Cambridge University Press, 1902, 1921).
Advisory Group on Citizenship, *Education for Citizenship and the Teaching of Democracy in Schools* (London: Qualifications and Curriculum Authority, 1998).
Alexander, John M., *Capabilities and Social Justice: The Political Philosophy of Amartya Sen and Martha Nussbaum* (Aldershot: Ashgate, 2008).
Allen, Anita L., and Milton C. Regan (eds.), *Debating Democracy's Discontent: Essays on American Politics, Law, and Public Philosophy* (Oxford University Press, 1998).
Altham, J. E. J., and Ross Harrison (eds.), *World, Mind and Ethics: Essays on the Ethical Philosophy of Bernard Williams* (Cambridge University Press, 1995).
Anagnostopoulos, Georgios (ed.), *A Companion to Aristotle* (Chichester: Wiley–Blackwell, 2009).
Annas, Julia, 'Comments on J. Cooper', in Patzig (ed.), *Aristoteles' 'Politik'*, 242–8.
'Plato and Aristotle on friendship and altruism', *Mind*, 86 (1977), 532–54.
Aquinas, St Thomas, *Commentary on Aristotle's Nicomachean Ethics*, translation by C. I. Litzinger, O. P., foreword by Ralph McInerny (Notre Dame, IN: Dumb Ox Books, 1993).
Summa Theologiae, cura et studio Sac. Petri Caramello, 3 vols. (Turin: Marietti, 1952).
Arendt, Hannah, *The Human Condition*, 2nd edn (University of Chicago Press, 1958).
On Revolution (London: Penguin Books, 1990).
Aubenque, Pierre, 'Aristote et la démocratie', in his *Aristote Politique*, 255–64.
(ed.), *Aristote Politique: Etudes sur la Politique d'Aristote, publiées par Alonso Tordesillas* (Paris: Presses Universitaires de France, 1993).

Ball, Terence, James Farr, and Russell L. Hanson (eds.), *Political Innovation and Conceptual Change*, Ideas in Context (Cambridge University Press, 1989).

Barber, Benjamin R., *Strong Democracy: Participatory Politics for a New Age* (Berkeley and Los Angeles: University of California Press, 1984).

Barker, Ernest, *The Political Thought of Plato and Aristotle* (New York: Dover Publications, 1959).

Bates, Clifford Angell, Jr, *Aristotle's 'Best Regime': Kingship, Democracy, and the Rule of Law* (Baton Rouge, LA: Louisiana State University Press, 2003).

Berlin, Isaiah, 'Two concepts of liberty', in his *Four Essays on Liberty* (Oxford University Press, 1969), 118–72.

Besson, Samantha, and José Luis Martí, 'Law and republicanism: Mapping the issues', in their *Legal Republicanism: National and International Perspectives* (Oxford University Press, 2009), 3–36.

Bevir, Mark, 'Are there perennial problems in political theory?', *Political Studies*, 42 (1994), 662–75.

Biondi, Carrie-Ann, 'Aristotle on the mixed constitution and its relevance for American political thought', in Keyt and Miller (eds.), *Freedom, Reason, and the Polis*, 176–98.

Bluck, R. S. (ed., with an intro. and a comm.), *Plato's Meno* (Cambridge University Press, 1961).

Blundell, Mary Whitlock, *Helping Friends and Harming Enemies: A Study in Sophocles and Greek Ethics* (Cambridge University Press, 1989).

Bobonich, Chris, 'Aristotle's ethical treatises', in Kraut (ed.), *The Blackwell Guide to Aristotle's Nicomachean Ethics*, 12–36.

Bock, Gisela, Quentin Skinner, and Maurizio Viroli (eds.), *Machiavelli and Republicanism*, Ideas in Context (Cambridge University Press, 1990).

Bodéüs, Richard, *Le Véritable politique et ses vertus selon Aristote* (Louvain: Editions Peeters, 2004).

Bookman, John T., 'The wisdom of the many: An analysis of the arguments of Books III and IV of Aristotle's *Politics*', *History of Political Thought*, 13 (1992), 1–12.

Bouchard, Elsa, 'Analogies du pouvoir partagé: Remarques sur Aristote, *Politique* III.11', *Phronesis*, 56 (2011), 162–79.

Broadie, Sarah, *Ethics with Aristotle* (Oxford University Press, 1991).

Bryan, Bradley, 'Approaching others: Aristotle on friendship's possibility', *Political Theory*, 37 (2009), 754–79.

Burger, Ronna, *Aristotle's Dialogue with Socrates: On the Nicomachean Ethics* (University of Chicago Press, 2008).

Cairns, Douglas L., *Aidōs: The Psychology and Ethics of Honour and Shame in Ancient Greek Literature* (Oxford: Clarendon Press, 1993).

Cammack, Daniela, 'Aristotle on the virtue of the multitude', *Political Theory*, 41 (2013), 175–202.

Canevaro, Mirko, '*Nomothesia* in classical Athens: What sources should we believe?', *The Classical Quarterly*, 63 (2013), 139–60.

Cartledge, Paul, *Ancient Greek Political Thought in Practice* (Cambridge University Press, 2009).

Charles, David, 'Comments on M. Nussbaum', in Patzig (ed.), *Aristoteles' 'Politik'*, 187–201.

'Perfectionism in Aristotle's political theory: Reply to Martha Nussbaum', *Oxford Studies in Ancient Philosophy*, supplementary volume (1988), 185–206.

Cherry, Kevin M., *Plato, Aristotle, and the Purpose of Politics* (Cambridge University Press, 2012).

Cicero, *De Re Publica, De Legibus*, with an English translation by Clinton Walker Keyes, Loeb Classical Library (Cambridge, MA: Harvard University Press, 1928).

Collins, Susan D., *Aristotle and the Rediscovery of Citizenship* (Cambridge University Press, 2006).

Constant, Benjamin, 'The liberty of the ancients compared with that of the moderns', in his *Political Writings*, translated and edited by Biancamaria Fontana, Cambridge Texts in the History of Political Thought (Cambridge University Press, 1988), 307–28.

Cooper, John M., 'Aristotle on the forms of friendship', *The Review of Metaphysics*, 30 (1977), 619–48.

'The *Magna Moralia* and Aristotle's moral philosophy', in his *Reason and Emotion: Essays on Ancient Moral Psychology and Ethical Theory* (Princeton University Press, 1999), 195–211.

'Political animals and civic friendship', in Patzig (ed.), *Aristoteles' 'Politik'*, 220–41.

Crick, Bernard, *Essays on Citizenship* (London: Continuum, 2000).

Dagger, Richard, 'Rights', in Ball et al. (eds.), *Political Innovation and Conceptual Change*, 292–308.

Denyer, Nicholas (ed.), Plato, *Protagoras*, Cambridge Greek and Latin Classics (Cambridge University Press, 2008).

De Ste Croix, G. E. M., *The Class Struggle in the Ancient Greek World: From the Archaic Age to the Arab Conquests* (Ithaca, NY: Cornell University Press, 1981).

Dover, K. J., *Greek Popular Morality in the Time of Plato and Aristotle* (Oxford: Blackwell, 1974).

Euben, J. Peter, 'Corruption', in Ball et al. (eds.), *Political Innovation and Conceptual Change*, 220–46.

Eucken, Christoph, 'Der aristotelische Democratiebegriff und sein historisches Umfeld', in Patzig (ed.), *Aristoteles' 'Politk'*, 277–91.

Farrar, Cynthia, *The Origins of Democratic Thinking: The Invention of Politics in Classical Athens* (Cambridge University Press, 1988).

Femia, Joseph V., 'An historicist critique of "revisionist" methods for studying the history of ideas', in Tully (ed.), *Meaning and Context*, 156–75.

Ferrari, G. R. F., *City and Soul in Plato's Republic* (Sankt Augustin: Academia Verlag, 2003).

Finley, M. I., *The Ancient Economy*, foreword by Ian Morris (Berkeley and Los Angeles: University of California Press, 1999).

'Aristotle and economic analysis', in Jonathan Barnes, Malcolm Schofield and Richard Sorabji (eds.), *Articles on Aristotle: 2. Ethics and Politics* (London: Duckworth, 1977), 140–58.

Democracy Ancient and Modern, 2nd edn (London: The Hogarth Press, 1985).

Frank, Jill, *A Democracy of Distinction: Aristotle and the Work of Politics* (University of Chicago Press, 2005).

'Integrating public good and private right: The virtue of property', in Tessitore (ed.), *Aristotle and Modern Politics*, 258–77.

Frede, Dorothea, 'Citizenship in Aristotle's *Politics*', in Kraut and Skultety (eds.), *Aristotle's Politics*, 167–84.

Fuks, Alexander, 'Patterns and types of social-economic revolution', in his *Social Conflict in Ancient Greece*, 9–39.

Social Conflict in Ancient Greece (Jerusalem: The Magnes Press, 1984).

'Social revolution in Greece in the hellenistic age', in his *Social Conflict in Ancient Greece*, 40–51.

Gadamer, Hans-Georg, *Truth and Method*, translation by William Glen-Doepel (London: Sheed and Ward, 1975).

Garver, Eugene, *Aristotle's Politics: Living Well and Living Together* (University of Chicago Press, 2011).

Gill, Christopher, 'Altruism or reciprocity in Greek ethical philosophy', in Gill et al. (eds.), *Reciprocity in Ancient Greece*, 303–28.

Gill, Christopher, Norman Postlethwaite, and Richard Seaford (eds.), *Reciprocity in Ancient Greece* (Oxford University Press, 1998).

Hamilton, Alexander, James Madison, and John Jay, *The Federalist Papers*, with an introduction, table of contents and index of ideas by Clinton Rossiter (New York: New American Library, 1961).

Hansen, Mogens Herman, *The Athenian Democracy in the Age of Demosthenes: Structure, Principles, and Ideology*, translation by J. A. Crook (Oxford: Blackwell, 1991).

'The mixed constitution versus the separation of powers: Monarchical and aristocratic aspects of modern democracy', *History of Political Thought*, 31 (2010), 509–31.

Polis: An Introduction to the Ancient Greek City-State (Oxford University Press, 2006).

Polis and City-State: An Ancient Concept and its Modern Equivalent (Copenhagen: Munksgaard, 1998).

Hanson, Russell L., 'Democracy', in Ball et al. (eds.), *Political Innovation and Conceptual Change*, 68–89.

Holmes, Stephen Taylor, 'Aristippus in and out of Athens', in Kraut and Skultety (eds.), *Aristotle's Politics*, 1–26.

Honohan, Iseult, *Civic Republicanism* (London: Routledge, 2002).

Humphreys, S. C., *Anthropology and the Greeks* (London: Routledge and Kegan Paul, 1978).

Irrera, Elena, 'Between advantage and virtue: Aristotle's theory of political friendship', *History of Political Thought*, 26 (2005), 565–85.

Irwin, Terence, 'The good of political activity', in Patzig (ed.), *Aristoteles' 'Politik'*, 73–98.

'The metaphysical and psychological basis of Aristotle's ethics', in A. O. Rorty (ed.), *Essays on Aristotle's Ethics*, 35–53.

Jackson, Timothy P., *Love Disconsoled: Meditations on Christian Charity*, Cambridge Studies in Religion and Critical Thought (Cambridge University Press, 1999).

Jaeger, Werner, *Aristotle: Fundamentals of the History of his Development*, translation by Richard Robinson, 2nd edn (Oxford: Clarendon Press, 1948).

Jones, A. H. M., *Athenian Democracy* (Oxford: Blackwell, 1957).

Judson, Lindsay, 'Aristotle on fair exchange', *Oxford Studies in Ancient Philosophy*, 15 (1997), 147–75.

Kant, Immanuel, 'On the common saying: "This may be true in theory, but it does not apply in practice" [Theory and practice]', in his *Political Writings*, edited by Hans Reiss and translated by H. B. Nisbet, 2nd enlarged edn, Cambridge Texts in the History of Political Thought (Cambridge University Press, 1991), 61–92.

Kenny, Anthony, *The Aristotelian Ethics: A Study of the Relationship between the Eudemian and Nicomachean Ethics of Aristotle* (Oxford: Clarendon Press, 1978).

Keys, Mary M., *Aquinas, Aristotle and the Promise of the Common Good* (Cambridge University Press, 2006).

Keyt, David, 'Aristotle's theory of distributive justice', in Keyt and Miller (eds.), *A Companion to Aristotle's Politics*, 238–78.

'The good man and the upright citizen in Aristotle's *Ethics* and *Politics*', in Keyt and Miller, *Freedom, Reason, and the Polis*, 220–40.

Keyt, David, and Fred D. Miller, Jr (eds.), *A Companion to Aristotle's Politics* (Oxford: Blackwell, 1991).

Freedom, Reason, and the Polis: Essays in Ancient Greek Political Philosophy (Cambridge University Press, 2007).

Knight, Kelvin, *Aristotelian Philosophy: Ethics and Politics from Aristotle to MacIntyre* (Cambridge: Polity Press, 2007).

Konstan, David, 'Reciprocity and friendship', in Gill et al. (eds.), *Reciprocity in Ancient Greece*, 279–301.

Kraut, Richard, *Aristotle: Political Philosophy*, Founders of Modern Political and Social Thought (Oxford University Press, 2002).

(ed.), *The Blackwell Guide to Aristotle's Nicomachean Ethics* (Oxford: Blackwell, 2006).

'Two conceptions of happiness', *Philosophical Review*, 88 (1979), 167–97.

Kraut, Richard, and Steven Skultety (eds.), *Aristotle's Politics: Critical Essays* (Lanham, MD: Rowman and Littlefield Publishers, 2005).

Kyrtatas, Dimitris J., 'Domination and exploitation', in Paul Cartledge, Edward E. Cohen and Lin Foxhall (eds.), *Money, Labour and Land: Approaches to the Economies of Ancient Greece* (London: Routledge, 2002), 140–55.

Lange, Lynda, 'Woman is not a rational animal: On Aristotle's biology of reproduction', in Sandra Harding and Merrill B. Hintikka (eds.), *Discovering Reality: Feminist Perspectives on Epistemology, Metaphysics, Methodology, and Philosophy of Science* (Dordrecht: Reidel, 1983), 1–15.

Lear, Jonathan, 'Inside and outside the *Republic*', *Phronesis*, 37 (1992), 184–215.

Lennox, James G., 'Nature does nothing in vain . . .', in his *Aristotle's Philosophy of Biology: Studies in the Origins of Life Science*, Cambridge Studies in Philosophy and Biology (Cambridge University Press, 2001), 205–23.

Lloyd, G. E. R., 'The idea of nature in the *Politics*', in his *Aristotelian Explorations* (Cambridge University Press, 1996), 184–204.

Lockwood, Thornton C., Jr, 'Polity, political justice and political mixing', *History of Political Thought*, 27 (2006), 207–22.

MacIntyre, Alasdair, *After Virtue: A Study in Moral Theory*, 2nd edn (London: Duckworth, 1985).

Ethics and Politics: Selected Essays, vol. II (Cambridge University Press, 2006).

'Moral relativism, truth and justification', in his *The Tasks of Philosophy: Selected Essays*, vol. I (Cambridge University Press, 2006), 52–73.

'Rival Aristotles: Aristotle against some modern Aristotelians', in his *Ethics and Politics*, 22–40.

'Rival Aristotles: Aristotle against some renaissance Aristotelians', in his *Ethics and Politics*, 3–21.

Whose Justice? Which Rationality? (London: Duckworth, 1988).

Mandell, David Paul, 'The history of political thought as a "vocation": A pragmatist defense', in Jason A. Frank and John Tambornino (eds.), *Vocations of Political Theory* (Minneapolis, MN: University of Minnesota Press, 2000), 118–42.

Manin, Bernard, *Principles of Representative Government*, Themes in the Social Sciences (Cambridge University Press, 1997).

Marrou, Henri-Irénée, *Histoire de l'éducation dans l'Antiquité*, 6th edn (Paris: Editions du Seuil, 1965).

Marx, Karl, *Capital: A Critique of Political Economy*, vol. 1, introduction by Ernest Mandel, translation by Ben Fowkes, Penguin Classics (London: Penguin Books, 1976).

Mayhew, Robert, *Aristotle's Criticism of Plato's Republic* (Lanham, MD: Rowman and Littlefield Publishers, 1997).

'Rulers and ruled', in Anagnostopoulos (ed.), *A Companion to Aristotle*, 526–39.

McCormick, John P., *Machiavellian Democracy* (Cambridge University Press, 2011).

McDowell, John, 'Virtue and reason', in his *Mind, Value and Reality* (Cambridge, MA: Harvard University Press, 1998), 50–73.

Meikle, Scott, 'Aristotle and exchange value', in Keyt and Miller (eds.), *A Companion to Aristotle's Politics*, 156–81.

Aristotle's Economic Thought (Oxford: Clarendon Press, 1995).

Mill, John Stuart, 'Considerations on representative government', in his *On Liberty and Other Essays*, edited by John Gray, Oxford World's Classics (Oxford University Press, 1991), 203–467.

'Grote's Aristotle', in his *Essays on Philosophy and the Classics* (University of Toronto Press, 1978), 475–510.

Miller, Fred D., Jr, 'Aristotle on the ideal constitution', in Anagnostopoulos (ed.), *A Companion to Aristotle*, 540–53.

'Naturalism', in Rowe and Schofield, *The Cambridge History of Greek and Roman Political Thought*, 321–43.

Nature, Justice, and Rights in Aristotle's Politics (Oxford: Clarendon Press, 1995).

Millett, Paul, *Lending and Borrowing in Ancient Athens* (Cambridge University Press, 1991).

'The rhetoric of reciprocity in classical Athens', in Gill et al. (eds.), *Reciprocity in Ancient Greece*, 227–53.

Montesquieu, Charles de, *The Spirit of Laws*, translation by Anne M. Cohler et al., Cambridge Texts in the History of Political Thought (Cambridge University Press, 1989).

Morrison, Donald, 'Aristotle's definition of citizenship: A problem and some solutions', *History of Philosophy Quarterly*, 16 (1999), 143–65.

Mulgan, Richard, 'Aristotle and the political role of women', *History of Political Thought*, 15 (1994), 179–202.

'Aristotle and the value of political participation', *Political Theory*, 18 (1990), 195–215.

'Was Aristotle an "Aristotelian social democrat"?', *Ethics*, 111 (2000), 79–101.

Mulhall, Stephen, and Adam Swift, 'Rawls and communitarianism', in Samuel Freeman (ed.), *The Cambridge Companion to Rawls* (Cambridge University Press, 2003), 460–87.

Nancy, Michel, 'Aristote devant les objections de Socrate à la démocratie (*Politique*, III, 4 et 11)', in Aubenque (ed.), *Aristote Politique*, 265–88.

Nehamas, Alexander, 'Aristotelian *philia*, modern friendship?', *Oxford Studies in Ancient Philosophy*, 39 (2010), 213–47.

Nussbaum, Martha Craven, 'Aristotle, politics, and human capabilities: A response to Antony, Arneson, Charlesworth, and Mulgan', *Ethics*, 111 (2000), 102–40.

'Aristotle on human nature and the foundations of ethics', in Altham and Harrison (eds.), *World, Mind and Ethics*, 86–131.

'Aristotelian social democracy', in Tessitore (ed.), *Aristotle and Modern Politics*, 47–104.

Creating Capabilities: The Human Development Approach (Cambridge, MA: The Belknap Press of Harvard University Press, 2011).

Frontiers of Justice: Disability, Nationality, Species Membership (Cambridge, MA: The Belknap Press of Harvard University Press, 2006).

'Nature, function, and capability: Aristotle on political distribution', *Oxford Studies in Ancient Philosophy*, supplementary volume (1988), 145–83.

'Non-relative virtues: An Aristotelian approach', in Martha Nussbaum and Amartya Sen (eds.), *The Quality of Life* (Oxford: Clarendon Press, 1993), 242–69.

'Reply to David Charles', *Oxford Studies in Ancient Philosophy*, supplementary volume (1988), 207–14.

'Shame, separateness, and political unity: Aristotle's criticism of Plato', in Rorty (ed.), *Essays on Aristotle's Ethics*, 395–435.

Ober, Josiah, 'Aristotle's political sociology: Class, status, and order in the *Politics*', in Carnes Lord and David K. O'Connor (eds.), *Essays on the Foundations of Aristotelian Political Science* (Berkeley and Los Angeles: University of California Press, 1991), 112–35.

'Democracy's wisdom: An Aristotelian middle way for collective judgment', *American Political Science Review*, 107 (2013), 104–22.

Mass and Elite in Democratic Athens: Rhetoric, Ideology, and the Power of the People (Princeton University Press, 1989).

Paine, Thomas, *Rights of Man*, edited with an introduction by Henry Collins, Penguin Classics (London: Penguin Books, 1969).

Pakaluk, Michael, 'The egalitarianism of the *Eudemian Ethics*', *The Classical Quarterly*, 48 (1998), 411–32.

Pangle, Lorraine Smith, *Aristotle and the Philosophy of Friendship* (Cambridge University Press, 2003).

Pateman, Carole, *The Disorder of Women: Democracy, Feminism and Political Theory* (Cambridge: Polity Press, 1989).

Patzig, Günther (ed.), *Aristoteles' 'Politik': Akten des XI. Symposium Aristotelicum* (Göttingen: Vandenhoeck and Ruprecht, 1990).

Pettit, Philip, 'Keeping republican freedom simple: On a difference with Quentin Skinner', *Political Theory*, 30 (2002), 339–56.

Republicanism: A Theory of Freedom and Government, Oxford Political Theory (Oxford: Clarendon Press, 1997).

'Reworking Sandel's republicanism', in Allen and Regan (eds.), *Debating Democracy's Discontent*, 40–59.

Pocock, J. G. A., *The Machiavellian Moment: Florentine Political Thought and the Atlantic Republican Tradition*, 2nd edn (Princeton University Press, 1975).

Polanyi, Karl, 'Aristotle discovers the economy', in Karl Polanyi, Conrad M. Arensberg, and Harry W. Pearson (eds.), *Trade and Market in the Early Empires: Economies in History and Theory* (Chicago: Henry Regnery Co., 1957), 64–94.

The Great Transformation, foreword by Robert M. MacIver (Boston, MA: Beacon Press, 1957).

The Livelihood of Man, edited by Harry W. Pearson (New York: Academic Press, 1977).

Polybius, *The Histories*, with an English translation by W. R. Paton, III in six volumes, Loeb Classical Library (Cambridge, MA: Harvard University Press, 1972).

Popper, K. R., *The Open Society and its Enemies*, Volume I: *The Spell of Plato*, 5th edn (London: Routledge and Kegan Paul, 1966).

Porter, Jean, '*De ordine caritatis*: Charity, friendship, and justice in Thomas Aquinas' *Summa Theologiae*', *The Thomist*, 53 (1989), 197–213.

Price, A. W., *Love and Friendship in Plato and Aristotle* (Oxford: Clarendon Press, 1989).

Rasmussen, David (ed.), *Universalism vs. Communitarianism: Contemporary Debates in Ethics* (Cambridge, MA: MIT Press, 1990).

Rawls, John, *A Theory of Justice*, orig. edn (Cambridge, MA: The Belknap Press of Harvard University Press, 1971).

Rée, Jonathan, 'The vanity of historicism', *New Literary History*, 22 (1991), 961–83.

Reeve, C. D. C., 'The naturalness of the polis in Aristotle', in Anagnostopoulos (ed.), *A Companion to Aristotle*, 512–25.

Rhodes, P. J., '*Nomothesia* in fourth-century Athens', *The Classical Quarterly*, 35 (1985), 55–60.

Roberts, Jean, 'Excellences of the citizen and of the individual', in Anagnostopoulos (ed.), *A Companion to Aristotle*, 555–65.

Rorty, Amélie Oksenberg (ed.), *Essays on Aristotle's Ethics*, Philosophical Traditions (Berkeley and Los Angeles: University of California Press, 1980).

Rorty, Richard, *Philosophy and the Mirror of Nature* (Oxford: Blackwell, 1980).

Rosler, Andrés, *Political Authority and Obligation in Aristotle*, Oxford Aristotle Studies (Oxford: Clarendon Press, 2005).

Rousseau, Jean-Jacques, 'Of the social contract', in his *The Social Contract and Other Later Political Writings*, edited and translated by Victor Gourevitch, Cambridge Texts in the History of Political Thought (Cambridge University Press, 1997).

Rowe, Christopher, 'Aims and methods in Aristotle's *Politics*', in Keyt and Miller (eds.), *A Companion to Aristotle's Politics*, 57–74.

'Aristotelian constitutions', in Rowe and Schofield (eds.), *The Cambridge History of Greek and Roman Political Thought*, 366–89.

'A reply to John Cooper on the *Magna Moralia*', *American Journal of Philology*, 96 (1975), 160–72.

Rowe, Christopher, and Malcolm Schofield (eds.), *The Cambridge History of Greek and Roman Political Thought* (Cambridge University Press, 2000).

Sandel, Michael J., *Democracy's Discontent: America in Search of a Public Philosophy* (Cambridge, MA: The Belknap Press of Harvard University Press, 1996).

Liberalism and the Limits of Justice, 2nd edn (Cambridge University Press, 1998).

'The procedural republic and the unencumbered self', *Political Theory*, 12 (1984), 81–96.

'Reply to critics', in Allen and Regan (eds.), *Debating Democracy's Discontent*, 319–35.

Schmitt, Carl, *The Concept of the Political*, expanded edition, translation, introduction and notes by George Schwab, with 'The Age of Neutralizations and Depoliticizations', translated by Matthias Konzen and John P. McCormick, with Leo Strauss's Notes on Schmitt's essay, translated by J. Harvey Lomax, foreword by Tracy B. Strong (University of Chicago Press, 2007).

Constitutional Theory, translated by Jeffrey Seitzer (Durham, NC: Duke University Press, 2008).

Schofield, Malcolm, 'Aristotle: an introduction', in Rowe and Schofield (eds.), *The Cambridge History of Greek and Roman Political Thought*, 310–20.

'Aristotle and the democratization of politics', in Benjamin Morison and Katerina Ierodiakonou (eds.), *Episteme, etc.: Essays in Honour of Jonathan Barnes* (Oxford University Press, 2011), 285–301.

'Aristotle's political ethics', in Kraut (ed.), *The Blackwell Guide to Aristotle's Nicomachean Ethics*, 305–22.

'Equality and hierarchy in Aristotle's political thought', in his *Saving the City*, 100–14.

'Political friendship and the ideology of reciprocity', in his *Saving the City*, 82–99.

Saving the City: Philosopher-Kings and Other Classical Paradigms (London: Routledge, 1999).

'Sharing in the constitution', in his *Saving the City*, 141–59.
Schumpeter, Joseph A., *History of Economic Analysis*, edited by Elizabeth Boody Schumpeter (London: George Allen and Unwin, 1955).
Schwarzenbach, Sibyl A., *On Civic Friendship: Including Women in the State* (New York: Columbia University Press, 2009).
Scott, Dominic, *Plato's Meno*, Cambridge Studies in the Dialogues of Plato (Cambridge University Press, 2006).
Sharples, R. W. (ed. with trans. and notes), Plato, *Meno*, Aris & Phillips Classical Texts (Warminster: Aris & Phillips, 1985).
Simpson, Peter L. P., 'Aristotle's *Regime of the Americans*', in Lenn E. Goodman and Robert B. Talisse (eds.), *Aristotle's Politics Today*, SUNY Series in Ancient Greek Philosophy (Albany, NY: State University of New York Press, 2008), 109–27.
Sinclair, R. K., *Democracy and Participation in Athens* (Cambridge University Press, 1988).
Skinner, Quentin, *The Foundations of Modern Political Thought*, vol. 1: *The Renaissance* (Cambridge University Press, 1978).
'Interpretation of the understanding of speech acts', in his *Vision of Politics*, 103–27.
Liberty before Liberalism (Cambridge University Press, 1998).
'Machiavelli's *Discorsi* and the pre-humanist origins of republican ideas', in Bock et al. (eds.), *Machiavelli and Republicanism*, 121–41.
'Meaning and understanding in the history of ideas', in his *Vision of Politics*, 57–89.
'The republican ideal of political liberty', in Bock et al. (eds.), *Machiavelli and Republicanism*, 293–309.
'The state', in Ball et al. (eds.), *Political Innovation and Conceptual Change*, 90–131.
Vision of Politics, vol. 1: *Regarding Method* (Cambridge University Press, 2002).
Sorabji, Richard, 'Aristotle on the role of intellect in virtue', in A. O. Rorty (ed.), *Essays on Aristotle's Ethics*, 201–19.
Stalley, R. F., 'Aristotle's criticism of Plato's *Republic*', in Keyt and Miller (eds.), *A Companion to Aristotle's Politics*, 182–99.
Striker, Gisela, 'Aristotle's ethics as political science', in Burkhard Reis (ed.), *The Virtuous Life in Greek Ethics* (Cambridge University Press, 2006), 127–41.
'Comments on T. Irwin', in Patzig (ed.), *Aristoteles' 'Politik'*, 99–100.
Swanson, Judith A., *The Public and the Private in Aristotle's Political Philosophy* (Ithaca, NY: Cornell University Press, 1992).
Tarlton, Charles D., 'Historicity, meaning, and revisionism in the study of political thought', *History and Theory*, 12 (1973), 307–28.
Taylor, C. C. W. (trans., with notes), Plato, *Protagoras*, Clarendon Plato Series (Oxford: Clarendon Press, 1976).

'Plato's totalitarianism', in Gail Fine (ed.), *Plato* (Oxford University Press, 2000), 762–78.

Taylor, Charles, 'Atomism', in his *Philosophy and the Human Sciences*, 187–210.

'The hermeneutics of conflict', in Tully (ed.), *Meaning and Context*, 218–28.

Philosophy and the Human Sciences: Philosophical Papers 2 (Cambridge University Press, 1985).

'What's wrong with negative liberty', in his *Philosophy and the Human Sciences*, 211–29.

Tessitore, Aristide (ed.), *Aristotle and Modern Politics: The Persistence of Political Philosophy* (University of Notre Dame Press, 2002).

Tully, James (ed.), *Meaning and Context: Quentin Skinner and his Critics* (Cambridge: Polity Press, 1988).

'The pen is a mighty sword: Quentin Skinner's analysis of politics', in his *Meaning and Context*, 7–25.

Urbinati, Nadia, *Mill on Democracy: From the Athenian Polis to Representative Government* (University of Chicago Press, 2002).

van Wees, Hans, 'The law of gratitude: Reciprocity in anthropological theory', in Gill et al. (eds.), *Reciprocity in Ancient Greece*, 13–49.

Viroli, Maurizio, 'Machiavelli and the republican idea of politics', in Bock et al. (eds.), *Machiavelli and Republicanism*, 143–71.

Vlastos, Gregory, 'Isonomia', *American Journal of Philology*, 74 (1953), 337–66.

'ΙΣΟΝΟΜΙΑ ΠΟΛΙΤΙΚΗ', in his *Platonic Studies* (Princeton University Press, 1973), 164–203.

Socrates: Ironist and Moral Philosopher (Cambridge University Press, 1991).

Waldron, Jeremy, 'The wisdom of the multitude: Some reflections on Book 3, Chapter 11 of Aristotle's *Politics*', in Kraut and Skultety (eds.), *Aristotle's Politics*, 145–65.

Walras, Léon, *Elements of Pure Economics: Or the Theory of Social Wealth*, translation by William Jaffé (London: George Allen and Unwin, 1954).

Walzer, Michael, 'Citizenship', in Ball et al. (eds.), *Political Innovation and Conceptual Change*, 211–19.

'The communitarian critique of liberalism', in his *Thinking Politically: Essays in Political Theory*, edited by David Miller (New Haven, CT: Yale University Press, 2007), 96–112.

Spheres of Justice: A Defense of Pluralism and Equality (New York: Basic Books, 1983).

'Michael Sandel's America', in Allen and Regan (eds.), *Debating Democracy's Discontent*, 175–82.

Warrender, Howard, 'Political theory and historiography: A reply to Professor Skinner on Hobbes', *The Historical Journal*, 22 (1979), 931–40.

Williams, Bernard, 'The analogy of city and soul in Plato's *Republic*', in E. N. Lee, A. P. D. Mourelatos and R. M. Rorty (eds.), *Exegesis and Argument: Studies in Greek Philosophy Presented to Gregory Vlastos* (Assen: Van Gorcum BV, 1973), 196–206.

'Pluralism, community and left Wittgensteinianism', in his *In the Beginning Was the Deed: Realism and Moralism in Political Argument*, selected, edited and with an introduction by Geoffrey Hawthorn (Princeton University Press, 2005), 29–39.

'Replies', in Altham and Harrison (eds.), *World, Mind and Ethics*, 185–224.

Wilson, James Lindley, 'Deliberation, democracy, and the rule of reason in Aristotle's *Politics*', *American Political Science Review*, 105 (2011), 259–73.

Wokler, Robert, 'The professoriate of political thought in England since 1914: a tale of three chairs', in Dario Castiglione and Iain Hampsher-Monk (eds.), *The History of Political Thought in National Context*, Ideas in Context (Cambridge University Press, 2001), 134–58.

Yack, Bernard, *The Problems of a Political Animal: Community, Justice, and Conflict in Aristotelian Political Thought* (Berkeley and Los Angeles: University of California Press, 1993).

Young, Charles M., 'Aristotle's justice', in Kraut (ed.), *The Blackwell Guide to Aristotle's* Nicomachean Ethics, 179–97.

INDEX LOCORUM

GENERAL INDEX

General index

Printed by Integrated Books International,
United States of America